Praise for *Last Chance Mustang*

"Through Bornstein's masterful storytelling, we understand, sympathize, and fall in love with his equine pupil, Samson. . . . *Last Chance Mustang* should be required reading in every high school and by every adult American until our wild Mustangs and burros are as revered as the American eagle. Bornstein brilliantly shows us how they deserve no less." —Jo Anne Normile, author of *Saving Baby*

"The most successful element of the book is Bornstein's intimate and vulnerable account of how he and Samson were able to bond and forge ahead despite the odds against them. Both found light, growth, stability, and dignity in their partnership, and that is truly inspiring." —*Horse Nation*

"Bornstein's story is far more than a tale of how one man tamed a wild horse. It is the story of man's dark history with horses and the heartbreaking consequences. Through his painstaking work with a traumatized wild Mustang named Samson, Bornstein reminds all of us that, when working with horses, we are among equals. It is this enlightened understanding that makes Bornstein's training techniques so successful. Three cheers for *Last Chance Mustang*." —Susan Richards, author of *Chosen by a Horse*

"Samson's is a story that all readers will be able to relate to: a story of survival, of trust, and ultimately, finding love. Readers will find themselves willing Samson to let down his defenses and let in his very last hope." —*Horsetalk*

MITCHELL BORNSTEIN

LAST CHANCE MUSTANG

The Story of One Horse, One Horseman, and One Final Shot at Redemption

St. Martin's Griffin ≈ New York

This is a work of nonfiction. However, the names and identifying characteristics of certain individuals have been changed to protect their privacy and dialogue has been reconstructed to the best of the author's recollection.

The Library of Congress has cataloged the hardcover edition as follows:

Bornstein, Mitchell.
   Last chance mustang : the story of one horse, one horseman, and one final shot at redemption / Mitchell Bornstein. — 1st ed.
      p. cm.
   Includes bibliographical references.
   ISBN 978-1-250-05941-3 (hardcover)
   ISBN 978-1-4668-6429-0 (e-book)
   1. Mustang. 2. Mustang—Training. 3. Wild horse adoption—Illinois.
4. Human-animal relationships. I. Title.
   SF293.M9B67 2015
   636.1'3—dc23

                                                                    2015012462

ISBN 978-1-250-10619-3 (trade paperback)

Our books may be purchased in bulk for promotional, educational, or business use. Please contact your local bookseller or the Macmillan Corporate and Premium Sales Department at 1-800-221-7945, extension 5442, or by e-mail at MacmillanSpecialMarkets@macmillan.com.

First St. Martin's Griffin Edition: February 2017

10 9 8 7 6 5 4 3 2 1

TO MY PARENTS, *who instilled in me the virtues of patience, acceptance, compassion, and understanding that I have carried with me through each of my sessions with Samson and through life. Your lifelong, unwavering devotion to each of your five children has taught me the true meaning of love and commitment.*

CONTENTS

ACKNOWLEDGMENTS

Writing Samson's story proved to be one of the most enjoyable experiences of my life. But all of that changed when the manuscript was completed and I entered the swamp of the literary world. Some claimed that I needed to be a world-famous horse trainer to get a publishing contract. Others advised that Samson's story was far too powerful to be left to an unpublished author wannabe like myself. After untold hours with Samson and years at the keyboard drafting his yarn, I was left deflated and dejected.

All of that changed when I spoke with Stephany Evans, agent at FinePrint Literary Management. When I questioned whether I was the proper person to write Samson's story, she responded that there was no one better. When I inquired if I needed to be a world-famous trainer to sell this book, she answered that all that was required was a good story and the desire to tell it. From that point forward, everything fell into place. Just days after the proposal was sent out, Samson's story had a publisher and a home. So it is with my gratitude and appreciation that I say thank you to Stephany, for taking a gamble on a no-name unpublished author and a lost, last chance Mustang, and making a dream come true.

When the proposal for this story went to St. Martin's Press on a Friday, I was convinced that it would get lost in someone's in-box and never get reviewed. But when Daniela Rapp, editor at St. Martin's, called Monday morning and said that she had read the proposal and wanted to talk with the author, my gut told me that Samson's story had landed where it belonged. The following day, Daniela and I spoke and I conveyed to her my one and only concern: that Samson's tale not be fictionalized, that the book had to stay true to Samson's saga, the plight of the wild horse, and the terrible predicament of any unwanted, abused animal. And when Daniela assured me that *Last Chance Mustang* would tell the real story of Samson's journey, the voice in my head told me that she meant it.

Dating back to that first conversation, Daniela, as promised, never strayed from her assurances to do justice to Samson's story. Through each step of taking this book to print, she kept alive my vision of what this book should be and guided this neophyte author through the long, arduous process. And thanks to Daniela's efforts, readers everywhere now have the opportunity to learn of Samson's strength, resilience, tenacity, and perseverance. Horse and animal lovers alike will, I hope, learn about the plight of our great wild herds and come to understand that every living thing, no matter how hated and despised, has value and worth.

Thanks to Daniela's belief in this author and this story,

Samson's tale was brought to life. For that, I will always be in her debt.

My thanks to Barbara Wild and Lisa Davis for all of their hard work and effort in moving this book through the production phase.

When I first started training horses nearly two decades ago, I unfortunately lacked the guidance of a seasoned mentor. So, I learned the hard way—through watching and learning the ways of the horse and through patience. I also served as a human piñata, being bitten, bucked, and kicked more times than I care to remember. Back then, without the resources of the Internet and search engines, many in the horse world were in the dark when it came to the proper methods to manage their unruly, obstructive, and damaged horses. Problem horses owned by well-intentioned owners were often excessively bratty; other steeds owned by unsavory characters were downright aggressive, violent, and terribly dangerous.

And so it was that many of my hardest cases came when I was just a fledgling in the horse world. It was trial by fire. And I survived, learned, and grew from each of these experiences. Many of these horses were downright nasty; all charged a premium to be my teachers. Though I lack warmhearted memories of much of their antics, I do look back with fondness for each and every horse who could have pulled the trigger on me but didn't. Back then, there were unquestionably many instances in which any number of horses could have put me down and finished me off. And yet they didn't. Perhaps they recognized that I had goodness in my heart; maybe they understood that I was only trying to help. Either way, they didn't go down that road even though they could have.

And so, it is with admiration and respect that I look back on and remember each and every horse who got me—still in one piece—to where I am today.

In the interest of full disclosure, Samson's tale wouldn't have made it to print without Alison, the hunter/jumper to my cowboy ways. Through the long, winding course of writing this book, she read every sentence, of every paragraph, of every page, of every chapter—time and time again without complaint. Her edits were dead-on; her input, invaluable. And through it all, she remained resolute in her conviction that Samson's story would find a publisher and steadfast in her belief in me. Samson knew a good apple when he saw one, and fortunately, so did I.

And last, I wouldn't have had a book to write without Samson, the true last chance Mustang. Since our very first meeting in that dark, dank stall to this very day, it has always seemed like that horse and this horseman were meant to be. From unchecked anger and unrestrained violence to unyielding loyalty and unencumbered emotion, our relationship has covered the spectrum. We have shared our highs and wallowed in our lows, and through it all this headstrong Mustang has remained my student, teacher, friend, and compatriot. In the end, my Samson Experience has enhanced my skills, enriched my life, shown me the power of hope, and taught me the true meaning of friendship. Samson the lost, troubled, wayward Mustang has touched me in a way that will never be equaled.

LAST CHANCE MUSTANG

THE BEAST IN THE STALL

*A woman needs two animals—the horse of
her dreams and a jackass to pay for it.*

—AUTHOR UNKNOWN

When Amy asked me to look at the Mustang she said
had torn apart her farm and ruined her life, I asked if
he was a refugee from the recent neighboring barn fire.

"Refugee?" she snorted as she averted her gaze and picked
at her fingernails. "His name is Samson, and he probably
started the fire."

For months I had heard the stories, how a wintertime
tragedy was averted when several horses managed to survive
a horrific barn fire. Though the sources were different, the
stories were all the same. Each focused on the crazed actions
of one horse in particular. One version told that this horse
had charged through the barn and in a matter of seconds
obliterated the sliding exterior wood door into little more
than toothpick splinters. Rumor had it that this Mustang
was a flesh-eating, fire-breathing monster.

By the summer of 2009, the story had weaved through
the local equestrian community and the horse had become

a legend. I had no way of differentiating truth from myth, but based upon what I was hearing on this day, it all seemed plausible.

A caring neighbor, Amy, had taken in several of the displaced fire refugees. As a board member for a local therapeutic riding center for children and adults with special needs and as a volunteer in charge of procuring and training horses, I had traveled out to rural McHenry County, Illinois, to evaluate one of the animals. Also a volunteer at the center, Amy believed that one of the horses would be perfect for the program, but my gut told me that she had something more in mind for me.

Approaching my fortieth birthday, I was single and by trade an attorney. But with fifteen years working with neglected, abused, and difficult-to-train horses, I had built a reputation rehabilitating horses who don't play well with others. Amy had mentioned that she had a second horse who more than fit the bill: a crazed and caged formerly wild Mustang who hated everyone and everything—the now-legendary barn fire horse.

The morning-heavy air held the smells of horse country—hay, manure, and livestock—close to the ground as the early July sun started to dry the prior evening's mist. Amy led me into the decommissioned dairy barn, down the dark barn aisle, past discarded, rusty mower blades, fan blades, a broken pitchfork, and rotting coils of rope. A scattering of a dozen or so very aged, rusted farm implements obstructed the path to the barn's prisoner retention section.

Picture a NASCAR twelve-car pileup on a rainy day; parts and chassis were everywhere. One machine looked like a MacGyvered motorized pitchfork. Another, with its long conveyor belt and sharp protruding blades, resembled a medieval torture device. If Freddy Krueger had a garage or machine shop, this was it.

The dark, dank, musty barn chilled the perspiration on the back of my neck. My Justin work boots sloshed through pools of rainwater unable to dry atop the damp concrete floor as shards of sunlight poked through holes in the exterior walls and spoke to the water's point of entry. Upon closer examination, the holes appeared hoof sized and the pockmarked walls resembled a shooting range backstop.

I stepped over a discarded metal bucket stomped on enough times that it now resembled a piece of sheet metal. A fractured wooden plank tattooed with hoof impressions leaned up against what little remained of a crimson-stained partition wall, the stains now dry and brown. This wasn't a barn; this was a war zone.

From down the aisle, the sounds of a hyperventilating animal caught and then monopolized my attention.

As we peered to the darkened milking stations now serving as makeshift stalls, Amy explained that she had rescued three horses from the fire: Studs, a large lumbering paint gelding whom I was there to evaluate, a two-year-old stallion, and the combative Mustang stallion. Over the years, I'd had nearly every client portray their uncooperative horse as the next Moby-Dick, only to have the animal turn around quickly for me. Amy would be no different.

She told me how one winter morning, before she locked him in a stall Samson had escaped his pasture and chased her back into her house as she tried to leave for work. He squealed high-pitched wails as if part pig and stomped his front legs on the porch steps, steam shooting out of his nostrils like a crazed dragon. When he ran up and down the length of the porch, blocking her exit, daring her to get by, she threw a shovel at him. Samson merely held his ground. When she tried to crawl out a bedroom window, he bit her on the ass and sent her tumbling back in onto the bedroom floor.

Amy stuttered her words and her rosy cheeks turned ashen. The mere thought of this Mustang had her stricken with fear. Yet it wasn't just fear that I observed. As Amy clenched her fists and paced around the barn, she seemed anxious, nervous, and jittery—as though she had just chugged a six-pack of Mountain Dew. If she was making me this nervous, I could only imagine what the caged Mustang must have felt. My assurances that Samson's actions were born out of a lack of familiarity were summarily dismissed.

Instead, Amy countered that though Samson and Studs had lived together for many months prior to their arrival, the significantly larger paint gelding bore the daily brunt of the Mustang's violent and contemptuous fits. Pointing outside to a thirty-foot stretch of wooden fence resting mangled on the ground like a pile of pick-up sticks, Amy told how Samson had galloped through the repeatedly rebuilt fence and into the adjoining pasture nearly three dozen times just so that he could pummel Studs with his hind-end barrages and sink his teeth into the paint's meaty, muscled neck.

"This horse hates anything and everything on two or four legs!" she shouted.

I glanced over to Amy, who at forty-something looked younger than her years. Recently relocated from the hustle and bustle of the Eastern Seaboard, Amy had sought out the refuge and serenity of McHenry County's quaint farms, rolling hills, and glacial valleys. Taxis, traffic jams, and power lunches were now remnants of her past life. Hordes of humanity moving on the sidewalks, like ants in an ant farm, had been supplanted by columns of cornstalks, which swayed beautifully, in unison, when fueled by the daily breezes. In this world, the closest thing to stress was inclement weather and a resultant poor crop season. The closest thing to gridlock: a slow-moving bright green John Deere combine.

Leaving the security of a metropolitan power center and her high stress job was Amy's change-of-life epiphany. Moving to the country was her *Eat, Pray, Love* moment—the farm was her Garden of Eden and walled fortress all in one.

Though Amy had pleaded with me to come out to the farm, from the moment that I arrived I had felt like an intruder. "I don't like people coming out here," she repeated several times. "I just prefer to be left alone."

Wind whistled in through a window frame in the east wall, the missing plastic pane evidencing numerous failed jailbreaks. I eyed the raised concrete flooring in all the empty stalls, a typical setup for a milking barn. Horses don't thrive on concrete, but Amy said that she had nowhere else to put him. After his daily cross-pasture attacks on Studs, Amy called Frank, Samson's owner, and with several men, ropes, intimidation, and brute force the unwilling Mustang had been forced into a stall.

Disgusted by the incident, and after learning that Frank intended to sell the horses at auction after which they would most likely end up on a truck headed to a slaughterhouse in Mexico or Canada, Amy had requested and was given title to the three fire refugee horses. From that point forward, the combative Mustang was officially her problem child. Concerned that Samson would be isolated and alone, she'd purchased two miniature horses. Ike, an older, abused mini, and Star, a plump and fresh youngster.

Samson would have neither as a neighbor.

With tears welling in her eyes, Amy recounted how nearly instantly Samson had crashed the wall separating the two stalls and punted each mini from their new abode. When Amy replaced the two minis with a mother-daughter pair of goats, the duo met the same unfortunate end, only this time Samson used his mouth, tossing each clear across the barn aisle.

Since that day, no horse—save the two-year-old stallion fire refugee—no mini, and no goat had entered or lived in Samson's barn.

At the last door toward the end of the aisle, the acrid stench of months-old manure and horse urine slammed me in the face testifying to one simple fact: no soul was brave or foolish enough to enter or muck this stall. Unlike the other stall doors, Samson's was buttressed with two heavy planks snugged down into metal brackets on each side and a bloody two-by-four vertically wedged down to the concrete floor.

This wasn't a stall door; it was the Siegfried or the Maginot Line, or the Great Wall of China. This was a last line of defense. Amy had effectively created a maximum-security prison to barricade Samson the beast inside.

For this Mustang, and thousands like him, Nevada's crisp sunrise and picture-perfect sunsets, craggy mountainside slopes, and borderless sagebrush valleys had given way to Midwest flatlands. His herd's mares, foals, and bachelor stallions—his family—were now nothing more than a distant memory's flicker, which with each passing day had lost its radiance. Freedom was now measured in feet and inches:

a small opening in his stall front through which he could peer across the aisle to horseless stalls and the aged dairy barn's long since decommissioned milking stations.

Samson's way of life, his entire existence, had been lost. This was now his prison.

From above the stall door, a muzzle tip appeared, then quickly retracted. The sound of deep, rapid breathing echoed off the walls and floors like the reverberating bass in a nightclub at 2:00 a.m. I thought Samson had just been running around outside, but this wasn't the sound of an animal exhausted from exercise. This was the sound of an animal in fear for his life. My mere presence had started Samson the time bomb ticking.

"Has he been gelded?" I wondered aloud. Like all animals, stallions are driven by two innate forces: the will to survive, and the desire to procreate. Round the clock, testosterone fuels a stallion's never-ending libido. This hormonally fed drive to reproduce induces dictatorial traits and violent behaviors that ward off potential competitors and enemies alike. These same aggressive traits and violent behaviors aid the stallion when it comes time to capture and retain—as a member of his harem—a mare in estrus.

A stallion's high-pitched screams will announce his presence, his bites will shred a competitor's skin and muscle, and his foreleg strikes can down a victim in a single blow. An instrument of warfare and an engine of reproduction, the stallion is a force like no other. With the earliest known reference to gelding dating back to 350 BC and Aristotle's *History of Animals,* for centuries since humans have gelded horses to remove these traits deemed harmful to herd or human safety.

"Yes," Amy answered, "he was gelded just prior to being locked away, but the process only made him meaner and left me deeply scarred."

From what I could gather, the vet bill, the chaos of the scene, the fact that gelding had done little to gentle her crazed horse had pushed Amy near the edge.

That I could understand. Most horses are gelded at a young age, when the drop in a stallion's testosterone levels will usually quash the desire to mate, to challenge, and to fight. But if gelded after puberty, engrained aggressive and alpha horse traits often remain a permanent component of the adult horse's behavior. Gelding Samson in his twelfth year failed to eliminate the behavior that had helped him survive in both the harsh wild and then the abusive domestic world.

No longer fueled by the combustible, lethal combination of testosterone and adrenaline, Samson had lost a degree of his hard-charging, chemically induced, consequences-are-irrelevant invincibility. But the behaviors, mannerisms, and actions that had matured a young colt into a fully fledged wild stallion would always be irrevocably hardwired into Samson's psyche. Wild or domesticated, gelded or not, free or caged, Samson was determined to live out his birthright destiny—his destiny as an American wild Mustang.

Amy had expected that after a snip or two the Terminator would become Mr. Rogers. In this case, the Terminator merely became Rambo.

Just like a stallion, Samson the gelding would still stand upright to attack. His hind-end kicks would shatter bones. His rump was a battering ram that would bodycheck a victim into submission. He would still establish his hierarchy, his domain, his rule, and extinguish any challenge to his authority. Samson was a walking, breathing, self-defense, self-preservation survival machine extraordinaire standing caged in an eight-by-ten-foot stall.

Something about the story I was hearing bothered me. If no one could handle this horse, then how did he make it to the farm in the first place? Frank and two of his gang, Amy recounted. They had surrounded, roped, and subdued him. And then, with two lines attached they dragged Samson down the road from the adjoining fire-ravaged property.

The thought of this perverse act, the mere image of a once-free wild horse dragged half a mile down the road, all the while being manhandled and disrespected, enraged me. This was an iconic American Mustang, a National Heritage Species that fell under the protections of the Wild Free-Roaming Horses and Burros Act of 1971. He and his cousins were, as proclaimed by Congress, ". . . living symbols of the historic and pioneer spirit of the West . . ." that ". . . enrich the lives of the American people . . . ," and should be considered ". . . an integral part of the natural system of the public lands."

This was a horse whose ancestors held a direct DNA link to the continent's first horses. His bloodlines had survived the harsh deserts of the East, discovered the Americas, and built the American frontier. He was a living symbol of America and a living, breathing piece of American history.

This horse deserved better. Any horse deserved better. I began to see why and how Samson had become so violent and so hateful.

I still had yet to look upon Amy's Mustang.

Now I peered into the shadows. Once my eyes adjusted

to the dim light, I could see the shape of Samson's head and neck, elevated by the thick concrete slab, piled manure, and soiled straw he stood on. Just my looking into the stall seemed to accelerate his breathing to an even more alarming rate. Tension and fear engulfed the stale barn air.

"Aren't you a big boy, Samson. Don't you worry; this stall is, and will remain, your safe place. I respect that, and there's no need for us to move hastily here," I told Samson calmly.

His right ear rotated to track the sound of my voice. Then his right eye turned to take my measure. Behind me, Amy froze against the wall. Most nervous horses would have snorted, danced in place, swooshed a tail, or at least raised and lowered their heads. But except for his ear and eye, Samson stood stock-still, silently strategizing, like an elk surrounded by wolves.

"It's nice to finally meet you," I said. "I was worried there for a while—I didn't think you were going to join the party."

While Samson and I sized each other up, Amy provided what little background she had on her troubled Mustang. Captured in the Nevada mountains in 2003 under the rotor blades of a low-flying helicopter, he became the property of the Bureau of Land Management (BLM)—an agency of the Department of the Interior charged with oversight of the majority of this nation's wild horse population. No longer wild and no longer free, this then six-year-old proud stallion was little more than a number and a statistic. A freeze brand bearing eight symbols of the International Alpha Angle System on his neck's left side, like all captured wild Mustangs Samson's mark identified him as BLM property. With the mark applied using a branding iron previously chilled in dry ice, the process permanently destroys the pigment producing hair follicles, leaving white hairs to grow at the branding site.

In Samson's case, the white symbols of his freeze mark told that he was one of 10,081 wild horses removed by the BLM from federal rangeland in 2003, one of 300,000 removed since 1972.

Horses purportedly are removed for their own good—to prevent starvation, dehydration, and death. In reality, wild Mustangs have been displaced to stave off alleged rangeland degradation. Once free, They are now homeless horses, chased from their land by hate, greed, and politics.

As Amy heard it from Frank, Samson had never received any training, was not worthy of any kindness, and was a real "willful son of a bitch." The instructions that Amy received from Frank had been passed down, from owner to owner, dating back to Samson's first days in the domestic horse market: beat this Mustang to get his attention, hurt him, and he will comply.

These were the Samson Rules. Instantly I understood that the last six years of this horse's life had been a dark, painful living hell.

For his first six years, Samson had survived in the harsh and unforgiving Wild West where he and other stallions each acted as judge, jury, and executioner. The stallion creed of justice was no doubt swift and decisive. At times Samson may have been the victim; other times he may have been the enforcer. Either way, Samson survived frontier justice and carried his stallion essence into the world of the two-legged predator.

There Samson's stallion ways had sustained him in what

proved to be a harsh, cruel, and sad existence. Undoubtedly, however, these attributes went unwelcomed by his new captors and brought down a world of pain and a torrent of abuse. Samson nonetheless knew what it took to survive: Be proud. Never show weakness. Strike first. And never shy from a fight.

It was Samson's credo; it was all that he had left. And so he fought and he defended himself.

While most attribute the concept of gentling to the modern practice of natural horsemanship, the idea that horses should be taught free of violence and coercion actually dates back to 350 BC and the Greek cavalry general Xenophon's treatise *On the Art of Horsemanship*. Advocating gentling techniques such as socialization and desensitization, Xenophon instructed that a horseman should always seek and encourage a horse's voluntary compliance. Violence, punishment, and abuse were to be applied in limited situations and only brought diminishing returns.

In the words of Xenophon, "The one best rule and practice in dealing with a horse is never approach him in anger; for anger is a reckless thing, so that it often makes a man do what he must regret. . . . To force him with blows only increases his terror. . . ."[1]

With guidance on how to select, groom, feed, and care for a horse and direction on how to properly lead, walk, control, mount, and ride, Xenophon's writings implicitly prescribed the formation of a reciprocal partnership between horse and rider. At the crux of this partnership, riders must assume a dominant command position with their horse while constantly evaluating its level of comprehension, fear, interest, and contentment. A horse who is content will absorb skills and techniques through praise and positive reinforcement, rather than force and brutality. Xenophon's suggested training techniques went widely ignored through the course of his era and on through both the Dark and Middle Ages, when horses were violently beaten to the point of total submission or death. Long forgotten, his teachings first saw resurgence during the Renaissance, when Italian monks recovered and disseminated his treatise. Centuries later, Xenophon's observations of equine behavior and his recommended education methods still remain widely applicable to the breaking, handling, and training of the modern-era horse.

These days, most untrained horses are handled with patience, firm direction, and understanding. By his twelfth year, Samson had been schooled with bullwhips, lariat ropes, anger, and pain.

With a wealth of hardcase trainers I knew of in neighboring communities, I just assumed that some had tried their hand at Samson. There had been, as Amy told it, vets, farriers, cowboys, and even a couple of neighbors—strangers who had invaded her fenced fortress. Everybody wanted a crack at and declared that they could gentle, change, or cure Samson. And with little more than a boot placed onto the pasture fence, each met Samson the terrible.

From deep within his pasture he would charge, ears pinned back, head lowered, upper lip curled back, and teeth in full view. One trainer was bitten, a farrier was kicked, and one unlucky soul was trampled. Samson didn't take prisoners. I realized that I wasn't the best trainer for the job but, rather, the only one willing to venture into Samson's domain.

I took a step closer. Samson's enormous structural system

and stay apparatus—the ligaments, muscles, tendons, and bones—remained locked. His midsection shook with each tachycardic beat of his palpating heart, as if being hit with a club. As his lungs moved air, his nostrils cycled open, then closed, faster than I could process. But instead of rearing, bucking, biting or thrashing about, he waited, marshaling his strength and plotting his defense to my impending intrusion.

Samson stood primed and ready to launch. This horse was a thinker, a strategist, a warrior.

I couldn't help but notice two distinctively sized sets of bloody hind hoofprints on what was left of the barn's interior walls, and once my questioning went ignored I knew there was more to the story. After a lengthy pause, Amy explained that the other stallion fire refugee, the two-year-old, had on numerous occasions entered the barn and done battle with the imprisoned Samson. The two had fought bitterly, tearing down entire sections of the barn to get at each other, knocking stall doors off their hinges, kicking out walls. They had kicked and reared and used their teeth like chain saws, shredding each other down to the bone.

Amy had no idea how stallions behave, and the fact that Samson was the stallion's sire, the thought of a father and son committed to killing each other, turned her stomach. The two-year-old had since been shipped off while the battle scars remained.

Bloody battles fueled by testosterone and machismo. A reclusive damsel in distress trapped in her living room. A horse who could dodge flying shovels faster than a speeding bullet. *Run,* I told myself. *Get away while you still can.* But my heart felt for this caged beast, and my brain and my ego were challenged.

Samson the Mustang was untrained and unabashedly un-apologetic. I was both amused and intrigued.

As we stood there, Amy's younger sister Lisa stormed into the barn and stood against the far wall a safe distance from the stall. Samson shuddered but held his pose. I avoided di-rect eye contact with him, to prevent coming off as a threat. I'd eventually use eye focus to my advantage, though; a fixed stare on a horse's hindquarters can move him forward, while a steely gaze at the shoulder can move him laterally. No force or intimidation, and no need to shout or strike.

Ordinarily, a milking stall was about the worst place I could think of to meet a horse like this. In the best of all worlds, a sixty-foot-wide round pen is my first choice, be-cause it gives me space to move an animal off, redirect his motion, or stop him dead in his tracks. Alpha horses like Samson are masters at using body posturing and visual cues to control a herd. For a trainer, the round pen sets up that same kind of dynamic.

But all I had was an eight-by-ten-foot sardine can, far from ideal for me yet perfect for Samson the warrior. He repositioned his body onto a diagonal, with his rump near-est to the door and his head in the far right corner. He clev-erly created just a small triangle of space for me to maneuver in. Stuck between his body and the wall, I could be pum-meled with his hind legs, bitten, or bodychecked at will.

I wondered if Amy's choice of name for her Mustang was my first warning to steer clear. This was Samson, the Book of Judges' epic biblical figure, conceived to an infertile mother through the divine intervention of God and his messenger angel. As he was destined from birth to possess tremendous strength by virtue of his long locks of hair and to launch the deliverance of Israel from the rule of the Philistines, Samson's life was fated to be both heroic and tragic. With deity-like strength, he slew a lion with his own hands and, in the rage of battle, single-handedly slaughtered one thousand Philistines.

This was a figure of biblical proportion who knew no fear and bore no visible weakness. Tragedy nonetheless followed Samson, as his wife-to-be was burned at the stake and his second love, Delilah, betrayed him and had his locks of hair cut while he slept. With his locks removed, Samson's power and strength instantly vanished—his capture and fate were irrevocably sealed. Samson's Philistine captors soon took both his eyes and his freedom. As his final act in life, Samson fulfilled his destined role and collapsed a crowded temple's pillars, felling himself and three thousand Philistines.

In life, Samson was a proud character, at times too proud. He was a figure without a home, roaming back and forth between the polarized Hebrew and Philistine societies. He was hunted and punished not only for his ego and vanity but also for his marked differences. In death, Samson sacrificed himself, fulfilled his destiny, and delivered his people from their oppressors' hands.

Not unlike the first Samson, Samson the wild Mustang now stood caged and denied his freedom. All that I had seen and heard told me that he too was proud and prideful, possessing both tremendous strength and fortitude. If he had any weakness, Amy claimed that he had yet to show it. Like his three hundred thousand fellow Mustangs, he was snatched from the mountains and plains of his homeland, separated from his herd, and relocated to a holding facility. There and thereafter, he was forced to submit to a people and a way of life of which he knew nothing. And upon his refusal to submit, he was punished and brutalized for not knowing the ways of a domesticated horse. Beaten down—like the biblical Samson—for his differences.

The winter prior, he was known simply as "the Mustang." Amy said that her choice of name for this hardcase Mustang had been random, but I had my doubts.

I knew better than to enter the beast's cage, but in retrospect I don't think that Samson and I could have met in any other setting or in any other way. Confined in that stall, we were both forced to believe that neither would turn violent, to hope that neither would inflict harm or injury. We were both forced to belay our fears and trust in the other before trust had even been established.

I asked the women to move back down the aisle, so Samson could focus on me alone. Also, if I had to flee the stall, I didn't want the door slamming into either of them. Above all, I wanted to avoid stressing Samson any more than he already was.

Hands raised, Amy backed off down the aisle, with Lisa in tow. I removed the buttressing planks and laid them aside, then opened the stall door a foot or so. Looking down, I observed that the step up from the aisle to the raised concrete stall would complicate things; if I had to exit fast, I might wipe out and get stomped. Or Samson could catch a hoof in the gutter and break a leg.

This was not the right place to do this, but it was where

we were. There was just one chance to connect with Samson, and this was it.

"Hey, big guy," I said quietly. "How do you feel about me coming in there?"

"No way!" Amy shouted. "No one has ever gone into that stall with him still in there."

I don't know what I was thinking. I tried to look past all of Samson's warnings—the manic breathing, pinned ears, and body posturing—for some sign, any sign that said that I could enter his stall. Looking through and past his hard stare, I thought I saw profound sadness and longing. I thought I saw an animal who was tired of going it all on his own.

I saw a horse who needed a place to call home.

"You can trust me, buddy," I reassured Samson.

But the real question was, could I trust Samson?

2

FIRST CONTACT

To me, horses and freedom are synonymous.
—VERYL GOODNIGHT

During his early years, Samson the wild horse had been, to borrow Bob Seger's words, "living to run and running to live." Locked away in a stall, Samson was now stripped of both his freedom and his very essence.

Out West, his wild cousins had been faring no better. Powerful special-interest groups, the cattle and hunting lobby and fuel and mining conglomerates that coveted wild horse land, had been taking it, acre by acre. With wild horse herds zeroed out from six states, millions of acres of Mustang rangeland leased to oil and gas interests, and 20 million acres of wild horse habitat and 111 protected herd areas forever lost, the wild Mustang was losing the battle and the war. After so many years of hardship and survival, Samson and his free-roaming cousins were still fighting for their freedom.

I had made up my mind; I was going into the stall. Those who know me would say that from this point forward there would be no turning back.

Samson shifted weight between his hind legs. He nervously danced in place.

"When you're done with that little two-step of yours," I said, "maybe I'll just come on in there and we can get acquainted."

He breathed like he had just galloped the straights at Churchill Downs. His body posturing said that he was enveloped in fear and consumed with the desire to fight.

I was intrigued by what I saw before me. Most horses who suffer years of chronic abuse avert their gaze, droop their head, and stand with a low, slouched back and shrunken profile. Everything about them says that they are broken in mind, body, and spirit. Samson, however, stared hard into my eyes, his neck stood upright and erect, and his back sat taut and rounded. This horse was anything but broken.

Samson the Mustang had me perplexed where I should have been gravely alarmed.

Standing outside the stall, I could easily see only what the others had. The bug-eyed hard gaze, the pulsating nostrils, and the body posturing that spoke of imminent threat and certain violence. The horse who had punted minis, tossed goats like they were beanbags, shredded his offspring, and defeated the most hardened cowboys.

But where others had seen contempt and hatred, I saw just cause. Samson was an untrained, unschooled wild horse and he was a monster created by six years of brutality and cruelty. Yet he didn't seem to want my pity or sympathy. He wanted something else, something more. He wanted to be understood, and in that moment I felt that I was the only person who could understand him.

I was the only person who understood that inwardly Samson was a still wild and free-roaming, proud Mustang stallion, where outwardly he was a brutalized victim.

"Here I come, Samson. Nothing to get worked up over," I said, committed to it, stepping up into his stall, making sure to leave the door open a bit for a quick escape.

Down the aisle, one of the sisters caught her breath. Samson and I were now sharing the same space, breathing the same thick, rank air, and wondering what would come next. Though mere inches separated us, our experiences, our worlds, had been miles apart.

Time and space stood still. Nothing else moved; nothing else made a sound; nothing else mattered.

Samson stood about 14.2 hands high —or four feet ten inches—and his dark bay coat appeared dull in the weak light. A compact and narrow frame sat veiled beneath his strong personality and firmly established Napoleon complex. His dark black mane, tail, and forelock fell in burr-filled tangles. By virtue of the limited light, the whites of his eyes glowed while the balance of the horse remained hidden in the shadows.

The little that I could observe said that he was a mutt of a horse, yet something about his look was natural, untouched, and pure. Unrefined features spoke to the fact that planned domesticated breeding was foreign to his world. Though the freeze mark branded on his neck at the time of capture estimated his year of birth as 1997, to me he more resembled Earth's first horse—dawn horse.

Standing hidden in the shadows atop his concrete pedestal, though he remained mostly a mystery, Samson was nature's horse and God's gift to man.

Even underweight, his body was muscular and elegant.

His watchful almond eyes seemed to say, *If you come close, puny man, I will put you down.* The choking smell of dung, urine, and Samson's yeasty breath forced tears from my eyes. Under these cramped, miserable circumstances, most horses would do anything to flee. But I could see Samson was different.

Unlike other horses, Samson would choose to stand and fight.

With his left front leg angled slightly out to the side, he could rotate on a dime and give me a lethal body check. His right hind hoof hovered off the ground, cocked and ready to shatter my legs. Standing parallel to and just inches from Samson's side, I knew it was imperative to keep in mind that horses have marginal eyesight alongside their body, and blind spots in front of the muzzle and directly behind the rump. Any movement on my part from within these zones would most certainly lead to an immediate defensive response.

I had to micromanage my moves. If I inadvertently swatted at a fly or scratched my chin, I could get trampled. If I sneezed, I might get cow-kicked or head-butted. I had to orchestrate every facet of my presentation to this horse to come across as respectful and calm.

"Easy, big boy," I said. The muscles in his right shoulder flexed and quivered; the air rushing through his muzzle sounded like the intake of a jet engine. Close now to his right side, I glanced into his eye and saw what I felt was profound, entrenched fear.

I knew I didn't have much time left. Like a wild animal with its foot caught in a trap, Samson was scared stiff. I was his enemy, and the last thing he wanted was help from anything on two legs. I had never felt this level of terror in all my years of working with traumatized horses—it was palpable, heartbreaking.

To relieve the tension, I decided to speak to Samson as if he were one of my legal clients. Having practiced as a litigator for the last fifteen years, I had dealt with many a difficult client. I enjoyed the law, but horse training had always excited me more. Reshaping a ton of maladjusted horse made me come alive.

Other than the fact that he could send me to my maker, Samson was no different from any of my legal clients: threatening, standoffish, and wearing a huge chip on his shoulder.

"Okay, Samson, what do you say we broker a deal? I'm a lawyer, so everything's negotiable. I won't hurt you if you don't hurt me. You trust me, I'll trust you. We'll have a meeting of the minds; we'll have a contract."

Samson blinked, then stared hard into my eyes, taking my measure, looking down into me. His gaze now seemed almost appreciative, so I made a decision and returned the stare, talking quietly. Our gazes locked, inputting information the way a computer instantly translates thousands of bytes of data. In a matter of seconds, it was as if we had each viewed the other's complete life story.

I hoped that he saw that I was a good person, that I cared for him, and that I meant him no harm.

The ball was in his court now. Something about this horse had made me go well past the point of safety; if he wanted to, he could unload on me, and he knew it. With just one ill-timed movement Samson would explode on me, and Amy and her sister would be left to mop up my gelatinous remains.

And then a remarkable thing happened; the hardened

Mustang let out a long, exhaustive sigh, as if he'd been holding his breath for the last six years. Previously wound taut as a rubber band, Samson's rigid frame softened ever so slightly.

"There you go, boy."

Moving as if underwater, I reached out to him. Only focus and predictability would keep me alive.

He whipped his head to the right and parked his nostrils directly in my hand's path. With his eyes focused square on my own, Samson blew out a torrent of hot air into my face.

I reached out the rest of the way and touched his shoulder. A violent shudder coursed through him; he recoiled and crow-hopped away from me.

I waited.

I watched him struggle within himself, his eyes wide, his chest heaving. "Come on, boy," I said, grinning.

Behind me, the women whispered. I ignored them. "Think about it," I said to Samson. He shifted his weight onto his right legs, leaned toward me, then shifted weight back onto his left limbs, returning to his distant position.

"He's thinking about putting you down," said Amy.

Back and forth he went, leaning in, then away, as if someone were rewinding and fast-forwarding him.

After what seemed an eternity, Samson shuffled back over, inches from where I stood. For the first time in six years, this wild horse was in something other than defense and dispatch mode.

Under Samson's bug-eyed stare, I again laid my hand upon his shoulder. This time he didn't recoil.

"Son of a bitch!" Amy yelled.

"*Shh.*"

I looked at his face. I was confused; was he wearing a halter? I could see straps running alongside his cheeks, a noseband. Then, horrified, I realized what I was actually seeing. The Mustang's face bore the seared imprint of a halter left on his face for years after it had grown too tight.

Our eyes locked. For an instant, it seemed that he was trying to tell me about what he'd been through for all those years—his capture, the terror of internment, the beatings—as if he wanted someone, anyone, to understand.

"Easy, boy." I rubbed him in tiny circles, mimicking the circular motions horses made with their mouths while grooming herd mates. Tracing the angle of his neck, my fingers found deep, embedded scars—more painful reminders of the rope and years of pain. His chest felt like a topographic map, with a lattice of raised scars, many inflicted by combative stallions, others by bullwhips, lariats, and other tools of man. There was barely a smooth patch of skin to be found.

"I don't know what you've been through since they caught you, old boy, but I know where you came from," I told him. "I know who you are."

Samson was supposed to be one of the lucky ones. He wasn't standing knee-deep in a BLM short-term mud lot corral or imprisoned in a long-term holding facility. He had snaked his way through the BLM's Adopt-a-Horse-or-Burro Program, but the adoption that was supposed to save him had instead damned him. BLM rules and guidelines designed to protect adopted Mustangs had failed Samson and thousands others like him. And now he was shut off, just wanting to be left alone.

The BLM claims that it has respected and followed the mandates of the 1971 Act when managing and culling this nation's free-roaming wild horses. Mustang advocates and animal welfare organizations alike disagree. Unlike an estimated 90 percent of captured wild Mustangs, Samson had not met his fate in a slaughterhouse. Yet despite this reprieve, his tale had been no less dark, no less sad.

As my hand ran across the ridges and divots, Samson flinched as if his scars were fresh again, as if my touch had reawakened memories of those long days of pain. But then, as if embarrassed by his moment of weakness, he quickly raised up his head, straightened up his posture, and stood tall, proud of who he was and what he'd endured.

He sported his scars like each was the Kentucky Derby's 564 red rose–laden Garland of Roses. Nothing, it seemed, could beat this horse down. I couldn't help but admire this proud and prideful Mustang.

The moment seemed right to try a test. "Can someone pass me the halter hanging over by Studs' stall?"

I reached up above the stall door and took the halter from Amy as Samson shot her a hard look. When she returned the gesture moments later, there was little left to the imagination—these two simply did not get along. As the halter came into view, Samson instantly rotated left and planted his face into the stall's far corner, hindquarters cocked and ready to kick. I quickly handed the halter back to Amy.

"You're okay, Samson. You and halters have quite the history, don't you?"

The halter now gone, Samson shuffled out of his corner and rejoined my company.

I gradually raised and then extended my arm out to him. For the next several minutes, I rubbed Samson's neck and shoulder until it came time for the day's second test. Slowly,

I removed my hand and left it suspended in midair, some three inches from Samson's shoulder.

For six long years this horse had fought and won countless battles with myriad enemies, and his herd would be proud. He was a survivor and he had held out for a long time—too long. Now was the time for Samson to drop his guard and make a new start.

After a moment of deliberation, Samson, like a cruise ship edging into its berth, lumbered right until my hand and his body met. Tremor after tremor shot through him. It was his head and heart, fighting again.

"Oh my god, he *came* to you," said Amy.

"Imagine that," I said, Samson's muscles pulsing beneath my hand.

Despite his imprinted fear of man, despite years in the domestic horse market where he had been subject to unimaginable abuse, this horse stoically and passively permitted the enemy to enter his world. With very little thought and even less effort, he could have put me down. Nonetheless, Samson didn't punt me through the door and he didn't trample me to the ground.

By twelve years of age, Samson had grown terribly alone and truly lonely. Exiled, solitary, and needing no one, he nonetheless still held out hope that man could be kind, caring, and compassionate. Samson's heart, close to dead for far too many years, had won out over his head's prudent warnings and caution. He, we, had both made a huge leap of faith.

Though I'd been in with Samson for twenty minutes now, I had yet to actually look him over in his entirety. With him now somewhat composed, I took the time to do just that.

Over the years, I had evaluated and handled other wild

horses. Just three years back, I'd spent several months training a Mustang gelding similar in size, shape, stature, and coloring to other horses. But his spirit and character were like
nothing I'd dealt with before.

And so it was with Samson, only there was more. It wasn't
his wild roots that made Samson so dangerous and unpredictable. It was the horrendous abuse he'd taken over the
years. That, mixed with the total lack of the companion-
ship horses need to feel right in their hearts, had turned Samson into an engine of hate and rage. Despite that, he let me
in, let me touch him, let me live. However deeply he had
buried them, he still held memories of being part of something bigger and better, something ordinary and familial.
The idea that he still grieved over the loss of these things,
after all the years of internment and abuse, broke my heart.

"He is a true Mustang." I said aloud. "And he's not crazy.
Just abused, scared, terribly sad, and angry at the world." I
rubbed his neck. "I bet you made those BLM contractors
earn their pay." He turned his head and stared at me. I lifted
my hand but kept it suspended. Reaching his muzzle over,
Samson took in the newfound smell of a gentling hand.

For perhaps the first time in his life, he felt something
other than the bullwhip's lacerating blows, the lariat's
choking constriction, and the pain associated with repeti-
tive blunt-force trauma.

Then, everything changed. Without warning, he leapt
straight up and slapped at the concrete floor with his right
hoof, the sound of it like a bolt of lightning cleaving pine.
He spun around and shot out two rapid-fire, dual-legged
hind-end kicks at me, both missing my chest by inches, the
wind from them fluttering my shirt.

He turned and stared, this time with the look of a man about to turn into a werewolf. *Get out while you still can.*

I backed out slowly and slipped through the door. Samson was still staring at me, breathing like Darth Vader. What had happened?

Then I heard the sound of an approaching helicopter. I secured his stall door with the planks as the sound of the helicopter slowly faded away.

"You almost got killed, and you're smiling," said Lisa.

I was. Though being trapped in Samson's stall during his meltdown was anything but enjoyable, it gave me the chance to understand one of this horse's many demons. His most feared and despised demon, in fact. It had chased him for miles through mountain passes, separated and destroyed his family, and ripped him away from the only home he had ever known. Samson knew to flee and evade, but locked in his stall he could do neither. He was a trapped soldier and a gladiator without armor as his greatest foe prepared to swoop down from the clouds and take away what little he had left.

Don Quixote had his windmills, Ahab had his whale, and Samson had the helicopter.

Samson stared at me, his face now vacant and hollow, without the light I'd seen in it when we'd connected. Now he seemed opaque, hopeless. His was a thousand-yard stare, weighted down by sadness and despair. Fleetingly intrigued by my attention, Samson was once again alone and caged. Like his brothers, sisters, and cousins—now near fifty thousand strong—confined in BLM holding facilities throughout the country, lifeless, listless, and hopeless.

They were all horses who had survived in their world only to suffer and die in ours.

"I can't give you back what you once had," I told him. "No one can. But you deserve to at least get out of this stall, and act like the horse you once were."

My brief time with Samson, Amy's accounts, and my observations told me that this was the most troubled and haunted horse I had ever come across. Samson was boiling over with rage, contempt, and fear. He was allegedly perpetually angry, socially dysfunctional, maladjusted, and hated anything and everything on two and four legs. And yet he spared me. For some reason, this horse still held out hope that he was wrong, that I, that we, could be so much better.

As Amy walked me to my truck, I asked what she planned for Samson. "There's only one plan," she said. "I can't keep a horse like this here, Mitch. Either he gets broke and mounted, or he'll have to go, and I don't think anyone out there will take him."

Her answer left me confused. I could understand if Amy wanted Samson to be taught the basics such as how to respect her space, walk under lead, and harness his temper. But as for this Mustang being mounted, that seemed highly unlikely. Yet Amy stuck to her guns; this lawless wild Mustang needed to have a saddle and rider atop his back. He needed to be normal, like every other horse, an all-or-nothing proposition for Samson.

The gravity of Amy's response shook me to my core. This was the last thing that I wanted to hear. My twenty years in the horse world had recently taken a toll: I had countless injuries that could be traced back to owners misrepresenting their horses' issues, and organizations taking advantage of my donated services had disillusioned me. I had become a disenchanted crash test dummy. The icing on the cake was when, just weeks before, a husband and wife had sold a horse who had been promised to me. The Quarter Horse had been like a brother to me and I was crushed.

For fifteen years, I'd been the only one who could mount him. For fifteen years, I didn't charge for my services and instead waited patiently to call him my own. He was an amazing and gifted athlete and a cantankerous, combative, and moody pupil. But after a neighboring horseman witnessed one of our rides, his fate was sealed. With ten thousand dollars in hand his owners trailered him off with not so much as a phone call.

I was fed up with horse owners, their dishonesty and deceit, and all the drama. I would not get attached to another hard case. I was done with horse training, prepared to give up my one true passion.

I wasn't there to rescue or rehabilitate Samson. I was there to evaluate Studs, and as I had finished my exam and concluded that a knee injury would delay his donation to the riding center, my responsibilities were now complete.

But what if Samson needed me?

As an aging, set-in-his-ways, stallion-like formerly wild horse, Samson would be a true challenge to even the most accomplished trainer. These attributes alone would make Samson nearly impossible to school. Factor in his abusive and oppressive last six years and the lethal mix had created an explosively violent, solitary beast. Samson seemed well past the point of reeducation, socialization, and training.

He was far from the elixir I needed to cure my ills. Was I even up to the challenge? I was torn.

Lacking the most basic of skills required to function in the domesticated horse market, Samson's survival had been cast in doubt the moment that the BLM placed him at auction. Samson now needed time. Time to let his guard down, time to breathe a first sigh of relief. Time to comprehend that he had finally found a true and safe home.

I counseled Amy to stay out of Samson's pasture, forget their rocky beginnings, and start anew. Since bullwhips and ropes were the only training aids familiar to this horse, I suggested that they avoid approaching him with any training equipment in hand—no matter how benign. Familiarity, comfort, and understanding would all come in time and with patience. For a horse like Samson, routines would bring stability and stability would bring security.

"Why don't *you* just work with him?" Amy questioned. "I really don't want anyone coming around here, but I guess I can manage with you."

It was a question I couldn't answer and so I let it go by. "Look—no horse should be locked away in a stall," I said, climbing into my truck. "Especially him."

Amy stood silent and expressionless. Though I couldn't quite put my finger on it, something was off. She appeared nervous, anxious, prickly, and at times awkward. My help had been requested, yet I was left to feel like a trespasser. She was there and conversing with me, yet her thoughts seemed a million miles away. Amy seemed spent. Minus the violence and intimidation, she came across as the two-legged version of her four-legged captive: alone, unhappy, and shut off.

As I gazed upon her, it was apparent that in her multiple acts of compassion, by making herself a modern-day version of Noah, Amy had thoroughly overtaxed herself and her resources. Her home had evolved into a veritable stockyard replete with geese and chickens, ewes, two sets of trip-let lambs, goats, a pregnant mare, a pony, and the three larger horses. A Noah's Ark, with the flood replaced with fire and a run-down dairy farm standing in for the ark itself. In no time, the fire refugees had overrun Amy's safe haven.

With scenes from *Wild Kingdom* playing out on her front lawn, somewhere between the bloody stallion battles and all the injured amateur horse professionals, Amy's dream of a tranquil home in the country had turned into a nightmare. I couldn't be certain, but a part of me believed that though she was the one who'd brought all on board, Amy now re-sented her animal charges for violating the serenity of her newly acquired rural sanctuary.

I couldn't bring myself to agree with Amy's assessment that she'd have no success in any attempt to find Samson a new home. Just as I didn't tell her that she and Samson were now stuck with each other. I slammed the door and drove off, leaving her there in the driveway. As I made my way back to the city, I thought of Samson in his milking stall, lonely, all alone, and without a future.

A description of the captured wild horse from J. Frank Dobie's book *The Mustangs* echoed through my head: "When he stood trembling with fear before his captor, bruised from falls by the restrictive rope, made submissive by choking, clogs, cuts and starvation, he had lost what made him so beautiful and free. Illusion and reality had alike been de-stroyed. Only the spirited are beautiful."

Despite all he'd been through, Samson was still beautiful. He hadn't lost his fire, his pride, or his spirit. It was something to see. It was something to look up to. It was a thought I could not shake.

This horse was something different. This horse was something special.

For the first time in my career, I saw a little bit of myself in a horse. Samson had his solitude and contempt, but a lonely life in his dark, cramped stall, his hate of other horses, and his disdain for humans now had him completely shut down. I had my legal career and my work with the horses, but something was missing. We both thought that what we had was working, but it wasn't.

My frustrations and injuries over the past months had curbed my desire to continue training. My years as a litigator had taught me to be calm, cool, and detached. But Samson had touched a chord in me, and I thought that, maybe, just maybe, I'd done the same to him. For a brief moment, the flame that had fueled my passion for training rekindled.

Amy, Samson, and I—we were all in search of something. Perhaps what we each needed was the help of the others.

3

THE RECONQUISTA

*Wherever man has left his footprint in
the long ascent from barbarism to civilization
we will find the hoofprint of the horse beside it.*

—JOHN MOORE

For decades, and despite its storied lineage and historical significance, critics have assailed the wild Mustang as a feral, invasive, and nonnative species. The policy favoring native over nonindigenous species can be traced to a 1963 report to the North American Wildlife Conference that directed government conservation efforts to only those animals that were present at the time of the Conquistadors' arrival—leaving all remaining nonnative and imported species to be considered "undesirable." As a result, state and federal agencies now follow a legal mandate that protects all native wildlife and natural ecosystems from all nonnative, invasive species.

Deemed by government officials as "reintroduced" rather than native, the North American wild horse has long since been considered one of these invasive species. It is now labeled by many as a feral interloper, a designation that not only defies logic but further disregards present-day molecular genetics studies that have established conclusive genetic equivalency between the equids that walked the continent prior to the Ice Age and the modern horse.

Wild or not, returned or reintroduced, the horse was one of North America's original inhabitants. In order to fully comprehend the debate over wild horse protection and conservation efforts, one has to first understand the history of the horse.

The first horse, "dawn horse"—otherwise known as *Eohippus*—walked this planet some 55 to 60 million years ago and bore little resemblance to the wild Mustang who remained locked in his stall. Fossilized remains unearthed in 1931 from Wyoming's Big Horn Basin depict the dawn horse as a twelve-pound animal measuring nearly fourteen inches in height. Its back arched, eyes centrally located in a small, short face, and with three molars implanted on each side of its jaw, dawn horse looked less like a horse and more like a small dog or fox. Unlike the modern horse, its legs were equally proportionate. With four toes supported by a pad on its forefeet, and three toes on its hind feet, *Eohippus* was well suited for movement in early Earth's tropical rain forest–like habitat.

Over time, *Eohippus* wandered from its natural environs and migrated across the existing land bridges to South America, Europe, and Asia. Whereas early theories proposed that the modern horse's earliest ancestors first evolved in Asia, generally accepted principle now dictates that the dawn horse evolved on, and traveled forth from, the North American continent. Like it or not, the first horses and all subsequent descendants were a species native to North America.

As millions of years passed and the habitat changed, evolution and natural selection were hard at work. Roughly 35 to 40 million years ago, *Mesohippus* evolved with disproportionate legs, three toes on the forefeet, premolar incisor teeth, and eyes located farther apart allowing for a greater lateral field of vision. With a longer muzzle, a prominent load-carrying toe, greater speed, and measuring close to forty inches at the shoulder, *Mercyhippus* walked the earth 20 to 25 million years ago and was the first of its kind to bear some resemblance to the present-day horse. *Pliohippus,* which lived roughly 6 million years ago and has been labeled by many as the "grandfather" of the modern horse, measured forty-eight inches in height at the shoulder, and was the earliest one-toed equid and the species' first true grazer.

Equus caballus, the "true horse," emerged 5 million years later. Standing near 13.2 hh (54 in) at five times the size of the dawn horse, in appearance *Equus caballus* most closely resembled a donkey. With a field of vision close to 360 degrees and an auditory system that tracked sound the way a torpedo zeroed in on its target, this was a living defense and survival apparatus. Able to reach a top speed of nearly 30 miles per hour, it was smarter, faster, and better equipped for life's rigors than the sum of its earlier versions. Following the path of its ancestors, 1 million years ago *Equus caballus* traveled across the land bridges to South America, Asia, Europe, and Africa. There, with the passage of time and the operation of evolution, the true horse gave rise to an additional twelve species, including Africa's asses and zebras and the Middle East's onagers.

Nearly 1.6 million years ago, the melting of the land bridge across the Bering Strait announced the arrival of the

Pleistocene era. The North American continent was cut off, isolated, and the Ice Age was prepared to claim its victims en masse. Then, roughly ten thousand years ago, countless species, including sloths, mastodons, and *Equus caballus* fell victim to climate change, food shortage, and a new predator— man. Death and extinction followed for all. With the equine population soon extinct on the North American continent, the species' survival resided with those horses that had previously migrated across the land bridges.

In order for the wild and feral ancient horse to survive, primitive peoples had to first alter their perceptions of the beast that danced with the wind. Fossilized evidence indicates that primitive cultures living around 10,000 BC viewed the horse as little more than a source of food. These early horses were run off cliffs or chased into walled valleys and beaten to death. By 9,000 BC, the formerly nomadic primitive populations of Iraq's Tigris and Euphrates river valleys had shifted to a static, agrarian subsistence. Wild feral horses were then tracked, captured, and penned and soon became an integral part of these agrarian-based societies.

With the dog previously domesticated in 12,000 BC, sheep in 9,000 BC, and goats, pigs, and chickens by 7,000 BC, domestication of the horse was not far off. One to two thousand years later, and predating the invention of the wheel by five hundred years, horses in Scythia's Dnieper River region were mounted and ridden. The wild, feral horse had entered a new era.

DNA tests published in 2009 reveal that by 3600 BC farmers in the Ponto-Caspian region had employed selective breeding to produce herds with predetermined colors, traits, and physical attributes. Horses with desired attributes were rebred; those less desirable were discarded. As the horse settled into its new role as a means of transport and as farmers became more proficient at selective breeding, the equine population skyrocketed. From this era forward, the modern horse was to carry primitive civilization's advance upon its back.

By the twelfth century, the horse of the Old World had galloped into its role as the pivotal factor differentiating between victory and defeat on the battlefield. Newly revered and esteemed, it first found preeminence when Genghis Khan and his skilled horsemen warriors conquered northern China mounted atop their trusted steeds. No longer a mere means to get from point A to point B, riding was now a learned, technique-driven skill set. As horses were ridden with increasing frequency and assigned greater responsibilities, the proficiency of those who rode atop their backs correspondingly improved. Preserved Assyrian illustrations depict that by the eighth century riders had transitioned from the "donkey position"—seated back at the loins—to the "modern position," seated forward at the horse's withers.

Initially a wild and feral beast, the Old World horse was now a vessel of sport, achievement, and subjugation. Gliding across foreign lands on four thinly sculpted legs carrying one thousand pounds of muscle and bone, *Equus caballus* was a conqueror and empire builder all in one. Once nothing more than a next meal, the horse had become a prized possession to kings and emperors alike. Ruins excavated in the 1930s at Siberia's Pazyryk Tombs reveal that the late-fourth- and early-third-century horse was a significant asset in both life and the afterlife. There archaeologists uncovered five tombs frozen in ice and perfectly preserved. Each tomb contained fourteen horses with braided tails, trimmed manes, bridles, harnesses, saddlecloths, and decorative headdresses.

Similarly, in perhaps one of mankind's greatest archaeological finds, excavation at the tomb of Qin Shi Huang—the first emperor of the Chinese Qin dynasty—unearthed a mausoleum containing life-size terra-cotta figures representing 500 chariot and 116 cavalry horses. Discoveries at both sites yielded the unmistakable conclusion that among the kingdoms of the Old World the horse had achieved elevated and preferential status. An essential possession in life, it was now a necessity in death as well.

While the societies of the Western world were slowly figuring out the complex interrelationship between horse and rider, the desert tribes of the East were busy breeding and inbreeding their herds—creating what was to eventually become the foundation stock for the present-day horse. These small yet sturdy horses—the Arabian and the Barb—bred and raised under the harshest of desert conditions and the strictest of man-imposed standards, proved unrivaled and unmatched in their endurance and strength, soundness, constitution, and conformation.

Arabia's Bedu tribes first chronicled the history of the Arabian horse in AD 786, successfully tracing breed pedigrees to 3,000 BC. Bedu legend, however, tracks the reign of the Arabian horse back to Adam, on to the era of King Solomon, then through to Mohammed's lifetime and beyond. By virtue of its 17 ribs, 5 lumbar vertebrae, and 16 tail bones—contrasted with an 18-6-18 ratio for all other horses—the Arabian, with its short, compact, and concave back and high-set tail, is readily distinguishable and uniquely singular from all other members of its species. In profile, its forehead is convex; the face, concave or dished. The refined Arabian head tapers to a small, delicate muzzle with large, flaring nostrils. Its eyes are richly dark in color yet soulful, expressive, and alert. When the Arabian moves out, it appears to be floating through time and space by way of invisible springs implanted in its legs.

The Barb horse, first bred by North Africa's Berbers, originated from a vast area that encompassed modern-day North Africa, Morocco, Libya, and Algeria. Also raised in the desert's unforgiving climate, the Barb's defining characteristics were its endurance, strength, agility, speed, and unstable temper. Similar to the Arabian, it required little food and water to sustain itself. Lacking the Arabian's floating gracefulness and delicate features, this desert steed was the workhorse of the pair. The Barb was easily distinguished from its counterpart by its long, convex head and face. Its shoulders were flat and upright, the chest deep and narrow. Its hindquarters sloped from the high point of the back down to a low-set tail. Crossbred with the Arabian during the eighth- and seventh-century Muslim invasions, the Barb nonetheless retained its distinguishing characteristics.

Beginning in the Early Middle Ages, these two similar yet different cousins were to immeasurably alter their species. By the arrival of the Early Modern Era, the Barb and Arabian's hot blood had crossed foreign territories, continents, and oceans and forever transformed the breeding, conformation, and bloodlines of the modern-day horse.

Following Mohammed's death in 632, Muslim armies set out on conquests and defeated enemies in the Middle East, the Byzantine Empire, Mesopotamia, Armenia, North Africa, the Indus Valley, and Central Asia. Years later in 711, ten thousand Moorish soldiers riding atop Arabian and Barb mounts crossed the Strait of Gibraltar, conquered the Visigoths, and took Spain. The large, slow-moving Spaniard mounts, European bred to carry armored knights, presented little challenge to the smaller, faster, and agile Arabian and Barb warhorses. Recognizing that their steeds were no longer suited to modern warfare, the Spaniards immediately bred the superior Arabian and Barb horses to larger Iberian breeds such as the Norse Dun.

The result, the Jennet, was fast, sprightly, and exceptionally intelligent. Over the course of the next eight centuries, the Spaniards continued selectively breeding and refining the highly sought-after characteristics of the two desert warhorses. By 1492, the year in which Spain conquered the last remaining Moorish stronghold of Granada, Andalusia and Seville were synonymous with the production of Europe's greatest and most sought-after steed—the Spanish horse. The horse destined to be the steed of the Conquistadors.

Desired by Europe's royalty and nobility, the Spanish horse would soon occupy a far greater and historically significant role than that of coveted breeding stock. Linked by DNA evidence to the horses that first crossed and then exited the North American continent near 1 million years ago, the horse of the Conquistadors was to follow in its ancient ancestors' hoofprints and embark on a historic journey. Horse hooves would once again grace North American terra firma. And in much the same fashion that the early equids had ventured across the land bridge and fathered various related species throughout Eurasia, the Spanish horse would father a new breed of horse—the North American wild Mustang.

When Spaniard Hernán Cortés landed in Mexico in April

of 1519, his force included 600 infantry, 250 Indians, and 16 Spanish horses. As the first horse disembarked and deposited its hoof in the soft, wet sand, *Equus caballus'* journey had come full circle. The horse of the Old World was now the horse of the New World. Having traveled across continents and oceans, survived inhospitable humans and bloody battles, having persevered through desert heat and mountain chill, the horse had returned to its land of birth and birthright.

On the hunt for huge stores of native gold, Cortés' equine force consisted of eleven stallions and five mares. The first sight of these hard-charging eleven-hundred-pound beasts— laden in armor from head to tail—left the native Aztec peoples terrified and bewildered. Mystified by the sheer size and power of the animals who carried the Spanish warriors, the Aztecs presented little opposition to their two- and four-legged invaders. In Cortés' own words, "next to God, we owed our victory to the horses."[2] Following Cortés' subsequent conquest of the capital city of Tenochtitlán and the defeat of the Aztecs, the Spanish Conquistadors set their sights on the continent's virgin interior lands.

Led by 558 Spanish horses and fueled by a lust to discover the legendary Seven Cities of Gold, Spaniard Francisco Vasquez de Coronado set out in 1539—traveling into the vast expanse of what was later to become Arizona, New Mexico, Texas, and Oklahoma. Coronado's expedition soon encountered the native Great Plains Indian tribes, and, in turn, the Plains tribes first encountered the horse. While some tribes feared this great and powerful beast, still others worshiped the horse—viewing it as a symbol and vessel of their holy spirits. As their apprehension subsided, many tribes turned to pilfering the Conquistadors' most prized possession—their Spanish mounts.

By the late sixteenth and early seventeenth centuries, the Spanish had established various horse farms in and around Santa Fe, New Mexico. When Don Juan de Oñate arrived in the Santa Fe area in 1598 accompanied by seven thousand animals, including horses, cows, and donkeys, the climate was ripe for conflict between the native Indians and the Spaniards. By the close of the seventeenth century, Santa Fe's horse population had swelled into the thousands. With this growth, the Indian horse raids grew increasingly frequent and successful. Eventually, the Indians overran Santa Fe and chased the Spaniards from their settlement. The thousands of remaining Spanish horses, subsequently acquired, ridden, and traded by the Indians, became the foundation stock for the Great Plains wild horse herds and the famous Indian Mustang warhorse.

As horses escaped from the Spanish expeditions and settlements and as countless others were stolen by the native tribes, the Spanish horse of the Conquistadors became an ever-present fixture on the unspoiled Great Plains. Spanish explorers and settlers identified these free-roaming horses by various terms imported from their homeland. *Caballos silvestres* and *caballos salvajes* translated to English as feral animals who belonged to the wilderness. *Cimarrón,* a term that in its original form was associated with a runaway slave, represented an ownerless animal.

While these and other expressions were utilized to describe the ever-increasing wild horse populace, each failed to gain widespread acceptance. Not a one seemed sufficient until the Spanish term *mesteño* took hold. As a Spanish idiom developed to identify animals lost in transit to their summer and winter ranges, *mesteños* were sheep who went missing from the Mesta—an organization of sheep owners. By the early nineteenth century, the free-roaming horses of the Plains were being identified by the English derivation of *mesteño*—"Mustang."

The New World now had a name for its newest, yet oldest, inhabitant—the Mustang horse.

Despite eight centuries of breeding, the Spanish horses of the Cortés expedition and those that followed bore a striking resemblance to their ancestors: the Arabian and Barb desert warhorses. After centuries of selective breeding, the defining Arabian and Barb characteristics had become synonymous with the Conquistadors' horses. While many Spanish mounts closely resembled the Arabian, still others carried the Barb's dominant characteristics. Countless remaining horses possessed features readily identifiable with both breeds. These dual-featured horses became known as the Spanish Andaluz Mustang.

It was a horse first bred on one continent destined for greatness on another.

The years 1640 to 1880 have been identified by anthropologists as the age of horse culture and the period of the Indian horse. During this time, the wild Mustang ruled the western frontier's grasses, prairies, ranges, and mountains. Galloping across these virgin lands, and gifted with superhero-like strength, speed, and resilience, it was an animal that would forever alter the Indian people and the Indian way of life. Over time, as the wild horse's numbers and skills increased, so grew the native tribes' fortunes. And once early American culture and society had advanced, the reign of the wild horse and the fortunes and prosperity of the native peoples would promptly recede. But to the end, the Mustang horse—a compatriot in life, battle, and death—would remain loyal and true to the native tribes.

In the years following the 1680 Indian-led raid on Santa Fe, the native warriors were hard at work figuring out their latest and greatest possession. If one ventured upon a mounted warrior, it was certain that his steed bore a Spanish brand. Out on the range, decommissioned Spanish mounts and free-roaming tribal horses soon populated the once barren and lifeless vast plains. In no time, these runaway and retired horses reproduced and the frontier soon had its first generation of ownerless, unbranded wild horses—the first true American Mustangs.

As the tribal herds increased exponentially, the Mustang assumed a vital and ever-present role in Indian life. The Great Plains tribes—the Cheyenne, Arapaho, Crow, Gros Ventre, Mandan, Arikara, Lakota, Dakota, and Blackfoot—quickly mastered the art of controlling and riding these spirited beasts. Many warriors possessed anywhere from fifty to two hundred horses; tribal herds often numbered close to sixteen thousand head. Among the swelling numbers, two horses were prized possessions: the buffalo-catcher and the Indian warhorse. So vital to a brave, these horses were often tied to a warrior's wrist or hitched to a tent peg during slumber. Well-trained and fine-tuned, both the buffalo-catcher and the warhorse were taught to respond to leg cues so that a mounted brave had complete use of his hands.

Depicted as early as the 1830s by artists George Catlin and Alfred Jacob Miller, the Indian horse and the wild Mustang were detailed with ". . . the compact body, graceful carriage, high-carried tail and refined head, with tapering muzzle and concave face, of the Arabian type."[3] Though the Mustang was a small horse, appearances were deceptive. In describing the Indian horse, one European cavalryman observed "only now and then noble animals of beautiful form." Still, he concluded, "it is unbelievable how much the Indians can accomplish with their horses, what burdens they are able to carry, and what great distances they can cover in a short time."[4]

While the Indian horse lacked beauty and size, the Native Americans knew that they had discovered something special: an animal that would hunt until its prey was downed, an ally in battle that would fight until the last enemy was defeated, and a companion that would run until there was no ground left to cover.

In short order, the Mustang horse became the focal point of Indian culture. Constant turnover and escape fueled the need for more horses as the Native Americans sought out and captured many of the frontier's free-roaming horses. According to Mustang chronicler J. Frank Dobie, the tribes with closest affiliations to the Spanish explorers were the first to develop the ability to rope and capture the free-roaming wild horse. On the hunt, groups of braves would target a wild Mustang, run it ragged, rope it around the windpipe, and then choke it down to the ground. Once the horse was incapacitated and tied, a brave would blow in its nose, allow it to rise, mount it, and then ride the bucks out of the crazed beast. Over time, the native tribes turned to other methods of capture, including pens, traps, and decoy mares.

As the Indian way of life and the Mustang horse became inextricably intertwined, the distinction between the two- and four-legged species started to blur. The buffalo-catcher held in its lungs the breath of deceased Indian ancestors. The great warhorse carried on its back the spirits of great chiefs and warriors long since lost in battle. An ever-trusted mount, the Mustang was a link to the past and a means of survival in the present.

All who subscribed to tribal life revered and respected the Mustang horse. As recounted by Chief Bobby Yellowtail of the Crow:

> They were called by the white men "old Indian Cayuses." That was a kind of impolite name for an inferior breed of horses. But we developed those kind of horses that could catch up with the buffalo and run right into the herd. It takes a real horse to do that! And he was a prince of a horse, and the Indians called him "his buffalo-catcher." Now that's the kind of horse we developed. He could go clear down to Nebraska country and come back. No oats! No hay! Live off of what he could pick up on the road. No shoes! Live on sagebrush . . . whatever he could find. We had a superior horse, although he had no pedigree. His pedigree was Indian Cayuse.[5]

Over the course of years and then decades, the great Indian tribes bore witness to the strength, power, and spirit of the great horse of the frontier. They learned to muster and then harness the strength, power, and spirit of the American wild Mustang.

For the native tribes, the only item more coveted than a buffalo-catcher steed was a warrior's warhorse, often one and the same, oftentimes not. The warhorse was a true prized possession. A warrior in its own right, the Mustang warhorse was not for menial tasks. Not mounted until the final moments before battle, the Indian warhorse was afforded all of the respect and care of a partner in battle. Gifted with speed, intelligence, and agility, this marvelous specimen was preserved solely and singularly for the rigors of combat. As such, the warhorse took part in a ritualized prebattle ceremony that turned it into an awe-inspiring walking, visual declaration of war.

Painted in bright colors, adorned with herbs, eagle and bear claws, and objects said to possess magical properties, the warhorse was a walking and breathing symbol of Indian cultural mores. Emboldened with painted symbols vertically from the poll to the hoof and horizontally from the sternum to the dock, it was a four-legged walking résumé of both rider and warhorse. Long stripes and paint specs on the chest and flanks represented tribal affiliation. A painted rectangle on the flank indicated that the mounted warrior had commanded a war party. Blotchy marks meant that the horse's owner had been lost in battle. A palm print said that the enemy had been killed in hand-to-hand conflict. Red and white circles around the eyes enhanced vision and accentuated the intimidating stare of the horse; lightning bolts represented speed and power.

Though the Plains Indian warhorse was a sight of beauty for foreigners, cavalry officers, and enemies alike, its painted symbols spoke to threat, violence, death, and power. When it arrived for battle it inspired awe—a medium of communication, a work of moving art and culture, and a method of intimidation all in one.

By the mid-nineteenth century, estimates approximated that 5 to 7 million wild Mustangs roamed the western frontier. Conservatively, Dobie estimated 1 million wild horses populated Texas and 1 million elsewhere. In the far West, horse ranches throughout California turned to castrating stallions deemed inferior breeding stock. Back on the Plains, though some tribal herds included castrated horses, not surprisingly many Native Americans, like the Spanish, viewed geldings as the virile stallion's lesser, substandard version. While many warriors shunned riding atop geldings, they did not, surprisingly, reject the use of saddles.

Composed of animal hides lined with hair and wood framing, the Native American saddles were a far cry from the bareback style of riding commonplace throughout the tribal world. Indian ways were changing, and in yet another sign of shift many tribes shod their steeds with mockersons— green buffalo hides—intended to protect a horse's soles through the rough and unforgiving terrain. By the mid-nineteenth century, tribal herds once solely comprised of 100 percent Spanish blood were now nearly dominated by un-branded, wild Mustang stock.

As the century progressed, the tide started turning for the buffalo and wild horse–centric tribal societies. Up to this point, with rich ancestral lands, millions of buffalo, and free-roaming Mustangs to sustain a nomadic, subsistence survival, life had been good. When Andrew Jackson penned his signature to the Indian Removal Act of 1830, the Native American tribes of the East were abruptly put on notice that they stood in the way of advancing westward expansion. Soon relocated to the Great American Desert west of the Mississippi, the tribes of the East had experienced the opening salvo in what was to be a century-long assault against America's earliest inhabitants: the Indian, buffalo, and wild Mustang.

By the latter half of the nineteenth century, ever-increasing cattle roamed the land once dotted with buffalo and wild Mustangs. When Joseph McCoy built stockyards in Kansas and started shipping steers to Chicago via railroad in 1867, the cattle business kicked into overdrive and the range swelled with bovine stock. Once the American Civil War had concluded, lust for property and gold deposits sitting atop and under reservation lands meant that yet again the native tribes would be relocated. Shortly thereafter, when the transcontinental railroad was completed on May 10, 1869, the death knell for the ranges of the great American West rang loud and clear.

The cattle business flourished in the latter decades of the nineteenth century and the era of the great cattle drives rapidly took hold. Once cowhands throughout Texas and the American West discovered that the wild Mustang made an excellent cow pony, thousands upon thousands were captured and put to work. With a never-say-die attitude, a thrill for the hunt, the awe-inspiring stamina of its desert ancestors, and the herding instincts of an alpha-oriented wild breed, the Mustang was a natural. The hard-charging, intelligent, adaptable, structure-seeking and imposing Mustang personality was on full display, but to those who knew this horse it was nothing new. As detailed by Washington Irving, "The Indian's steed, well trained to the chase, seems as mad as the rider and pursues the game as eagerly as if it were his natural prey, on the flesh of which he was to banquet."[6]

The 1870s saw the slaughter of thousands upon thousands

of Mustangs as the tribes lost skirmish after skirmish to government soldiers. The Great Plains tribes—the Sioux, Cheyenne, and others—stood hopelessly by as the frontier's tribal and wild horse herds were decimated under the aim of cavalry rifles. With the native tribes laying claim to thousands of head, the resulting carnage was unfathomable, and the worst was yet to come.

Between the years 1850 and 1900, the U.S. government ratified 363 treaties with two hundred Native American tribes. The vast majority were either blatantly ignored or flat out violated. There was no secret when it came to the plan for the Indians: to transition the tribes from a nomadic, migratory lifestyle to a static, agricultural-based existence. The native peoples were being forced to reject their way of life and adopt a lifestyle that mirrored that of the white settler.

As highlighted by a report prepared by General William T. Sherman, Native American culture was a continuing threat to westward expansion: "All Indians who cling to their old hunting grounds are hostile and will remain so until killed off. . . . We must take chances and clean out Indians as we encounter them."[7] The buffalo and the wild Mustang, both integral to the nomadic tribes, became the instant target of this government policy to resocialize and indoctrinate the native peoples. A telegram sent by General Sheridan to the War Department addressing the wild horse didn't mince words: ". . . the main objective is to get them away from the Indians."[8] It was the first but certainly not the last time that the political establishment would declare all-out war on the free-roaming American Mustang.

The final years of the nineteenth century saw the cattle population explode across the West. Range degradation was inevitable and extensive as 22.5 million foraging head of cattle roamed the frontier. The rich and palatable wheat-grass, bluebunch, giant wild rye, dropseed, and oat grass, along with the protective topsoil, were all destroyed and replaced with unpalatable sand, sage, yucca, and winterfat. As the government slaughtered thousands of wild horses and pursued its overt war against the native tribes and their herds, the range degradation problem provided justification and validation for the eradication of the wild horse. Identi-fied as an enemy of the land, the destroyer of the range, and a feral and unwanted beast, the Mustang quickly became public enemy number one.

By the close of the century, the scourge of the West, the previously ownerless free-roaming Mustang was under the control of newly created state stockmen associations and subject to state "estray laws." The wild horse that had roamed the North American continent for three centuries, the steed that had discovered and then built the great Amer-ican frontier, was now legally identified as a "maverick," "estray," and "unbranded stock." The wild horse of the West was now the property of its greatest foe—the stockmen who raised and grazed cattle. Wild Mustangs were now under the control of those who needed and wanted their land. And by operation of law, the stockmen were now empowered to remove the single greatest obstacle to un-hindered cattle grazing—the free-roaming wild Mustang.

Extending well into the latter half of the twentieth cen-tury, state "estray laws" and stockmen associations presented a looming legal obstacle to those who sought protection for this nation's free-roaming wild herds. By the time public out-cry was finally acknowledged and received, the state estray laws, the stockmen associations, and their members had very nearly annihilated the free-roaming wild Mustang. And as a telltale sign of the dark times yet to come, by the close of the nineteenth century the State of Nevada authorized the killing of all wild horses within its borders.

The era historically identified as the period of the horse brought together a steed as wild as the plains and a people who knew of no borders. Over the course of decades and then centuries, the Native American peoples forged a complex, interdependent relationship with this fiercely independent and then fiercely loyal wild horse of the frontier. Together, the native peoples and the wild Mustang rose in numbers, developed skills, and became a formidable force and an integral part of early American history.

By operation of time and destiny, for better or for worse, over time the fortunes and the fate of the wild Mustang and the North American Indians became invariably and inevitably forever intertwined. And as fate eventually turned on the native tribes, the fortunes of the wild horse quickly soured. Nevertheless, there can be little disagreement, during the heyday of the tribes the native Indians were a great and proud people graced in battle and in life with a fierce and loyal companion.

Standing locked in his stall, and not unlike the Indian horses chased down by the cavalry, Samson had nowhere to run and nowhere to hide. He was, like so many great Mustangs before him, born wild, free, and proud. But where Samson's freedom had been taken, his wild ways could not and would not be tamed. Like his ancestors that roamed the virgin plains, similar to the great warhorses and buffalo-catchers, the will to fight, the desire to survive, was inside of him.

Samson would not go down without a fight.

4

THE WARHORSE WITHIN

*The essential joy of being with horses is that
it brings us in contact with the rare elements of
grace, beauty, spirit, and fire.*
—SHARON RALLS LEMON

As an alumnus of the BLM's Adopt-a-Horse-or-Burro Program, Samson the stallion found little quarter in the domestic horse market. Nevertheless, to an extent he had fared better than many of his 235,700 fellow graduates. While 36,000 fellow adoptees disappeared in the months following their placement, Samson was neither MIA nor KIA. Unlike three to five hundred other wild horses each year, Samson was not labeled as unmanageable and returned to BLM authorities. And though a U.S. Government Accountability Office (GAO) report found that untold numbers of adopted horses died from abuse and inhumane treatment during their initial year of domesticity, Samson had somehow survived his first twelve months of terror.

Weeks and then months passed without any news and I couldn't stop thinking about Samson the maladjusted Mustang. He was the abandoned dog you see walking along the side of the road. He was the feral cat who snakes through your yard and keeps going. Samson was the lost and hopeless animal you wanted to help, but you just didn't. I felt like the older brother who had failed to take responsibility for his younger sibling, the best friend who had let down his buddy.

Was Samson still alive, had he been freed from his incarceration, who had been his latest victim?

When Amy phoned nearly three months to the day since my first encounter with Samson, I was determined to right my wrong. Hindsight instructed that I had been selfish where I should have been selfless. I had turned my back on a horse truly in need and I would not make the same mistake twice. While guilt had ruled my thoughts, there was a stronger emotion that I couldn't quite identify. It had felt like a part of me had been missing for the last several months.

Through all of my years working with others' horses, this was a first.

Though Amy called to discuss Studs' rehabilitation, our conversation quickly turned to Samson. "He's outside, just as you instructed, but other than that, nothing else has changed. He is still bitter, violent, and mad at the world," she advised. Frustration and anger permeated her tone.

Over the last several months, Amy had shopped Samson around and there were no takers. Samson the marauding Mustang had run out of track; there was nowhere left to run.

"I've decided he can go to the rodeo and be a bucking horse," she continued. "That will suit his temperament just fine. He can break bones, mangle a cowboy or two, and I'll bet they'll cheer him and make him a celebrity. And if that isn't an option, well then . . ."

I didn't know if Amy was serious or not, but I instantly recognized that Samson was in the fight of his life. Too far gone for the reputable rodeo circuit, he would end up at some illegal backyard rodeo where his debut performance would be his final performance. And if he wouldn't be gentled and he couldn't go to the rodeo, then he would most likely be put down—Amy's farm was Samson's last and only hope.

As our phone conversation continued, Amy pulled back the veil ever so slightly and told of her recent woes. A serious health scare, a failed relationship, and the daily grind of a demanding job had sent her packing for the country. She was tired and spent and needed a break from it all. Samson was not part of the plan.

For over a century, wild horses in the tens of thousands had been hunted, brutalized, and slaughtered. And with the once-iconic American wild horse now forgotten and displaced, I was determined to find this Mustang, this homeless horse, a place to finally call home. I was going to make a difference; I was going to make Samson and Amy work.

Samson wasn't just a Mustang; he was every Mustang.

Thrown together by a strange twist of fate, horse and human had more in common than each thought. Samson had been locked away from the world; Amy had run from it. Neither had anywhere to go; both needed to hit the reset button and start anew. And though neither realized it, they were perfect for each other.

One was a damaged horse, the other a damaged soul. Neither was totally broken.

"I'll come out this weekend," I uncharacteristically blurted out, "and we'll see what we can accomplish."

As I drove west from Chicago, congested suburban multilane thoroughfares gave way to two-lane ascending and descending country roads. Rural Illinois' green valleys, hilly terrain, and endless yellow cornstalks provided a stark and quieting contrast to the overbuilt and overpopulated metropolitan area. Riddled with moraines, kettles, glacial lakes, and knob and kettle topography, McHenry County's glacially sculpted landscape was geologically atypical for the Chicagoland area. Ironically, Samson's new home sat in a valley once covered by the Pleistocene ice sheet—a remnant of the Ice Age that had temporarily eradicated his species ten thousand years earlier.

Whether or not he knew it, whether or not Amy recognized it, Samson had returned home. The sight of a hulking shiny green John Deere combine creeping down the highway announced that I was nearing my destination.

Years of training hard cases had instructed that there was only one strategy: I needed to convince the battle-tested Samson that he could be schooled and handled without threat, violence, and pain. I would have to turn his world upside down.

Upon my arrival, I scanned Amy's property. If viewed from above, the farm would appear as a perfectly proportioned square. Fifty yards of driveway cut the acreage into two equal north-south halves. The ramshackle dairy barn occupied the southern acreage; a dilapidated red siding–framed farmhouse sat to the north. Two pastures bordered the barn. On the east side, a small pasture with mostly concrete footing stretched all the way to the road. To the west sat a small grass pasture with a corncrib once used to house the season's take. A football field–sized "south pasture" and an equally vast "north pasture" rounded out the far west half of the property. Horse-unfriendly heavy-gauge barbed wire enclosed each of the pastures.

The "roadside" pasture and its concrete was a definite no; the north and south pastures were far too large to tighten the net on Samson. For our first session, the "corncrib" pasture with its limited green space and small structure would have to suffice.

Gazing across to the fence that separated the roadside and crib pastures, I observed Studs and the two miniature horses calmly sunning and snoozing. In nearly an instant, and with much greater speed than I believed any of the three possessed, they were off and running to the pasture's far corner. With the wind in this valley an ever-constant force to be reckoned with, I assumed that loose roof shingles or a dust devil had panicked the threesome and sent them packing. When a dust cloud appeared moments later and engulfed the area where the three last stood, my assumption seemed correct.

Once the dust cloud dissipated, I realized that a different force of nature, one not previously considered, had caused the commotion. It was not high winds and debris; it was not a dust devil; it was Samson. Like a warrior fresh from victory, Samson—chest out and head held high—pranced back and forth along the fence line as his body language spoke volumes. *Ah, yes! The thrill of victory and the agony of defeat; there is nothing better.* It did me good to see that Samson the wild Mustang was once again free and his domain's king. I probably shouldn't have been so pleased, for I was both his next victim and his next conquest.

Samson peered over the fence rail, and after three months of separation our gazes locked. Though bloated from parasitic worms and covered from muzzle to tail and poll to hoof in burdock burrs, he looked regal. No longer caged and no longer confined, his stiff neck, pointed ears, rounded back, and fluttering tail all spoke to this fact.

His eyes were no longer dulled from the monotony of confinement, and I was happy for Samson. This was not to say, however, that he wasn't in full threat detection mode. True to his ways, Samson stood stationary; he didn't run and he didn't flee. Other than his tail, the only part of his body that moved was his ears—repeatedly rotating forward and then pinning backward.

Samson's facial expression signaled recognition; his hard stare suggested that he knew my purpose and that the game was on.

Still seated in my car, I looked Samson over from top to bottom and front to back. On this, my first true opportunity to view him in full daylight, I took in all that I saw. Like most true Mustangs, he was small, proportional, and sturdy. In a true exhibition of natural selection's wonders, his eyes protruded wide from his skull, thus affording him the greatest field of vision with which to view the wild's many predators. His long, narrow legs stood for speed and strength; his deep chest delivered endurance and stamina.

Black points, including a dark black muzzle, mane, and tail, highlighted his bay coloring. The hue of his legs gradually transitioned from bay to black from just above the knees and hocks on down. In the dim light and low contrast of Samson's stall, these black points had previously escaped my detection. Now apparent, this two-tone coloring painted Samson in light and dark tones and empowered him as conspicuous in the day and stealthy at night.

He was a true horse of the wild and a true wild horse.

Like his Arabian ancestors, Samson's short, markedly concave back sloped to a high-set tail. His broad, slightly convex forehead tapered to a concave face and slanted, flared nostrils. His wide-set, dark, rich, introspective eyes said that he had a tale to weave. Conversely, his distinctively long face, flat and upright shoulders, and narrow chest spoke to his Barb ancestry. And lest we forget, from all accounts Samson had most certainly inherited the unstable and famously unpredictable Barb temper.

I could see in Samson the characteristic blend of his Arabian and Barb ancestors—the Arabian swift and sure, the Barb rough and tough—both desert horses, both proud. With Spanish traits recognizable in horses with as little as one-thirty-second Spanish ancestry and bloodlines, the dominant genetic code of the Conquistador horses still canters across the West in the American wild Mustang.

I shifted the gear lever into drive and turned up the driveway.

My truck advanced a mere ten yards before coming to an abrupt stop. Two horned goats, one larger than the other, stood in my path seemingly preparing for battle. I inched forward and honked the horn, but the pair refused to budge. Suddenly the impromptu greeting party's smaller half took to flight, landing squarely atop my truck. With four freshly minted hoof-sized divots on the hood in plain sight, I unleashed an expletive-laden tirade. In turn, the small female responded verbally with what I imagined was a mix of reciprocal profanity and bravado. Concurrent with this animated, high-decibel response, a flurry of dark pellets exited from her hind end—bouncing across the hood like marbles on pavement.

On the spot, I forgave Samson's prior trespasses against the goats. They deserved what they got. Moments later, reinforcements arrived.

Three dozen chickens and roosters—darting about as if they had lost their heads or ingested crack—scurried beneath my car. Nearly twenty ducks and geese followed and huddled together directly in front of my vehicle's grill. With this ragtag assembly of fowl squawking in high pitched tones and wildly waving their wings, my poor truck and my patience had taken enough abuse. Just as I was preparing to floor the accelerator and create a week's worth of duck a l'orange, what I believed to be my rescue party arrived on scene.

A gigantic yellow Lab who looked as if he was a cross between a horse and a dog led the charge, leaping directly into the huddled masses. A medium-sized black mutt covered the flanks, chomping at any unfortunate critter who dared to cross her path. Coming up the rear, a geriatric but no less crazed shepherd mix raced after the stragglers.

With the rebellion quashed and the insurgents dispersed, the three canines turned their attention to my truck. In a scene reminiscent of *Cujo,* the yellow Lab stood tall on his hind legs and slammed his face hard against the driver-side window—leaving behind an opaque glaze of drool. The black mutt mauled my oversized Goodyear tires while the old-timer took to christening my muffler with a lifted leg. Within seconds, the wild pack of dogs was running circles around my vehicle and howling as if they had captured a Grade A sirloin dinner.

From a distance a familiar voice called out, "Now you guys stop that. You know that isn't the proper way to greet our guests." Carrying what appeared to be an entire library's worth of books, Amy walked down the driveway.

As I watched the hounds race to greet their master, I realized that these rabid dogs, insolent goats, antagonistic ducks and geese, clueless chickens and roosters, and the horses all shared one common thread. Some had wandered onto the property from adjoining lands, others had been dumped by their owners under the cover of darkness, many had been rescued by Amy and Lisa, but all had been unwanted and homeless. Instantly I realized that this nondescript little farm in the middle of nowhere housed the animal kingdom's rejects and society's outcasts.

Like it or not, I was living a modern-day version of Orwell's *Animal Farm*. My dinged hood, the sonata of fecal pellets, the unwelcoming fowl, and the bloodthirsty dogs announced the cold, hard truth: I hadn't even confronted Samson the hateful Mustang and I was already losing the war. Animal rejects one, helpless horse trainer zero.

Amy approached with books in her arms and books strewn across the lawn marking her path of descent from the house. "I have a dozen books here," Amy announced "and not a one helped me reform that beast out there."

She then continued, "One of these books advised reading poetry each day. This paperback training manual said that I should try to locate and connect with Samson's inner self. The hardcover book—here it is—instructed that I sing to him each and every evening."

Unfortunately, Samson and Amy possessed widely divergent tastes in both music and poetry. Amy's new-age training techniques had been a total bust.

Glancing back over my shoulder, I observed that Samson was staring at me, studying me. I also noticed that he was wearing a halter. When I learned from Amy that a friend of hers had used a pole to drop the halter down over Samson's face, I instantly became agitated. The incident had been ripe with fear and violence and no doubt erased our previous successes. Despite our earlier advances, Samson once again had cause to hate and fear his captors.

It was early October, and the colder temperatures and change of season would have Samson pumped, rank, and primed for a fight. But I didn't care; Samson the forever wild Mustang and I were going to be reunited. I felt energized.

I placed my foot on a strand of barbed wire, grabbed a post, and leapt over the fence. Samson and I, horse and trainer, squared off amid the corncrib pasture's seventy-by-fifty-foot fenced confines. No longer caged and imprisoned, Samson was statically charged and primed for battle. Standing upright on his hind legs, he unleashed a flurry of foreleg strikes, which found nothing but air. Like a fighter shadowboxing moments before a bout, his blows were intended as both a prefight warm-up and a message to his opponent.

Bring it on!

From a distance, I glanced upon Samson. The first lesson was always about where you looked and how you looked—how you carried yourself and the message that you conveyed. Was your posture upright and dominant, or were you slouched and submissive? Did you approach on a direct straight line like a predator, or did you meander and move in on a less threatening diagonal? Was your gait assertive and confident or slow and timid? Did your body language communicate confidence, or did it speak of threat and intimidation?

Confidence gains command and control of a horse; threat and intimidation gets you punted across the pasture.

As I slowly angled toward the center of the pasture, Samson's entire disposition shifted. In mere seconds, his respirations turned shallow and rapid. His spine tightened and his back rounded as he first extended, and then lowered, his neck and head. He flared his nostrils while his eyes seemed to bulge out from his face. His tail circulated feverishly in complete 360-degree motions as he pinned his ears hard against his skull and slammed his right foreleg into the ground.

Samson's actions and reactions said that he feared for his very life.

The entirety of Samson's behavior—the sights and the sounds—could, would, and certainly did evoke a flight response in those of the two- and four-legged persuasion. To an untrained eye, Samson's actions might have appeared as the manifestation of anger, threat, and contempt. In reality, though, Samson's central nervous system was merely trying to keep pace with his fear-fueled, raging circulatory and respiratory processes. The "Samson Experience," as I later coined the phrase, was this creature's most potent tool in his vast and impressive weapons arsenal.

This fear and threat–induced response, Samson's automated last line of defense, permitted him to conserve enormous stores of energy, which he otherwise would have expended via preemptory actions such as bucking, kicking, spinning, and charging. He was, in effect, storing up for the battle. Natural selection, Darwin's theory that first went to work on this species' dog-sized ancient grandfather some 60 million years earlier, was now at work on Samson—the dawn horse's modern-day descendant.

The impressive nature of Samson's exhibition made it no less heartbreaking and disheartening. These were behaviors born out of years of pain, abuse, and suffering. This was a train wreck created by man and a horse who seemed beyond repair.

It was then that I realized that while Samson had been spared the confines of a BLM long-term holding facility, he nevertheless had spent years locked in a cage. Samson's cage didn't have bars and it didn't have walls. His cage was a mental prison, and he was sentenced and then delivered there by those tasked with providing his care and instruction. After years of abuse and brutality, whatever hope Samson held of being handled humanely had long since vanished.

Or so I thought.

The only required equipment for the day's training session was my fifteen-foot training lead line. While I possessed no intention to clip on to Samson, coiled in my hands the lead would provide a useful tool to visually stimulate movement and present a deterrent should Samson charge. But when Samson caught sight of the lead line, he pinned his ears, violently tossed his head, and fled in an all-out, wild, disjointed gallop. As he pounded his legs into the grass, he released a good dozen bucks. Each buck spoke to his dire enemy.

With the lead line closely resembling a bullwhip and with scars covering his body, it wasn't hard to read his thoughts. It was an easy decision. On this day, I would be working without my lead line.

With twenty-five yards separating horse and horseman, I took one step forward.

Samson abruptly rotated his head, locked on my position, cocked his neck, and bolted away with the speed of a pinball shot off a bumper. Through plumes of low-hanging, lingering, and choking dust clouds, my eyes scanned for and then located Samson. He stood along the fence line panting heavily, camouflaged among the trees and brush.

As a free-roaming Mustang, Samson had been all wild horse. Thrust into the domestic horse market, he became first a brutalized victim and then a mutual combatant. Locked away in a stall, he evolved into a caged beast that communicated threat with little more than a hard look. And now he was a horse determined to keep his newfound freedom and his autonomy.

Samson the lawless Mustang had identified his spot, and now it was time to assert myself and apply some herd psychology. Like an alpha horse repositioning submissive herd members, I needed to relocate him to a location of my choosing. I opted for the grass ramp that led up to the barn's second story. Yes, I would be surrendering the higher ground. But the safety and security of the ramp would only help to calm Samson's off-the-charts panic response.

Once again, I took one step forward.

My approach from across the pasture sent Samson into a galloping frenzy. He raced alongside the perimeter fence and violently tossed his head in frustration as he considered crashing the razor-sharp barbs that prevented his escape. We were thirty yards apart and Samson was willing to risk life and limb to get away. The barbed-wire fence could bring serious harm, but in Samson's eyes the same could be said for my close proximity.

He had to make a decision. Was he going to vault the fence, stand and fight, charge, or yield to my pressure?

Samson drifted off the fence line and darted toward the center of the pasture concurrently galloping and bucking. I took two steps backward, releasing my mild pressure and rewarding his movement away from the fence. He in turn slammed on the brakes and came to a sliding stop as a dust cloud engulfed his position.

Several minutes elapsed and I again moved forward. Samson in turn bounded for the fence line. This time I followed in hot pursuit.

"No," I yelled, "the fence line is off-limits!"

Angered and threatened by my pursuit, Samson, while at a full gallop, unloaded a double hind-leg barrage on an innocent oak tree. The tree splintered and I was officially on notice that this Mustang meant business. Head down and pounding his forelegs into the ground, Samson crisscrossed the pasture leaving deep hoof-sized indentations in his wake.

Our ritualistic battle continued for sixty minutes. Samson relied upon his tremendous speed and strength to make it to the fence line. I employed pressure, angles, and swift diagonal movements to cut off each of his attempts. It was a choreographed ballet of sorts, a beautiful thing to see and experience. Man versus beast, rational thought pitted against primal instinct. There could be, in my opinion, only one victor.

As the minutes ticked by and his disposition eased ever so slightly, so did Samson's gait. He was no longer pounding his hooves into the ground, no longer running for his life. His weight now properly centered back on his hindquarters, his head raised to the vertical position, Samson's all-out dash was now a graceful, gliding canter. I was amazed by his elegance and gripped by his grace. Samson was floating on air. There was little doubt; this was the highly coveted Arabian gait.

Samson was truly a blend of breeds, the rightful heir of his wild ancestors.

With respirations akin to a horse who had just galloped twelve furlongs, Samson finally found his way to the ramp. Nearly instantly I averted my gaze, softened my posture, stepped backward, and turned away from my panting, wheezing student. This retreat and the subsequent rest break was Samson's reward. He had yielded to my cues and followed my direction.

This was textbook pressure/release of pressure training. Since horses lack the ability to learn through deductive thought and logic, most trainers rely upon this tried-and-true training method. It is a technique premised upon the horse's ability to learn from the release of mild pressure and the trainer's ability to instantly recognize and reward compliance. When employed properly and appropriately, it is a method that works.

I allowed Samson several minutes to digest what he had learned and then it was time to get back to work. Only in this instance, Samson was not going to wait for my approach. After shooting me a steely gaze, he bolted down the ramp and headed toward the fence line. Samson was making his statement; he was letting me know that I was not his boss. Where others had punished him for being stubborn and willful, I had nothing but respect for this prideful beast. With a slight grin on my face, I took off in pursuit.

Thirty minutes later, Samson begrudgingly ran up the

ramp and parked out. I backed off. He had returned to my place of choosing, but now I wanted him to remain there. Several minutes passed, and I once again initiated my approach. In the wild, predators travel in a straight line toward their prey. So in this instance, I moved slowly, meandering diagonally toward Samson as he lowered his head and, like a sundial, tracked my every move.

Twenty yards, fifteen yards, ten yards, and then in an instant he was gone. With mud and dust flying in his wake, Samson galloped across the pasture.

When Samson slowed, I stepped forward and kept him moving. We had established rules and a system; he was now expected to follow both. Until he returned to the anointed spot, there would be no rest. He rounded the far corner and came about; I moved in closer and cut off his angle of retreat. The instant that he averted his eyes to the ramp and slowed his gait, I retreated. Back and forth we went, repeating our little tango over and over.

Samson understood what I was asking for; he was just not willing to give it.

Forty minutes later, Samson returned to his perch atop the ramp. I stood amazed by our progress and shocked that the Mustang had yet to exhibit the one true act of aggressive conduct that had become his calling card. He had yet to charge. I had already heard the countless stories. With curled upper lip, teeth fully exposed, lowered head, pinned ears, and a brakeless gallop, Samson's charge would garner the attention of even the toughest cowboy.

But on this day, I sensed that something was different.

Samson was a horse who had never been shown compassion, let alone handled properly and humanely. At the ripe age of six years, his introduction to man came by way of low-flying pursuit helicopters, mounted cowboys with lassos, holding pens, and stock trucks. In the six years that followed, he had been roped and dragged, surely on repeated occasions, and forced to acquiesce under unremitting pain and certain injury. As he had been violently coerced to submit since his first moments with man, voluntary submission was an unknown and foreign concept.

And now I was asking him for just that. But unlike those who had come before me, I was asking and not telling. I was requesting that he voluntarily acquiesce to my direction, my will, my authority. This October afternoon, Samson the formerly wild Mustang and his two-legged nemesis were engaged in a mutual and reciprocal battle of wills. On equal footing, Samson was finally able to challenge the predator who took him from his home and his family, the antagonist who mentally and physically had habitually beat him down and forever scarred his psyche.

On this day, Samson was afforded the respect he was due.

As we repeated our little dance, Samson's fear and anxiety soon gave way to minor intrigue and reserved interest. His decision not to charge communicated a message that Samson himself could not speak. Though he was terrified, a small part of Samson trusted in my approach and my intentions.

As he had been alone and solitary for so many years, Samson's decision not to charge was a sign. It was a green light to proceed. I threw caution to the wind and decided to expand the day's lesson beyond what was planned.

Samson's willingness to accept my touch, hold his stand, and not flee would test both our bond of trust and his ability to keep his volatile emotions in check. Though I had the option to clip on to his halter and manage his movements, there would be no compulsory compliance during this exercise. Samson would not be forced and he would not be cornered. If he felt the need to run off and seek safety, he would have a direct avenue to do so.

From twenty yards away, I angled toward Samson at an agonizingly slow, nearly idling amble. Each halting stride covered mere inches. At ten yards and closing, Samson, with ears pinned back, started to nervously dance in place. At five yards and closing, he engaged the Samson Experience and all corresponding defenses. Wide-eyed and breathing like a marathoner, he appeared nervous and anxious.

While fear was present, it was not evident to the extent of our previous encounter. There was, I felt, a small degree of trust and curiosity.

Just three feet off the point of Samson's right shoulder, I came to an abrupt halt. I remained there, idle, facing him, as we each gazed at and then through the other. Slowly I raised my arm to a position perpendicular to his shoulder. Instantly and without hesitation Samson reared up. Standing upright on his hind legs, he deposited a right foreleg strike into open air and then bolted down the ramp.

I now had full warning of Samson's destructive capabilities.

I retreated back to the center of the pasture as Samson returned to his mandated and prescribed perch. Again I angled toward him, this time with more speed. He knew the drill—there was no need to baby him. With outstretched arm I moved in and gently placed my hand atop his withers.

Tremors surged through him as though he had stepped

on an exposed electric line, but he held his ground. Our contract, our bond, forged months prior in that dark, dank stall, was still in full force and effect.

We had contact.

"Gooooood boy!" I spoke to him in an excited but hushed tone. "I just knew you had it in you. I'm sooooo proud of you!"

I meant my words. I had asked Samson to belay his fears, hold back his violent responses, and he complied. I had asked him to believe and trust in me where trust was a new and foreign concept. I was truly proud of this old boy and I believed he sensed and knew it. As he had always been feared, oft despised and hated, this was a new emotion. It was a first sense of accomplishment for a horse deemed for far too many years hopeless, unwanted, and worthless.

My hand slid across Samson's lower neck, right shoulder, and even part of his chest. After a mere two minutes, anxiety got the best of him and he walked off. I had no objection. When he returned, we repeated the entire process, with Samson departing after roughly three minutes. Though he refused to show it, I was certain that Samson relished both the attention and the physical contact.

Our lesson had lasted longer than planned and it was time to conclude the session. From ten yards away I made one final approach. I rubbed Samson's withers, his neck, and then started to work my way up to his head. It was a mistake—an apparent huge mistake.

Samson threw his weight back on his haunches, rocked forward onto his forelegs, tossed his head left, then right, and crashed his forehead into my elbow. Bone impacted bone; Samson reared up and then galloped away. Like a horse out of the gate, he was off to the races and gone in an instant. Samson the terrible was back in the house.

It was just the start of what was to come.

Perhaps I pushed the envelope a little too far, but that was okay. Before Samson's issues could be remedied, they had to be identified. My failed attempt to touch Samson's head provided much-needed insight into this dark and complex animal. Samson not only guarded his head, but he had also repeatedly jerked away from the slightest intimation of physical contact. The stories and my worst fears were now confirmed: Samson had been struck repeatedly in the head, face, and body.

Sadly, in the weeks to follow, I would learn firsthand that Samson's head and face–related issues were unlike those of any other horse I had ever handled.

As Samson's list of issues continued to grow, so too had the list of crimes committed against this Mustang since his arrival in the domestic horse world. The two were no doubt correlated. Samson was a walking and breathing crime scene. And as our first training session came to a close, I recognized that Samson's past life had left profound scarring and he now viewed, with no exception, each and every person as a dire threat.

While I understood what motivated Samson to strike, I could not condone his actions. He had communicated through ways and means learned and perfected as both a wild horse and a frequent victim. He didn't know any better and thus I could not impose punishment. I could, however, impose discipline, order, structure, and expectations.

Over the years, I have preached to countless horse owners to "expect, demand, nothing until you teach something."

In other words, there is no place for expectations until you have first properly introduced your ways and your rules. When Samson exploded, he believed that I had crossed a line—his line of comfort. If I had punished him for what was a yet-to-be-defined infraction, I would have both negated the day's successes and placed myself in a category with all who had come before me. I would have been no different from those who had punished Samson for being and acting like an untrained wild horse. So for the time being, Samson received a free pass.

This pass, however, would soon expire.

Samson circled the pasture and tried to calm his nerves. His mad dash over, he came to a halt, chest heaving, at the ramp's edge. Since every trainer knows you never end a lesson on a bad note, our dance card was not yet complete. For what I hoped was the final time, I slowly angled in toward Samson and placed my hand upon his shoulder. Seeking to reinforce the positive, I briefly rubbed his neck and then gradually stepped away.

With a foot separating us, I looked upon Samson and spoke, "You are succchhh a good boy. I think we are going to work things out."

Samson and I had sparred for two hours and faced each other with mutual respect and mutual restraint. It was a battle that both sides fought free of overt aggression and unprovoked violence. Samson sought to demonstrate that he would not be controlled; I was determined to establish my identity as the alpha. Like herd alphas of the last 60 million years, I had communicated my dominance by initiating and controlling Samson's movements.

The skirmish was over; the war was just getting started.

I left Samson standing at the ramp, returning moments later with knife and apple in hand. The fundamental principle at the core of my training regimen is P & P: praise and punishment. Praise anything that nears or resembles attempted compliance; punish or deter anything approximating threat, intimidation, or violence. Over the years, however, I have given a great deal of thought to renaming my training motto something other than "praise and punishment." Not because the terms don't fit, but rather on account of the fact that many in the horse world attach very different meanings to the word "punishment."

Yes, in very rare situations, if threatened with violence and injury, I will strike a horse. But such corporal punishment is extremely rare and the instances few and far between. The remaining 99.9 percent of the time, punishment in my training regimen translates to providing discipline, structure, and order, rechanneling unacceptable actions, and redirecting energy. In all instances, punishment in my world requires that I provide either significant incentive for a horse to comply or sufficient deterrence to prevent the undesired behavior.

For many horsemen, though certainly not for all, punishment means a lip chain, a skipped meal, or an ass whooping. I can't say that I understand these methods, nor can I claim to have observed long-lasting, permanent results when they were employed. But just as you can't tell an adult how to parent a child, it is very difficult to counsel a horse owner on how to properly deter his animal's unacceptable behavior. Ultimately for me, punishment is synonymous with and translates to deterrence. If, for example, a horse has decided to jog rather than walk home, then he in turn has bought himself a nice extended day out on trail. When he decides to walk at my speed and pace, then he can proceed directly home.

Compliance should be easy and inviting; obstruction, costly and unappealing.

It was now time for Samson to receive his first lesson in praise. He had worked hard—his efforts required both physical control and mental focus, and he was entitled to and deserved a reward.

As I quartered the apple, Samson stood puzzled. Seconds later, nerves and anxiety got the best of him as he engaged what were now his standardized defense mechanisms but held his ground. With an outstretched arm, I slowly moved the apple toward Samson's muzzle.

He instantly recoiled as though confronted with the forbidden fruit from the tree of knowledge. *How sad,* I thought to myself, *that a twelve-year-old horse has never been treated to an apple.* I placed the apple on the ground and departed the pasture under Samson's watchful gaze.

Having observed the entire lesson from the safety of the driveway, Amy broke her silence as I jumped back over the fence, "I was in awe of everything that you accomplished up until a few minutes ago. But after seeing that head butt, I really don't know why we are bothering. I just don't know that there's any hope for him."

Amy had it all wrong; hope was the one thing that Samson actually had going for him. Hope instructed him not to drop-kick me when I trespassed into his stall. Hope advised him not to run me over when I pressured him in the pasture and placed my hand atop his quivering back. Life had taught Samson to distrust, hate, and preemptively put me down, but hope had counseled otherwise.

If Samson held out hope for those who had brutalized him for more than half his lifetime, then I most certainly could hope, believe, that he could be gentled, trained, and eventually mounted.

Deep down, in Samson's dark, intelligent, and expressive eyes, I saw that fierce and loyal companion long known to the native tribes. Buried beneath layers of contempt, there existed the markings of a buffalo-catcher that would tirelessly chase and pursue its prey until capture. Hidden under six years of justifiable distrust, I saw the nineteenth-century Indian warhorse that rode into battle without fear—a painted, breathing, and galloping résumé of conquest, tribal history, and tribal pride. Obscured by a lifetime of unwarranted punishment and pain, there lurked an intelligent, innately and instinctively driven cow horse and herder extraordinaire.

The problem was how to get through to the greatness that lay beneath, how to locate and tame the illustrious and esteemed Indian pony and cowboy cow horse obscured by years and untold layers of damaged horse.

After witnessing Samson's crime, Amy was nearly convinced that he was not worth the effort. But I had seen the warhorse within and my rekindled flame was now aglow. My passion for training was returning, my love for horses making a comeback. Everyone, including Jamie, my girlfriend of six months, thought that I was wasting my time and risking my life. But I had a plan. If Samson and Amy could each learn to tolerate, understand, and accept the other, then together they could make a new start. Together they would have a home.

Several moments of silence passed before I answered Amy, "Today was very hard for Samson. He had to disregard all that he knew and start fresh, and he did just that. It's in there; underneath all that fear, all that contempt, all that doubt and insecurity. Underneath all those bad memories there is a horse."

Back in my truck, I shifted the gear lever into reverse and started down the driveway. For some reason, I stopped and looked out to Samson. He stood motionless—head outstretched, surveying the apple. Seemingly aware of my gaze, he raised and cocked his head to the right as our eyes met. And then, with what from a distance appeared as a mild nod, he lowered his head and hurriedly picked up an apple quarter. His head back to the vertical position, Samson once again cocked his head to the right and gazed upon my position. In an instant, the bright red chunk that hung from his lips and reflected the afternoon sun, disappeared.

Now that's being a horse.

5

CATCH ME IF YOU CAN

As a horse runs, think of it as
a game of tag with the wind.

—TRE TUBERVILLE

In Samson's lifetime, timing was everything.

During his early years, good timing allowed Samson to avoid the BLM wranglers and helicopters. Bad timing sent Samson to a myriad of abusive homes and cruel owners. Good timing first brought Samson and me together, and after it seemed our time together had come and gone good timing then reunited us. And strange as it may seem, good timing framed Samson's capture in 2003. Had he been captured a year later and not subsequently adopted, Samson would have been a "three strikes" horse subject to the "Burns Rider;" a 2004 amendment to the Wild Free-Roaming Horses and Burros Act.

As a "three strikes" Mustang—a wild horse passed over three times for adoption—Samson would have been eligible for outright sale to any interested party "without limitation." Unlike Mustangs funneled through the Adopt-a-Horse-or-Burro Program, once sold Samson would not have had the protection of the twelve-month probationary period during which his owner would have been subject to random BLM inspection. Since Samson was willful and all "wild at heart," his sole purchaser would have been a kill buyer—one who buys auctioned Mustangs at bargain basement prices and ships them directly to slaughter. Samson's bill of sale would have been a one-way ticket to the slaughterhouse.

Where fortune had closed doors on Samson, fate had opened gates.

By the second week of October, my thoughts were any-thing but so philosophical. After the advances of our first training session, most horses would have understood that I was the boss, they were the student. But Samson was not most horses. In the lessons that followed, we repeated our choreographed dance and pursuit. I pressured; he sought an escape route. I advanced; he violently retreated. At times, fear seemed to drive Samson's flight. In other instances, he was a headstrong former warrior stallion determined to cement his role as the alpha.

One side of Samson needed my patience, understanding, and a degree of compassion. The other required firm direc-tion, disciplined behavior, and structure. Both were in need of a complete overhaul. Deciphering who I was dealing with and figuring out how to teach, train, and reshape each would prove to be the greatest challenge of my career.

The four-hour round-trip drive from my downtown Chi-cago apartment to Amy's farm meant that I could only work Samson on the weekends. Foul weather was just around the corner and anyone and everyone who had a horse with some problem wanted it resolved prior to winter's onset. Between my other horse clients, my commitments to the therapeutic riding center, and my legal work, I was beginning to feel the strain. Catch-up time soon became between the hours of one and three in the morning.

No longer a twentysomething law student able to pull off all-nighters, I questioned how long this lifestyle could continue before I crashed and burned. Making matters worse, I had little time for Jamie and when we were together she claimed that I was distracted.

After my second session with Samson, Jamie made her feelings known: "Let's be clear on one thing: I will not compete with a horse."

Just two weeks into my war with Samson, both of our worlds had been turned upside down. Something soon would have to give.

By the time I was ready to catch Samson the uncatchable horse, I had identified an issue that would complicate the already-monumental task at hand. Whenever Samson faced me, he did so by exposing the right side of his body, while consistently guarding and shielding the left. Between Amy, Lisa, and those before me, explanations were aplenty. Some believed that Samson suffered from poor eyesight on his left side. Others were certain that his brutal tormentors had favored striking him on the left.

My rationalization was far more elemental and profoundly more telling.

Moments after the BLM wranglers captured Samson, the wild Mustang stallion was forced into a cage and branded with his permanent freeze mark. The mark identified his year and place of capture but couldn't tell of the fear and trauma that he experienced. Though the branding was classified as painless and harmless, to an alpha stallion such as Samson the process left scars of a different variety. These scars spoke to unwanted submission, a loss of family and freedom, and, ultimately, defeat.

Tattooed on the left side of his neck, the BLM freeze mark was Samson's scarlet letter. It was forever a reminder of his life stolen away. The totality of Samson's behaviors, his level of contempt and disdain for his new world, said that it was a life that Samson had cherished.

The left side of his body foreclosed to my approach, from twenty yards away I slowly angled in toward Samson's right side. Gradually, I fished the lead line through the mane and up to his neckline. Samson leapt away, then doubled back and faced me. Standing upright on his hind legs, he threw two foreleg strikes targeted directly at my face. I dove to the ground as his left hoof nicked my baseball cap—sending it tumbling to the ground. Tossing his head and throwing bucks, Samson bounded off to the far side of the crib pasture.

As he harbored deep-seated issues with the lead line, the left side of his neck, and capture, Samson's obstructive behavior continued unabated for an additional sixty minutes.

Eventually, I was able to fish the lead line up over his right side, down the left, and firmly grab both ends of the rope underneath his throat. Samson took a moment to consider his options. His eyelids narrowed, his gaze hardened, and his lip curled upward. And then, without warning, he blew.

I yanked hard on the lead line; he, in turn, reared up and threw a right cross that missed my jaw by inches. I was exercising control over Samson and he was fighting back. I wasn't schooling a damaged and brutalized victim; I was battling a proud and willful former wild Mustang stallion.

I spoke in a reassuring tone to try to calm this horse who was barely holding it together, "Eaaaaassssyyyy, boy . . . whoa . . . and hold your stand."

For the next twenty minutes, I comforted and stroked Samson until his anxiety seemed to ease. Both ends of the lead line still in hand, I slowly walked a semicircle around Samson's muzzle—coming to rest parallel with his off-limits left side and the BLM freeze mark. This was too much, too soon for Samson, and he immediately sought flight. Only now, with him properly secured and under lead, flight was no longer an option. With each of his many attempts to gain momentum and run, I pulled Samson back into a tight 360-degree circle and spoke to him.

"Sorry, buddy, those days are gone."

Unable to escape, Samson engaged his hindquarters, swinging his hind end around like a wrecking ball zeroing in on its target. His head veered right as his rump rotated left. Full impact was imminent. I was a hockey player about to receive a body check into the boards from a one-thousand-pound opponent.

As his pendulum-like mass of muscle swung into me, I dug my right elbow into the flank—the fleshy area located between his midsection and hind end. The impact launched me into the air and then sent me hurtling to the ground. Dazed and winded, but still holding the lead line, I jumped back to my feet.

With nowhere to run to, Samson appeared defeated.

With the realization that I was not going away and he was not getting away, with the recognition that I had not struck, yelled at, or punished him, Samson soon eased up and the fight that had previously permeated his every muscle

and tendon soon wafted away with the dust cloud that engulfed our struggles. This skirmish, this back-and-forth
battle of wills, was nothing more than a war of attrition and
I was well versed in how to win both the battle and the war.

Rather than punish Samson for doing that which came
naturally and instinctively, I quietly and patiently waited him
out.

And then moments later, for the very first time, I ever so
gently placed my hand upon the left side of his neck and
the BLM freeze mark. My fingers passed through the hairs
of his neck—permanently tinted white from the freeze-
branding process—revealing various hieroglyphic-like symbols that told his long and storied journey: his estimated year
of birth, registration number, and state of capture.

Borne by all captured Mustangs, the BLM tattoo provides the sole means of identifying and tracking each culled
and captured wild horse. Under his approving hard gaze, like
a blind person reading braille, I slowly reviewed Samson's
life story.

I couldn't help but chuckle. Like so much in this modern era, Samson, a horse born to the wild, was a living and
breathing barcode.

My hand moved across his left shoulder, back, and left
flank. Samson mustered every pound of muscle he could call
upon to maintain his composure and hold his stand. For the
second time since our introduction, I found myself admiring this Mustang's willingness to shun his better judgment,
disregard his inner voice, and cast aside years of distrust to
ever so slightly trust in a stranger's touch.

While this was an opportune moment on which to conclude the day's session, the reality was that Samson's hooves

were growing longer and, like it or not, a quickly approaching date with the farrier was inevitable. This was as good a time as any to start Samson's leg training. There was little doubt; it was going to be a slow and violent process.

Moving back over to his more comfortable right side, standing off the point of his right shoulder, I ran my hand over the humerus, across to the elbow, and then slowly down the forearm. Instantly Samson reared up and attempted several foreleg strikes. With the lead line looped over his neck, I promptly aborted Samson's takeoff.

Samson's reaction communicated that which he could not speak: *Steer clear of my legs.*

Annoyed by the fact that I had checked his vertical aspirations, or perhaps put off by my control over his actions and reactions, Samson's anger meter jumped directly into the red zone. Wildly and violently, he threw his head right, then left, and attempted several head butts and body checks while I firmly controlled the lead line.

"Noooootttt," I firmly told him as I spun him around in a tight circle, "that is no longer acceptable behavior."

With him frustrated and suddenly enraged, Samson's intemperate anger returned for a second performance as he attempted to reach me with a right hind leg forward strike. It was something you don't see every day and a warning that he was on the verge of losing it. The fight—bucks, body checks, foreleg and hind-leg strikes, and rearing—continued for thirty minutes with Samson not even winded.

Once Samson realized that I would continue to touch his leg so long as he continued to object, he slowly calmed himself and his nasty little temper soon receded. Again I ran my hand down his upper foreleg to the knee, and though clearly agitated and put off, Samson kept his anger and wrath in check.

Immediately I stood up, moved away, provided verbal praise, and patted his neck. Samson had complied and he had earned a release of pressure. Horses possess a relatively un-developed corpus callosum—the neurological tissue that connects both hemispheres of the brain—and thus the equine mind learns and processes skills just one side at a time. In order to touch Samson's left foreleg, I had to repeat the en-tire process from that side. Slowly, I arced around Samson's face making my way toward the left foreleg.

Ever the warfare strategist, the Mustang combatant was way ahead of me.

From a complete standstill, Samson vaulted forward in a vain attempt to get away. He made it as far as the length of the lead line—fifteen feet—before being yanked back to reality. He could have put his body into it and dragged me off, but he didn't. Slowly but surely, through control of his actions and movements, I was establishing myself as the al-pha of our small herd. Once again, I pulled Samson in close and made him trot tight circles around my position. Over the next thirty minutes, he bucked, reared, and kicked, but eventually he lost. Able to finally rub Samson's left foreleg from the point of the elbow to the knee, I immediately heaped praise upon my crestfallen subject.

"Don't be too hard on yourself, buddy; you may have lost this battle, but the true war lies ahead. I still have yet to handle your hinds, and then of course we have to lift and pick out all four of your hooves. You will have opportuni-ties aplenty to put me down and finish me off."

I could act all macho and say I was primed for the challenge, but the reality was that I dreaded the prospect of handling Samson's hind legs. The day's lesson successful and complete, I pulled the lead line back across Samson's neckline and in a puff of dust and mud he was gone.

"Hopefully, we can still be friends," I announced to a somewhat dejected and deflated Samson as I placed a quartered apple a few yards from his location. "I'll see you next week."

After I exited the pasture, Amy approached with a concerned expression. "Mitch, I'm amazed and so thankful for everything, but I simply can't afford to pay you for any of this."

"Don't worry," I answered. "This is my way of giving back to an animal that has brought me so much over the past twenty years. So, consider us square."

Among local horse enthusiasts, it is widely known that I have never turned away a hard case on account of money or lack thereof. Maybe Amy didn't know this fact; most likely she did. Samson would just be another of the many horses I had trained free of charge. And yet this Mustang wasn't just another charity case; something about our relationship, our bond, was unique.

Despite our struggles, I started to sense that I was getting under this loner's skin, as he was already under mine. I was drawn to Samson, as he seemed drawn to me.

The training plan for the following weekend included Samson's further socialization to the lead line and, more significantly, removing and replacing his halter. During our initial sessions, he had remained standoffish and doubting at his best and violent and explosive at his worst. Like every other damaged and maladjusted horse, this Mustang needed a healthy dose of time and patience. My hope was to have Samson halter broke by the end of the weekend, but in light of his significant head and face issues, I had absolutely no idea how to go about it. I had a tentative schedule for our sessions, but I would have to go hands-on and face-to-face with my pupil and just let the lesson plan evolve.

Samson's ability to forgive and forget as well as my horsemanship skills would be put to the test.

The schedule for both weekend days was identical: to work Samson in thirty-minute intervals, release him for twenty minutes so that he could rest and contemplate that which he had learned, and then return to repeat the process. This work/rest method had proven successful in countless similar situations over the years and would prove integral to Samson's training regimen.

Alerted to my approach from the driveway, Samson, in full bravado, put on quite the exhibition. He launched himself several feet in the air. He threw a dozen wild bucks. He galloped across the pasture taking hard, sliding turns.

Samson understood what my presence meant. I was the alpha who was controlling his behaviors, actions, and reactions. As my authority had increased, Samson's had correspondingly decreased, and he was less than pleased.

While Samson's demonstration of machismo unfolded, I yelled out to him, "Just remember what I whispered to you in the stall that day, 'You trust me, I'll trust you.' You and I, we have a binding contract!"

The first order of the day was to handle the area between Samson's ears—the poll. As my hand ran up the right side of his face, he squealed and attempted yet another head butt. Instantly he met my right elbow—his new and most intimate best friend. Verbal reprimand and tight circles at a trot were immediately imposed.

Standing still, breathing hard, and dazed, Samson shot me a piercing gaze. It was the look a criminal would give a cop after a foot chase and subsequent capture. If looks could kill, I would have been down on the spot.

Samson's hard gaze spoke to me. *Now why'd you have to go and do that? You know how I feel about my head and face.*

That I did. The fact was that Samson was so neck protective, so head and face shy, that I could have waited weeks, if not months, for the same result. His reactions were now and had long since been rote and reflexive. In much the same fashion that you or I kick a leg out when given a reflex test at the doctor's office, Samson turned to impulsive, automatic blows when anyone ventured near his neck, face, or head.

And thus, under my student's watchful gaze, I returned my hand to the spot that angered Samson most and, yet again, gently rubbed his head.

I repeated the process from the opposite side, and to no surprise, violence ensued. Once Samson bilaterally abstained from attempting to crush my skull, I released him. Twenty minutes later, I returned to the pasture and turned my focus to his face. Before I even made contact, Samson threw his weight back on his haunches and went ballistic.

Three hard tugs of the lead line on his neck and Samson's forelegs were back on the ground. The fight, however, was just getting started. As every part of his body twisted, kicked, and objected, I rotated Samson in tight circles and, implored my stubborn brother, "Just try it."

Several minutes passed before Samson eased back on the throttle. And then, with a gentle hand, I rubbed the wide, convex expanse—the characteristic Arabian forehead—between his eyes.

At first, Samson fought the new, warm sensations that suddenly enveloped him. His eyelids became heavy, started to buckle and close, but Samson jerked his head in both directions and shot to attention.

Fight it, he told himself. *Never show weakness; never let your guard down.*

It was too late. Like Mikey in the famous Life cereal television commercial from the 1970s, he had tried it and he liked it. And then, with his eyes half-shut, half-open, Samson seemed, for a brief moment, to be a horse at peace. Slowly, my hand moved up across his forehead toward his ears before I abruptly halted all forward progress. The combined expression in Samson's eyes, his pinned ears, and the fact that he literally held his breath told me that for now his ears would remain off-limits.

I would only later learn the true depth of Samson's ear-related issues.

His ears a no-trespass zone, my hand journeyed south, down Samson's mildly concave face. My fingers then happened across Samson's saddest, darkest attribute—the full face-sized scar left behind as he grew into and then out of a constrictive, fastened halter. Hair no longer grew where the unyielding and painful halter once sat, making Samson's aged wound visible and apparent from a significant distance.

Samson's previous life had left scars both seen and invisible.

I had to wonder who, in this instance, was the real monster. Was it Samson, the combative Mustang, who only sought to defend himself? Or was it those who induced and produced this torture? The answer, for me at least, was visibly apparent.

Under Samson's unblinking observation and with his silent yet tacit approval, my fingers traveled across the wide, deep, and perfectly symmetrical lines—scars that bilaterally traversed Samson's cheeks. Slowly, my hand moved across the bridge of Samson's nose where I saw and then felt a dip—a permanent divot that forever instilled this horse with a unique profile. This was the spot where Samson's halter grew most taut and restrictive. This was the spot where the halter ate through the soft tissue until nothing was left but nasal bone.

It was a spot that Samson guarded with his deepest fervor and maximum wrath. A wound years since closed that when touched still caused Samson to brace and stiffen as if it were still open, still bleeding, and still horribly painful. A wound forever exposed; a perpetual gaping reminder of man's and life's cruelties.

Just inches from his eye, I turned into Samson and spoke to his steady gaze, "I can see and feel why you act the way you do. I get it. I get every part of it. Those days are long since passed and they will never return. But you and I will both forever remain cognizant of those times, for those days have shaped and molded the horse which you are today."

My fingers ventured down Samson's long, narrowing muzzle to the very tip, just above his nostrils. There, for a brief moment, I felt Samson's head drop as his eyes closed. I had found his special spot.

Ever under Samson's acute and unwavering surveillance, this was the first instance in which I observed Samson closing his eyes and shutting down his perimeter defenses. For a brief moment, I was no longer a threat. For a brief moment, the outside world was no longer one big overwhelming, menacing hazard. Fully aware that he was vulnerable and altogether exposed, Samson abruptly opened his eyes, returned his head to the vertical position, and reassumed his now-characteristic defensive posture.

"I think you just found his G-spot!" Amy called out from her position in the spectator gallery. "Can men have a G-spot? Do horses? Because I definitely think you just found his!"

Six years, more than half of his life in the human world, and Samson had finally experienced, for the very first time, the sensations associated with being thought well of and cared for.

Samson greeted my arrival the following afternoon with the eagerness of a pupil ready to learn and an athlete ready to start practice. Having spent the last several months terrorizing and doing battle with Studs, Ike, and Star, Samson had been endowed with a wide buffer zone compliments of his three cousins. My newfound attention, my schooling, was now providing purpose to this otherwise apathetic and withdrawn Mustang. As he was a quizzical, intelligent animal, Samson's brain had started to decay and slow from a dearth of proper stimulation.

But now, together, we were both challenged and stimulated.

I pushed forward and for the first time successfully rubbed Samson's hind end and haunches—the loin, croup, pelvis, and hip. Under his cautionary gaze, my hand traveled south past the thigh as Samson checked his pressing desire to strike. Once my hand moved across the stifle and headed toward the gaskin—the upper hind leg and the tibia bone—the safeties that Samson had put in place that curbed his anger, whatever they were, instantly failed.

I had both violated Samson's space and touched a hind leg. Either act alone would have amounted to a minor misdemeanor. Both acts together equaled a felonious assault.

"Noooottttt!" I sternly yelled out as Samson repeatedly kicked at my tibia and fibula. "That is *unacceptable* behavior!" The kicks were vicious; if he had made contact, the fractures would have been severe.

If forced to address Samson's violent tendencies, I was not going to beat, lip/nose-chain, twitch to submission, hobble, or whip him. These were not my methods and this was not my style. Any use of physical force was to be strictly responsive, immediate, swift, and instantly concluded. There was no room and no place for hard feelings, grudges, or escalating tempers. Samson had to first learn my rules and expectations before I could expect, demand, his voluntary compliance. Up to this point, the verbal reprimands and tight circles at a trot had failed to deter his violent behavior. In much the same fashion that a herd lead horse or alpha instantly and violently corrects unacceptable behavior, 99 percent of the time a quick, single blow will arrest a horse's testing, probing, and challenging behavior. This of course was the goal, to emulate and employ that which was known and familiar to a herd-oriented horse such as Samson.

I was smart enough to avoid getting sucked into prolonged fisticuffs with a one-thousand-pound animal. Both the battle and the message would be lost in any and every such instance. When applied appropriately and sparingly, corporal punishment can be an instrument of deterrence and punishment. It should never, however, be thought of as a tool or means to create an alpha-submissive relationship. Before you impose discipline upon a horse, you must have the horse's respect. A strike when appropriate and warranted reinforces respect; it does not create it. Strike a horse prior to earning its respect and you are guaranteed a visit to the nearest emergency room.

Respect must be gradually taught and reinforced through one's presence, through one's command and control of the horse's movement, actions, and behaviors. Respect is a two-way street; if you desire respect, you must in turn give respect.

Horses like Samson present a real challenge to the use of corporal punishment. At our first and then subsequent encounters, Samson had sadly anticipated and expected immediate and unprovoked physical abuse. When it was not delivered, he had ever so gradually dropped his guard. But our work together had demonstrated the immediacy with which he turned to instinctive, involuntary, and extreme violence.

I certainly sought to avoid, with all my efforts, becoming the two-legged predator that Samson so innately feared. Yet, as I had gradually imposed rules, discipline, and restraint upon my pupil, periodically his anger and temper had flared uncontrollably. At times, his reactions were knee-jerk and borne out of his dark past. In other instances, his aggression was a reaction to my ever-increasing control. Either way, the violence had to stop, preferably before I was seriously injured.

I had given this subject much thought and was conflicted. So conflicted and doubting that I hesitated in the moments following his hind-leg strikes. Within seconds, the opportunity to act was lost.

Was I letting Samson off too easy? Did I need to strike him to put an end to the violence? Frustration quickly set in as I questioned whether I was the right trainer for this horse.

Once I was able to successfully touch both of Samson's hind legs, I released him. After a twenty-minute breather, I reentered the pasture and, to my complete surprise, Samson, for the first time, permitted my approach and his capture from the left side. This was nothing short of groundbreaking. It was an act that indicated that Samson's trust was growing, a sign that our bond was strengthening.

Mere weeks with Samson had already established that this horse viewed anything and everything as a dire threat. My hat perched upon a fence post was undoubtedly hiding a sinister danger. The jacket draped across the fence was an enemy waiting to spring and attack. But now my problem child was dropping his guard; I couldn't let this pass. I seized the moment and grabbed the body brush.

Samson reacted as if it were an instrument of death. But then, after the third stroke down his neck and across his back, he warmed to the sensation. He wasn't going to overtly acknowledge and evince his pleasure, but did this horse ever relish his first brushing. Instantly grooming jumped to the number one spot on Samson's top ten list.

Halter breaking was next on the agenda and it was destined to be a jarring experience. My ultimate goal for the afternoon was to minimize and control Samson's fear and his fight. The first step in the process was to remove Samson's halter and do so without mortal injury to myself. In light of his patently obvious issues, I decided to release the poll strap—the part of the halter that sat behind the ears—rather than pull the halter over Samson's forehead. This would permit the halter to fall to the sides of Samson's neck and bypass his sensitive and guarded ears.

Getting things started, I gently handled Samson's throat-latch, cheeks, face, and forehead. Hundreds of burrs fused together the black hairs of his mane and forelock. Not just unsightly, these burrs could be terribly dangerous to Samson's eyes—causing inflammation and ulceration to the cornea and ultimately potential blindness. A smart person would have left this problem to a pair of scissors and another day.

I saw an opportunity.

Samson's newfound adoration for the brush and grooming gave me the idea that he might enjoy having his mane and forelock cleaned up. Removal of the burrs could both calm him and help to socialize this otherwise terribly head-shy horse. Once I introduced Samson to my red-handled hoof pick, I tried, unsuccessfully, to insert the pick's pointed edge into a strand—any strand of hair that wasn't endlessly and hopelessly balled and matted.

Beads of sweat fell from my forehead like water droplets from a leaky faucet—me and my great ideas. Eventually, I made progress and slowly but surely removed countless tennis ball–sized burr clumps.

As Samson stood motionless and transfixed, I observed, to my surprise, that he was both content and at ease. Seemingly transported to a far-off place, a happy place, Samson had, for the second time of this day, discovered a newfound pleasure. His first beauty salon appointment was a rousing success. This agonizingly slow process of removing the hundreds of burrs that inundated Samson's mane, forelock, and, later, his tail instantly developed into a ritualized, mandated component of our weekly training sessions.

To my amazement, burr removal duty, as I came to call it, did more to foster, enhance, and strengthen my bond with Samson than any other single event or training activity.

With Samson calm and somewhat relaxed, it was time to remove his halter. The fence provided an excellent inanimate object to block any forward flight efforts and hinder any attempts to rear. Parked in front of the fence, Samson, forever conscious of his space and surroundings and ever the thinker, quickly realized things were amiss. Not wanting to waste any time and provide my astute pupil an opportunity to figure things out, I moved my right hand up the left side of his face to the halter's buckle while my left hand, tucked under the throat, secured the ends of the lead looped over Samson's neck.

Similarly wishing to avoid delay, Samson dismissed with all formalities, turned his head inward and hard left, and executed a nearly perfect head butt with no advance posturing or warning. It was a catastrophic blow that should have broken or dislocated my shoulder.

Mr. T would have been proud.

When stallions engage in warfare, they will often lock heads in the moments before all hell breaks loose. Perhaps Samson was doing what came naturally. Or maybe he was seizing the opportunity to take me out before I could inflict any harm or injury to his all-too-oft-targeted head. While I understood his motivations and did not take his aggression personally, enough was enough.

During his dark years, Samson had been forced to defend

himself against the unwarranted abuse that frequently rained down upon him. The head butt and head tossing, leg strikes, rearing, blind galloping charges, and body checks were defensive tools gifted to this wild creature by way of both nature and nurture. As for those who beat down this horse, I can only hope that they experienced his true skill in wielding these God-given defensive tools. For once his fight started, Samson was like the Energizer bunny—he kept going, and going, and going. But now was the time for Samson to retire his tools of the trade. He was in a good place and a good home. While he had yet to realize it, pain and abuse were now realities of his past, not his present and not his future. Several weeks of warmth, compassion, and patience had failed to teach this haunted horse that violence was no longer necessary and no longer appropriate. The time had come to push the reset button and teach this horse right from wrong, acceptable from unacceptable behavior.

This time I didn't hesitate.

I drove the flat part of my right palm directly into Samson's freeze mark. For a moment that seemed to last a lifetime, Samson did nothing but stare at me out of the corner of his left eye. *Et tu, Brute? You! You are no different than all the others who came before. Our contract is null and void. I am out of here.*

It was a decision that I had agonized over and an act that would haunt me.

Unable to go forward, Samson in a strategically adept move lunged to his left, pushing me out of my centered stance. Still secured by the lead line draped over his neck, he jumped into what I have affectionately called the teeter-totter. He rocked back and forth throwing a good dozen violent and purposeful bucks. Samson, unbeknownst to me, was a true specialist, a third-degree black belt buck master.

Little did I know at the time, or perhaps I did know, that months later I would experience the sheer power and wrath of this professional bucking horse.

I spun Samson around in tight circles using his momentum and my control over his neck to guide his force and movement. Standing face-first in front of the fence, Samson braced for what he believed would be an inevitable and calamitous beating.

"You took your shot; I took mine. We're done." I told the combative Mustang as his pupils bulged from the sockets and he fought to catch his breath. "I'm not looking to have my face rebuilt or my skull caved in, so get your act together."

Reading Samson the proverbial riot act, I stood close enough to provide him with the opportunity to take a second shot, if he so desired. Only Samson didn't take a second shot. And that, simply put, is the way in which I handle violence and threat: Find out what a horse is capable of, what it can do. Let the pupil put it all out there and then address it appropriately, promptly, and sparingly.

Samson braced for impact as my hand neared. Gently, I rubbed his neck and his freeze mark. I spoke to him as if he were a defendant standing before a judge for sentencing, "Now, my determined little student, you are fully versed in the simplicities of our legal system. There will be no beat-downs, no devices of torture, employed here. Punishment or praise, you get to decide which it is. If you need time with something, you are welcome to all the time in the world. Just don't object with violence and threaten my safety."

Having read Samson his terms of probation, I moved in to unlatch the halter's poll strap. The subsequent release of Samson's halter went off without a hitch: no fight and no interference to his ever-sensitive ears. For several seconds, Samson stood completely motionless, seemingly shocked and doubting of what he had witnessed.

With the realization that I had indeed removed his halter, Samson launched himself toward the stars. While in midair he turned sideways toward the fence, pummeled it with several hind-leg strikes, and made a run for it. Lacking a boarding pass for this particular flight, I released my grip on one end of the lead line, and Samson was gone.

"I'm sorry!" Amy yelled out from the cheap seats of the peanut gallery. "I don't mean to intervene while you are doing your thing . . . but . . . what the hell are you doing? You just turned a perfectly haltered horse into a free, uncatchable crazed beast. Just remember, you break it, you buy it."

Armchair quarterbacks, every sport has them.

I turned my gaze to Samson, who interchangeably galloped and bucked wildly as hoof-sized chunks of mud vaulted from his hind legs like clay targets launched in a skeet shoot. Covering yards of pasture with each powerful stride, the ever-stoic Mustang squealed in high-pitched tones. *I'm free,* he declared. *Free at last. I'm free.*

Something was different this time. Samson wasn't angry, marauding, or running for his life. He was happy; he was joyous; he seemed to be smiling. And with that observation, I came to the realization that moments before Samson hadn't wrenched away from my grasp and control. Rather, he had escaped, escaped from the clutches of the omnipresent halter. Samson's ever-growing list of mortal enemies continued to grow: the despised helicopter, the hated rope and whip, and now the loathed halter.

Samson knew of the halter's power. It could limit, control, and restrain his every action and movement. Resting ever present on his face, it was a minute-to-minute, day-to-day reminder of his captivity, his defeat by the two-legged predator, and his freedom lost. Like a convict who takes off running upon the realization that he has broken free of his leg shackles, Samson too, with the removal of his halter, had struck out for freedom.

As he pounded his hooves in the McHenry soil, as he galloped passionately with the exuberance of a youthful horse and freely with the reckless abandon of a once-wild stallion, in the foreground I saw a bay Mustang. In the background, I saw the plains, valleys, and mountain ranges of Nevada. For an instant, a fleeting moment, Samson was transported back home and I was his journey's guest.

In describing the legendary pacing white stallion of the American West, J. Frank Dobie seemingly depicted Samson as he galloped free of the halter's restraint: ". . . his fire, grace, beauty, speed, endurance and intelligence were exceeded only by his passion for liberty."[9] After a lengthy absence, Samson the once-wild Mustang had rediscovered his liberty.

I let Samson run with the wind and savor his newfound yet short-lived freedom. To expect this horse to change overnight would speak to ignorance as to not only who he was but also what he was. Samson was no youngster. He was determined in his ways and resolute in his beliefs. He was a rigid leader and a traumatized victim. He was damaged goods. Over the course of the next hour, I repeatedly released Samson from his halter and then subsequently caught him. This pattern continued until the point at which the entire process went off without Samson's physical objection or obstruction.

As our first month of training neared an end, I was exhausted and spread too thin. Due to my weekend Samson commitment, a looming legal brief filing deadline had me go without sleep three nights in a row and a canceled apple-picking excursion with Jamie had me in hot water. And when the therapeutic riding center held its quarterly board meeting, I walked in and then promptly and acrimoniously walked out. With twenty years working in special needs, I had long since known that not-for-profits were as much about board member personal agendas as they were about helping those in need. Nonetheless, my tenure had soured me and it was over.

Now with more time for my pupil, the center's loss had been Samson's gain.

My resignation from the riding center probably would have been the final straw—the last excuse I needed to walk away from the horse world—but for Samson. Horse and horseman had made progress and we'd started to trust in each other. But our successes had come at a price. Amy had witnessed Samson's aggression and wanted nothing to do with her volatile Mustang. More time spent with Samson meant less time for my girlfriend, my legal career, my life. And then there was the violence; without even intending it, Samson could kill or maim me, Amy, or any innocent person.

As October waned, the cost of my commitment was adding up. My pledge to break Samson was now having a ripple effect on other aspects of my life. Buyer's remorse occupied

my thoughts. I questioned my abilities. I doubted my decision to break this unbreakable horse.

The one thing that kept me going was that Samson's life
was in my hands.

The work of the weekend complete, I offered Samson his
apple. This time, after great contemplation and deliberation,

ny grasp a quartered sec-
ew and swallow so that
piece. But Samson did
ly gaze moved up from
ked on each other. His
ok the apple from you, as

1 to keep me going.

6

A GAME CHANGER

*A stubborn horse walks behind you,
an impatient horse walks in front of you,
but a noble companion walks beside you.*
—AUTHOR UNKNOWN

In 1961, Hollywood cast its bright lights on the plight of
the wild Mustang with the feature film *The Misfits*. Star-
ring Clark Gable, Montgomery Clift, Eli Wallach, and
Marilyn Monroe, the film followed a trio of aging cowboys
as they hunted their one last chance at fortune—a band of
Mustangs that lived high in the Nevada desert. With the aid
of an airplane, the Mustangers first chased the wild horses
from their mountainous home and then pursued the horses
by truck across the dry, arid Nevada wastelands. Startled and
sickened to learn that the captured horses would be slaughtered and processed into pet food, the character played by
Marilyn Monroe eventually convinced the trio of broken
men to release the detained Mustangs. Free once again, the
wild horses galloped off into the Nevada highlands.

While Hollywood's fictionalized Mustangs received a reprieve, in the many years since *The Misfits* there has been

no such happy ending for the real wild horses who roam Nevada's vast open spaces. Notwithstanding decreasing numbers and ever-shrinking lands, the Mustang is still blamed for range degradation, still allegedly overpopulating the frontier, and still being culled, captured, and relocated.

By our second month of training, and despite his untold and countless demons, Samson had allowed my approach and accepted my touch. He had permitted my entry into his dark, lonely, and solitary world. With each encounter, Samson had checked his instinctive desire to strike first and ask questions later; only Samson wouldn't have asked questions later. It seemed incomprehensible that up to this point Samson had not met his fate at what I termed a "quad b end"—a bullet backyard backhoe burial. The only thing that had kept Samson alive was that he was a stallion and could produce valuable Mustang offspring. But this was no longer the case. Samson's violent ways and antisocial tendencies would no longer be overlooked.

In the days following my resignation from the therapeutic riding center, various organizations sought me out. I first started working with children my junior year in college when I spent time in a high school special needs classroom. Since then, I had worked with pediatric cancer and burn patients, Special Olympics, and hippotherapy and therapeutic riding clients. I would miss working with the kids, but in order for me to do this right Samson would have to be my one and only focus.

As the last signs of summer faded and fall's leaves fell, November's first sessions brought change, success, and violence. Samson's feedings were increased from two to a more evenly spread out three feedings per day. His sweet feed ration was changed to a small amount of nutritionally balanced, commercially prepared concentrate. When it came time to handle his mouth and prepare him for deworming and later the bit, Samson balked. With the help of a syringe filled with applesauce, he relented. The once perpetually melancholic Mustang could have been the poster horse for a CLIO-awarded Mott's advertising campaign.

It would be nice to say that Samson was settling down and had dropped his explosive and violent ways. But this perfect ending was not to be. His demons permeated him to the core and he remained as tightly coiled and unpredictable as a jack-in-the-box toy primed to explode. The question was not if Samson was going to detonate but when.

As the days turned shorter and winter's chill grew closer, Samson struggled to stay warm. While his body produced sebum—oil that would help warm him—and though he could, similar to cats and dogs, fluff his coat and trap air required for insulation, he was waging a losing battle. The time had come to start socializing Samson to his winter blanket.

For weeks, the bright blue insulated blanket had been sitting on the fence during each of our sessions. It started at thirty feet away and was now within five feet of the four-legged sentry. With its noisy nylon, puffy insulation, and ever-threatening leg straps, this was a code red, and Samson was mobilized for action. The first two times that it was placed atop his back, he had squirmed, danced, and wiggled his way out from under it. But for some reason, he didn't detonate.

A week later, however, Samson's "rule of three" kicked in and he bucked wildly until the blanket waved the white flag, slid to the ground, and was trampled to its near demise.

Samson's rule of three was premised upon the concept that each time a new task or tack item was introduced Samson would object, but not excessively, for the first two encounters. He would take in and digest all that he could observe and then by the third encounter he would strike violently, pointedly, and determinedly. And he would continue his barrage until the particular item was no longer on his body and the particular task was no longer a threat.

This was without fail Samson's rule of three and he engaged it with the lead line, the halter, the bridle and bit, the saddle pads, when his hooves and mouth were handled, and of course when the saddle was introduced. It was frustrating, it was aggravating, but it was simply Samson. Take him or leave him.

Among horse professionals, countless opinions exist as to what act truly signifies and communicates a horse's complete submission. Some believe that a horse has fully submitted once it accepts the saddle. Conversely, others assert that a horse has acquiesced to human control only after it has allowed a rider atop its back. In both instances, the animal has exposed itself and diminished its ability to seek unhindered flight. The last thing that any prey animal wants is a predator seated atop its back or a heavy object slowing its escape.

Yes, a horse's acceptance of a saddle and then subsequently a rider should each be considered monumental and ever important. But in allowing a saddle or rider on its back, and though it has relinquished control, the horse has yet to make a sacrifice. If the horse wants the saddle or rider gone, then it can buck each off. If it wants to flee, it can certainly do so with rider in tow.

In contrast, when a prey animal such as the horse lifts and

places its leg in your hand it is making both a huge leap of faith and a tremendous sacrifice. Instantly its sole means of flight are disabled and one of its very limited methods of defense is left immobilized. With a leg up in the air, a horse has indeed surrendered its very lifeline. For a horse on four legs is a spectacle of speed, strength, and agility; a horse on three legs is easy prey.

Samson must have agreed with my rationale. When his forelegs were lifted for the first time, he—like the Texans at the Alamo—made quite the last stand. And once he had complied and was offered his peppermint reward, he lowered his head, inhaled its aroma, turned his head hard to the right, and rejected the overture. *What?* his narrowed gaze seemed to say. *You really think that little sphere of compressed sugar is a proportional reward for giving up my legs?* As he was always a character, this was certainly not the last time that Samson, ever proud and prideful, would defiantly reject a reward.

In much the same fashion that Samson fought when I lifted his forelegs, he flew into a jarring rage when I handled his ears. He bucked, reared, and flung his forelegs out like he was Rocky Balboa pounding cow carcasses. He pitched his head from left to right and back again looking for a target. While Samson guarded both ears with a crazed fervor, it was the right one that truly set him off.

Standing along his right side, I spoke to my pupil, "This just gets worse by the week, doesn't it? They ear-twitched you, didn't they? You have truly seen it all and then some, my friend."

Employed when handling overly excited, difficult, or unruly equines, twitching is a process that when utilized properly allows a handler to manage an otherwise-unruly horse. With pressure applied to parts of the horse's anatomy by either hand or a tool called a twitch, the ensuing endorphin release calms the animated and unmanageable animal. When they think of this process, most horse people envision nose twitching applied via the upper lip. In these instances, a loop of rope or chain is placed on to and then slowly tightened around the horse's upper lip until the animal turns compliant. Ear twitching, on the other hand, thankfully remains mostly unknown.

Those horse owners who still resort to the ear twitch as a method of restraint do so by grabbing the horse's ear in their hand, tightly squeezing, and then twisting it until the animal is subdued. These days, most in the horse world reject this method of control since it often leads to head- and ear-shy horses. Yet even old-school horsemen—those who manually ear-twitch—reject the application of a mechanical chain or rope twitch to the sensitive tissue of the equine ear. When a rope or chain is affixed to and tightened around a horse's ear, it is a procedure that is almost always applied incorrectly and more likely than not results in permanent nerve and cartilage damage. Ultimately, a horse who has been ear-twitched with a chain or rope ends up physically and emotionally scarred and combative to any who venture near its head.

As I stood next to Samson and gazed upon his outer ear—the pinna—cartilage damage was plainly visible. I suddenly understood why Samson acted as he did, and thus withheld punishment.

One step forward, two steps back.

Looking into his right eye while whispering into his right ear, I spoke to the victim, "We'll get through this, Samson. Slowly but surely, we'll get through this."

Now that Samson and I were working up close and personal, it was time to clip on to his halter and teach him the release and yield to pressure. If correctly taught and properly learned, the yield to pressure is arguably the single most significant skill in a horse's vast training repertoire. A horse who yields to pressure will follow under lead, submit to the bit, and respond to and move out from leg pressure. The horse who doesn't will drag a handler, violently fight the bit, refuse leg cues, and ultimately take its rider for the ride of his or her life.

The plan was simple—clip on to the halter, put some distance between us, and then apply intermittent pressure to the lead line until Samson yielded, released, and moved forward toward me. After the lead line was attached to Samson's halter, I slowly walked backward. I had fifteen feet of lead line to play with but never had the chance to use nearly any of it. Having been roped, yanked, and dragged his entire life, Samson instantly knew the game plan and understood what needed to be done.

With the slightest hint of pressure applied to the lead line, he lifted his head, straightened his neck, and leaned back against the halter. I wasn't concerned—this was a standard response for any and every unschooled horse. Nevertheless, I had no intention of engaging in a tug-of-war with a one-thousand-pound horse where the outcome was certain. I resituated Samson so that his rump abutted the barn's west wall and his head faced the open pasture. If Samson was going to shoot back in reverse, which he no doubt was, then he had nowhere to go. This horse was tough, but not tough enough to emerge victorious against the barn's concrete foundation wall.

Samson turned his head to the left and shot me a hard look. *You suck!*

I had removed his best defense to the pull and control of the lead line, but that didn't mean Samson was going to wave the white flag. This was a horse who was well versed in how to fight and resist the pull of the rope. Yet this time, there was no unrelenting pressure, no hard jerks, and no constriction of his airway. There was only alternating pressure and a denied back-door escape. I played out the lead line and increased the distance between teacher and student.

And then something strange happened.

Already simmering and nearing his boiling point, Samson turned nervous and unsure. He seemed afraid. Without warning, he took several abrupt, hurried steps forward and parked out alongside my right shoulder. And to my surprise, that was all it took.

Needless to say, I was ecstatic and praised him accordingly. Aware that he had displayed what he believed amounted to a show of weakness, Samson stood chisel faced and indifferent to my commendation.

That afternoon, I didn't take the fight away from Samson. That afternoon, Samson chose not to fight. Left standing alone, attached to his greatest foe, the rope, Samson was overcome with an emotion that was not anger, contempt, or disdain. He was overcome with fear. Though he hadn't realized it at the time, Samson had slowly come to rely on me for his safety and his security. And when he timidly stepped forward to me, he found the very safety and security that he had sought. The process had started. Samson was showing the first signs of voluntarily seeking out my protection.

He had, ever so slightly, started to trust in me.

While Samson's actions were monumental, they were, nonetheless, borne out of panic. If our progress was to continue, Samson's decisions would have to be fueled by something more than fear. It was time for Samson to decide whether or not he needed my guidance and direction. It was time for Samson to decide whether or not he needed, wanted, his first friend.

As Samson and I spent more time together, his inventory of learned skills increased, as did my list of permissible actions. Each new skill meant more of my time, more of my investment. In order to ensure Samson's survival, I needed to prove that he could change. But as our bond was strengthening, the Mustang continued to shun all others. Though Samson held a glimmer of hope that I could be different, he had made his mind up about all the rest. He needed only me. No one else could stand him; no one else would even go near him.

I was the Mustang's only ally and apologist.

Each week, week after week, Samson had some form of a meltdown. Every advance was met with obstruction, violence, or a combination of the two. And as luck would have it, Amy just happened to be present on those days when Samson lost it. Having time and time again observed Samson at his worst, Amy was growing increasingly frustrated and impatient. His successes were her highs, his failures her lows. It seemed there was more here than an owner who wanted her horse rehabilitated. It seemed that Amy had some other interest in Samson's successes and failures.

The gap between Samson and Amy was growing into a schism. My concern that Samson would be shown the door—or in this case the gate—grew greater. We needed results, and soon.

Every training session now included and followed a fixed order of routines and practices. Predictability would be the best tool to impose order and control upon this horse. Provide a horse like Samson a routine and you in turn remove his fear of the unknown. Fear of the unknown and fear of change are traits that all horses carry and, when combined, together they present the greatest impediment to a successfully trained mount. Make the horse your partner in the training process, key it into what is going to happen and when, and the sky is your limit. Keep the horse guessing and in the dark, and you only sustain its anxiety and doom your hopes for a well-trained and receptive steed.

Through the years, Samson's fear of the unknown had kept him rigid, on the defense, and primed to strike. If he could predict anything, it most likely involved a whip, lariat, or beat-down. The associated anxiety made it nearly impossible for him to function and carry out the most basic of tasks. But now things would be different.

Week after week, Samson was caught, his halter removed, his legs picked up, and he was brushed—same order, same routine, same thing, time after time. For certain actions, he received praise and reward. For other specified behaviors, he was punished and made to work. He and I were to be equally informed as to what was going to happen, when, and why. As Xenophon instructed, we would be partners.

No longer anxious and fearful, Samson could eventually willingly assent to my dominion, my control, and my teachings. It was a theory and a practice that works. A theory and a practice, with a horse like Samson, easier said than done.

It was a theory and practice that soon yielded results.

When I arrived at the farm in mid-November, Samson greeted my appearance with a series of perfectly executed concentric circles. He wasn't pounding; he wasn't bounding; he was prancing. Fluid and aristocratic, Samson was showing off. *I'm ready to work,* he seemed to announce. As I unloaded my gear, Amy made her way down the driveway.

"You mentioned the other day that you wanted pictures of Samson, right?" I questioned her. "Well, I recommend you get your camera." I don't know exactly what I saw, but something told me this was the day that Samson would "join up."

Minutes later, I had Samson under lead as I brushed his coat, removed the burrs, and lifted his forelegs off the ground. Together, we walked in unison as I taught him the verbal commands of "walk up" and "whoa." We covered the entire expanse of the crib pasture, traveled through the gate, and entered the roadside pasture. "Whoa, stand, and hold your stand," I told my focused student as we came to rest on the concrete pad that encircled the barn. As Samson held his stand, I gently rubbed his neck, face, and muzzle. Several minutes passed while the sedate Mustang took in the entirety of his massage.

And then, without warning, he slowly turned his neck to the left, closed his eyes, and buried his head deep into my chest. Instantly the warrior's body—permanently taut and tense since our first meeting and for years before that—suddenly went limp. I didn't know what to do and for fear of ruining the moment did nothing. He then released a long, exhaustive sigh that when combined with a single inhaled breath resembled the sound of a foghorn. It was a sigh that seemed to discharge years of fear, contempt, and doubt.

Samson had finally voluntarily submitted—he had "joined up" with me.

Samson's face remained tucked in my chest for a good two minutes. Once he removed it and returned his head to the vertical position, I turned my attention to Amy. "Please tell me that you got that shot?" I asked.

I waited for a response, but there was none. Seated on a water bucket with the camera on the ground beside her, Amy remained silent. I stood shocked, relieved, and reenergized as she cradled her head and sobbed. Like her Mustang's long, exhaustive sigh moments before, Amy's sobs seemed to release years of bottled-up stress, doubt, and pressure. Samson's breakthrough moment had been cathartic for both this dysfunctional Mustang and his emotionally spent owner.

Samson the reticent Mustang had exposed a side of himself that no one had ever seen and in doing so he had earned a reprieve. He was safe, for now.

Amy and I chatted for thirty minutes while Samson stood perfectly still. Ten minutes into the conversation he dropped his head and dozed off to dreamland. "Who would have figured it?" I declared to Amy. "Your perpetually troubled, socially dysfunctional Mustang has made his first friend."

Sadly, the bliss was short-lived. In just days, the bond that had developed between Samson and me, all that he had learned and digested, would be cast in doubt and placed in jeopardy. In a heartbeat and in an instant, a traumatic encounter would return this horse to his dark past and the old Samson would once again emerge.

• • •

Rejuvenated by Samson's actions, I returned days later. As I unloaded my gear, I observed Amy conversing with the driver of a truck that had pulled up the driveway behind me. Minutes later, I was introduced to Frank, Samson's previous owner. Staring in the direction of his farm, he told me of the devastating barn fire, how he came to own Samson, and what he knew of the Mustang's past.

"When I bought this horse, I was told to not even waste time trying to be nice," Frank explained. He then continued, "This horse is a real son of a bitch and if you have any hopes of handling him, then you need to put a pretty good beat-down on him so that he has no choice but to submit. Also, make sure that you always have at least two other guys with you so that you can get one or two ropes on him and muscle him down. I can't really see that the women here are going to help you with that, so I can always lend you a hand."

"Really," I responded, "a pretty good beat-down? Is that every time, or just initially?"

"Every time. Always," Frank answered without a moment's hesitation. "And if you approach him one-on-one, my friend, I don't think you'll be coming back."

After a lengthy pause, Frank continued, "You'll probably need a good piece of wood."

"Some wood?" I asked incredulously. "You mean like a two-by-four?"

"It works like a charm," Frank replied with an air of bravado.

I had heard enough. I now had the final piece of the puzzle. In legal jargon, a preponderance of the evidence convinced me that Samson had been unjustly battered and beaten. Proof beyond a reasonable doubt said that this Mustang's abusers were guilty of chronic and systematic abuse. While I held no personal animus toward Frank, it was obvious that we each held manifestly differing opinions on how to treat not only this horse but all horses. My worst fears regarding Samson's past were no longer conjecture; my fears were now conclusive fact.

Through the course of my training career, the horses I have worked with can be segregated into one of three categories. Type I horses are young, untrained, and green and fall into two subcategories: normal and difficult dispositions. For whatever reason, I have always gravitated to the difficult, aggressive personalities. Experience has shown that if trained properly during their youth, wayward and headstrong type I horses make fearless and steadfastly obedient companions under saddle.

Type II horses are horses who are older and have yet to be broke, trained older horses whose schooling has omitted particular critical elements, or trained horses who have developed certain unacceptable behaviors or vices. Examples of type II horses include a saddle-broke horse who has yet to learn how to yield to pressure, a horse who body bashes a handler under lead, kicks when its legs are handled, or walks off from under a rider during mounting. Horses who are chemically fueled, overly aggressive, or violent and horses who have been traumatized, mishandled, or abused in any way round out the third category, type III problem horses. Type III horses can range from a horse who needs to overcome its fears to reenter a trailer following an accident to any horse who has suffered through malnourishment, isolation, or physical or mental cruelty.

As a combination of type II and III horses, Samson was the sum of all my fears. He was the perfect storm. And on this quiet Sunday afternoon, I was about to witness firsthand the damage left behind from a lifetime of abuse.

"My friend," Frank interjected as I climbed over the pasture fence, "you're not even carrying a lariat to rope the beast. I think it is best if I give you a hand."

"No thanks. I'll find some way to manage!" I yelled back over my shoulder with a hint of sarcasm and contempt.

Since my arrival, Samson had remained parked on the far side of the corncrib—hidden from view. With all of the activity and people, I thought nothing of it. When he was confronted by either commotion or strangers, this was Samson's modus operandi. As I closed in on his position, I felt a strange sensation and turned to observe Frank following close behind.

"No, I'm sorry," I declared as I stepped right up into Frank's face, "you can't be in here."

"I know this monster better than anyone; trust me, you will want my help. Hey look, there's the beast now," Frank responded as he pointed over my shoulder toward the corncrib.

A glance over my left shoulder revealed Samson's head—and only his head—as he peered around the corncrib's far wall. He looked as though he had been napping, but as his clouded eyesight turned clear his eyes confirmed what his ears had heard. It seemed obvious that Frank wasn't this horse's first sadistic owner, but he was certainly the last and Samson remembered him well. Awakened from a slumber to a wash of painful memories, the beast inside Samson exploded.

Charging forward, Samson took out the high-tensile electric line that cordoned off the pasture's dangerous terrain, darted through the open gate, galloped across the roadside pasture, and disappeared. Like the dust cloud from his crazed frenzy, our progress, all that Samson had learned, quickly evaporated.

"You should have listened to me, my friend; I tried to warn you!" Frank yelled as he took off in pursuit. "Now we really need to teach him a lesson."

Before I could respond, I heard a loud crash—the undeniable sound of high-speed impact between horse and fence. My worst fear had now become reality. Samson had crashed the split-rail perimeter fence, injured himself, and escaped. He was willing to risk it all to get away. The only person who could capture the fugitive was me, and I already knew, long since understood, that there was no way to capture this Mustang if he was truly crazed, frenzied, or injured.

Enough was enough. Incensed by what had just occurred, I focused my wrath on Frank. "I understand your interest in helping here, but you signed Samson over a long time ago and he is no longer your horse. So leave, now!"

My heart down at my ankles, I assumed Samson was gone, long gone. If this was the case, then his fate was sealed. He would most likely run as far and as fast as he could and wind up under the wheels or in the windshield of a pickup truck coming around the valley's countless blind curves. If fortunate to avoid such an end, Samson would nevertheless happen upon a neighbor, his dog, cattle, or horses, then attack, as he was prone to do, and wind up felled by a shotgun round. Either way, he would not be coming back.

Once I passed through the open gate, to my shock and amazement, I saw Samson standing in the far corner of the roadside pasture. His respirations were off the charts, his body trembling, muscles twitching, and his eyes bulging out from the sockets. This was not the horse I had worked with the last several weeks. In fact, he was unlike any horse I had ever observed. In twenty years I had seen and worked with the best of the worst at their worst, and at that very moment they had nothing on Samson.

Samson, the horse I believed held no weaknesses, was stricken to his core with terror.

As I made my approach, it was clear that Samson was still intent on attempting another prison break, so my movements were kept slow and deliberate. From fifteen yards away, I observed clumps of hair tangled in the barbed wire strung across the wooden fence's now-shattered top rail. At ten yards and closing, Samson spun, faced me head-on, and stopped my approach dead in its tracks. Drops of blood trickled from sections of his chest previously covered with hair. He raised his neck higher than I had ever observed, violently shook his head up, down, and back again, and repeatedly slammed his right hoof hard into the dense soil.

His message was undeniable: *Approach no further.*

Without moving my legs, I leaned forward to test the waters. Samson met my ever-so-minimal movement with his own. He rotated hard to his left, showed me his hind end, and delivered three pounding double hind-leg kicks. If this were any other horse, I would have addressed the unacceptable show of violence and force. But it was Samson. I understood where he was coming from and what he felt.

In an instant Samson's dark past and vivid memories had reappeared and resurfaced. Witness protection had relocated the chronically victimized Mustang and now his safe house was both discovered and violated. This was all my fault. Weeks prior, I had made Samson a pledge. I promised him that the darkness and abuse of his past was just that—the past. I assured Samson that he could put those days and those memories behind him and that he would be forever safe and protected.

I was clearly wrong.

While Samson faced the road and mapped out his escape, his right eye wildly darted back and forth between the rolling hills in the distance and my position behind and off to his right. *Freedom,* he must have thought to himself, *that is the only way I will forever be safe.* I arced around Samson's right side and came to rest alongside the damaged perimeter fence. There horse and horseman stood parallel to each other and ten yards apart.

"No, buddy, this road and those rolling hills do not hold the solution to your problems; your new life will be over before it even has the chance to get started." I told Samson as he plotted out his new exit strategy. "This is my fault; I made a promise and I broke that promise. I will fix this."

Samson didn't hear a word I said. Like a soldier suffering from shell shock, he just wasn't all there. After nearly an hour of standing beside and talking to my frazzled four-legged friend, I was able to finally approach and clip on to Samson. Together, inch by inch, we made our way back to the crime scene—the corncrib pasture—where we rejoined Amy.

Though I had no control over the ghosts that had taken up residence in Samson's head, I did have control over the demon who had just reappeared. Seeking to keep the discussion short and simple, I dispensed with the usual emotional and moral arguments and went right for the jugular—dollars, cents, and liability.

"You know," I spoke to Amy while gently rubbing Samson's special spot, "next time Samson won't run away and Frank won't get away. As Samson's owner and the holder of this property, you will be on the hook both financially and legally. My suggestion is that you go out of your way to make sure that Frank never goes anywhere near Samson, or Samson's pasture, again."

It took mere seconds for Amy to digest and respond to my comments, "Samson has already done enough damage. I simply can't afford, nor do I even want to deal with, any more problems resulting from his psychotic breakdowns. I will tell Frank that you have stated that *no one* is permitted anywhere near Samson's vicinity. You can be the bad guy, not me."

I didn't really care if I was the bad guy or not. All that mattered was that Samson once again felt safe and protected and that he had a home. All that mattered was that Samson was able to put and keep his dark days in the past where they belonged.

I then realized that while Samson and I had been making great strides together, the damage inflicted from his earlier life had continually hindered, if not wholly impeded, our advance. Working with Samson was like standing on the ocean's edge as the tide came in; our progress advanced, then retreated, advanced, then retreated. No two of our training sessions ended with the same progress; no two of our sessions concluded with the same retreat. It would have been overwhelming had Samson not been making such grand efforts. At that moment, I understood that while most of my horse clients eventually shed the majority of their demons, Samson would never shed any of his. There was no way around it; Samson would forever bear the scars—physical and emotional—of a harsh and unforgiving life.

I was Sisyphus, doomed to push the rock up the hill only to have it eternally roll back down.

As November came to a close and winter zeroed in, my focus shifted from Samson to the obliterated barn. With temperatures inside the structure hovering nearly ten degrees below those outside, the barn provided little safe haven from the elements. My years working as a carpenter in college and graduate school would now come in handy as I broke out the circular saw, level, hammer, and nails and went to work. Over the course of two weeknights, I boarded up the missing windows, resheeted the aerated interior walls, repaired the shattered exterior door, insulated the stall area, and rebuilt the stalls. When I arrived home well after 1:00 a.m. on the second night, the barn was warm and cozy and the task complete.

The following morning, I slept through my alarm, stumbled in late to a court call, and nearly caused a client's case to be dismissed. After being lambasted by the judge and embarrassed before my peers, I took a few minutes to catch up with a mentor from my early practice days who had witnessed the public flogging.

"I've never known you to once arrive late for court,"

Charles correctly observed, "and while I'm sure that the fury of a screwed-up horse can no doubt be severe, I would have to think that it pales in comparison to the wrath of an irate judge and a disgruntled client."

Charles was correct; I had a lot to lose. I was gambling with my livelihood and my future. Later that evening when I turned to Jamie for a sympathetic ear, one was not available. "Mark my words, you are going to regret all of this," she said as she cut the conversation short and hung up the phone.

The price of working with Samson was on the increase. Amy's growing impatience, a mentor's valid concerns, and Jamie's ever-increasing list of grievances—none of it mattered. The more I was criticized, the more my tunnel vision further narrowed. I was committed to Samson, at any cost.

At a time when most Americans were celebrating Thanksgiving and giving thanks, I was certain that Samson was thankful for my attention, my care, and, ultimately, my friendship. At the most basic level, I was thankful for being uninjured and still mostly intact. But on a more profound level, I was thankful for having Samson in my life. He was learning from me; I was learning from him. The fact that I understood a horse no one else seemed to get, the reality that I had given him direction and purpose and that he had chosen me as his friend, filled me with a sense of pride, worth, and accomplishment.

Though I hadn't realized it before this point, we both were affecting each other's lives.

7

FROM EXALTED STEED TO EASY TARGET

A dog may be man's best friend,
but the horse wrote history.
—AUTHOR UNKNOWN

Once the BLM captured Samson, he was one of 3,938 wild horses removed from Nevada in 2003, one of the 10,081 rounded up nationally that year. With 40 percent of the nation's wild horse population gathered in the first decade of the twenty-first century, he was dumped into an overburdened, mismanaged system. As one of the 6,165 Mustangs adopted nationally that year, Samson then found himself in a strange new world. Through no fault of his own, he had been torn from his free-roaming, wild ways. And despite his innocence, for this horse and those like him there would be no going back. The reasons and justifications for their removal had been a century in the making.

The start of the twentieth century saw 230,000 wild horses removed and shipped to service in the South African Boer War and 15,000 Mustangs shot dead in Nevada. Life would never be the same for the free-roaming wild herds. In twenty short years, overgrazing cattle had severely depleted and irreparably damaged the frontier's great grasslands. The West's vast ranges were dry and barren; modernization and industrialization were just around the corner.

The Mustang horse—once prized for its endurance, fortitude, speed, and adaptability—soon found itself an essential ingredient in pet food and a necessary component in the production of glue, conveyor belts, clothing, and mattresses. Young men from across the nation quickly made their way west—seeking riches hunting and capturing the great, untamed American wild horse. They were called Mustangers, and at six cents per pound the free-roaming wild horse stood in their crosshairs. The famed horse of the frontier was now a ticket to instant fortune.

The great American war against the Mustang had officially begun. No quarter was to be given and no compassion shown. The once majestic symbol of the frontier and the American way was under all-out attack.

In the American West, the number of free-roaming Mustangs was on sharp decline. With two hundred thousand shipped to and having perished in Europe during World War I and the U.S. government successfully carrying out its eradication policy against the Indian herds, the onslaught against the wild horse was just getting started. When P. M. Chappel and his two brothers opened the nation's first major meat-processing plant in 1923—Chappel Brothers Corporation in Rockford, Illinois—the canned food industry was officially up and running and the wild horse was in serious straits.

In little time, two hundred similar plants opened across the country and an industry that processed 150,000 pounds of horse meat in 1923 soon processed 23 million pounds in

1930, followed by 50 million pounds in 1933–34. Along the Western Seaboard, towns that once raised chickens started accepting daily arrivals of railroad stock cars full of wild horses. Packed in like sardines, transported under special low "feed" rates, and not subject to humane transport requirements, the Mustangs suffered all the way to the processing plants. Industry was growing and building, and the Mustang horse was its bricks and mortar. Once praised by the explorer, the Indian warrior, and the cowboy, the Mustang was now nothing more than a commodity, a resource, a carcass.

As demand for the Mustang as a tool of industry grew, "Mustang Fever" gripped the nation. Magazine articles published in the 1920s depicted Mustang hunts as exciting, challenging, alluring, and enthralling. Chasing down a Mustang horse was not just sport, but it was also a business, and a profitable one at that. Mustangers could make a name and fortune for themselves and rid the range of the feral, invasive, outlaw wild horse. By 1925, the State of Montana had placed a bounty on all free-roaming wild horses and four hundred thousand Mustangs were dispatched in short order. The verdict had been handed down—Mustanging was glamorous, lucrative, and a public necessity. Fueled by profit motive and driven by machismo, the Mustangers showed little respect for their four-legged victims.

On the hunt, many old-time Mustangers often employed creasing to down their prey. An act that entailed shooting at and grazing the spinal nerve, which runs along the neck, creasing temporarily stunned and incapacitated a wild horse long enough for it to be roped. As recounted by Frank Dobie, the Mustanger had to be an expert shot: "Creasing, too, was a kind of sport—without sportsmanship. If a rifleman wanted to kill a horse, he did not aim to crease it; if he aimed to crease, he frequently killed."[10] If the Mustanger was a crack shot the horse was off to slaughter; if he was anything less than a marksman the downed animal was left behind to die a slow, painful, lonely death.

Still other Mustangers relied upon snares that fastened around a horse's neck or leg. With broken legs and necks more oft than not the norm, felled Mustangs were left behind to yet again suffer an agonizing end. While creasing and snares were commonplace, other Mustanger techniques included shooting fleeing horses in the eyes, using trip wires to sever tendons, poisoning water sources, and constructing traps around water holes. Often, herd mares were captured and then released with nostrils sewn shut and horseshoes bent around their lower legs as a means to slow a herd's movement. With a 25 percent fatality rate during the chase and inevitable mortality upon capture, whether transported to slaughter or not a pursued Mustang was doomed to a painful and gruesome demise.

By the 1930s, the Great Depression gripped the nation. With 67 percent, near 25 million acres, of range destroyed by cattle and overgrazing, the once-rich western grasses no longer provided a viable forage source. Grasslands that had a cattle-carrying capacity of 22.5 million head in 1880 were now able to service no more than 10 million livestock. Concern for the fate of the American range was growing and Congress responded by passing the Taylor Grazing Act of 1934. Named after senator Edward Taylor, the Act established grazing districts, land allotments, and a permit system, while classifying 143 million acres of public land according to its suitability for crop development. The Taylor Act further established a government agency—the U.S. Grazing Service (the first incarnation of the BLM)—that supervised all land allotments, livestock permits, and animals grazing upon public lands. At the time, cattlemen paid mere pennies in fees for each grazing animal; today, stockmen pay a meager $1.35 per head.

Local advisory boards were established in each grazing district to help the Grazing Service manage and supervise land allotments and permits. Comprised entirely of cattlemen, the advisory boards were anything but Mustang friendly. These stockmen, long since searching out validation in their quest for the annihilation of the wild horse, finally had justification and the force of law to support their crusade. The Mustang—not the sheep and cattle—was to blame for the destruction of the frontier's rich and plentiful grasses. It had ravaged and raped the range; the feral horse of the West had to go.

The Grazing Service's position on the free-roaming Mustang was apparent when in 1939 then acting director of grazing Archie Ryan declared, "A wild horse consumes forage needed by domestic livestock, brings in no return, and serves no useful purpose. . . . ."[11]

Long since identified as a feral and invasive species, the free-roaming wild horse lacked the protections of the safe harbor provisions of Section 9 of the Taylor Act, which mandated the allocation of forage for all local "native" wildlife. With the knowing consent of a newly formed and powerful government agency, the assault on this nation's wild herds was ratcheted up to a new level. The cattlemen now had carte blanche to rid the range of its one true companion and an army of destitute and homeless young men to fight their crusade. The time had come: the time to replace the free-roaming wild horse with cattle and sheep and to wage an unchecked, all-out attack on the American Mustang.

By the close of the 1930s and start of the 1940s, the assault on the Mustang was at full tilt. In Arizona one thousand horses were shot dead in Sitgreaves National Forest, and in Oregon four thousand Mustangs were removed from the equation. As America fought in and ended a second world war, wholesale "range clearance" was in full force and effect. Scapegoated for range destruction and degradation, Mustangs across the West dropped in the tens of thousands as water holes were poisoned and Mustanger bullets felled entire herds. In Nevada, an additional one hundred thousand Mustangs were dead and fewer than four thousand remained. The offensive against the American Mustang was at a fever pitch, and with the aid of modern technology things were about to get worse.

In its ongoing battle with the Mustangers, the already-undermatched Mustang found itself pitted against a new foe from which it had no defense: airborne fixed-wing assault. With the advent and initiation of aerial roundups, Mustang hunters could trap entire herds with far less human labor and effort. The continued survival of the nation's free-roaming herds seemed cast in doubt until one fateful day in 1950 when a young woman pulled behind the tailgate of a stock truck trailing a steady stream of blood down Nevada's Highway 395.

Her name was Velma Johnston and she was a woman who had spent a lifetime battling adversity. Diagnosed with polio and fitted into a three-quarter, nearly full-body cast at the age of seven, Velma knew the meaning of pain and suffering. "Here comes Humpy!" the kids would shout as she passed by with drooped eye, drooped jaw, displaced teeth, and uneven shoulders.[12] As Velma recounted, it was a terrible existence for anyone, let alone a child: ". . . there was always the pain. And the adults who discovered my 'pitiful' condition and wondered what on earth would ever become of me, as though I was deaf, too, and not able to wonder myself what would become of me, since they mentioned it."[13]

Those who ridiculed Velma and callously trampled her feelings had no idea of her fortitude and tenacity and what she was destined to accomplish. Velma would soon wage all-out war against the Mustangers, the cattlemen, and all those who had Mustang annihilation in their sights.

Velma followed the bloody stock truck to the slaughterhouse, where she watched the unloading of horses with buckshot wounds, missing eyes and hooves, and bloody stumps where their legs once were. It was a sight that would have sickened the hardiest of souls. When she inquired as to what had caused the gruesome scene, Velma was given a very matter-of-fact response: "Oh, they were run in by plane out there. . . . No point in crying your eyes out over a bunch of useless Mustangs . . . they'll be dead soon anyway."[14] Velma had grown up with animals and they had provided her with comfort from a cold and reclusive existence. Her father, Joe Brown, often sang the wild horse's virtues: "Mustangs are born in the wind. . . . They drink it, that's why they can run so fast."[15] The harsh, apathetic explanation provided at the slaughterhouse was like dropping a bucketful of bloody fish into shark-infested waters. It was a huge mistake and a call to attack.

Velma was prepared to pounce; her crusade to save the wild Mustang had officially begun.

Gravely troubled by the plight of Nevada's Mustangs, Velma first took her concerns to the BLM's Reno district office. There officials told her that the Mustang was an inbred, mongrel, feral creature that proliferated like vermin. Even worse, the officials advised Velma that the Mustang posed a serious threat to forage resources, sheep, and cattle grazing. The only good that the Mustang served was as chicken feed and pet food. In other words, the only good Mustang was a dead Mustang.

Sadly, to this day these sentiments and beliefs still echo throughout various parts of the country.

The BLM officials' words were cold, harsh, and eye-opening. Velma was on notice: her fight was going to be a one-woman crusade. In search of knowledge and facts, she sought out local ranchers who provided her with critical information. Sheep, and not wild horses, ravaged the range, the ranchers advised. Long since blamed for rangeland degradation, the Mustangs were actually good for the frontier's vast grasslands—their manure reseeded it. As for the purported ever increasing and uncontrollable Mustang population, inclement weather and natural predators would continue to keep mortality rates high and reproductive numbers low. The BLM, it turns out—not the ranchers—wanted the wild horses removed from the range and knew exactly what to say to raise the local population's ire.

Armed with facts and educated by firsthand accounts, Velma's advocacy campaign kicked into full swing. In no time, opponents had labeled her "Wild Horse Annie." She responded by insisting that her friends and colleagues start addressing her as Annie rather than as Velma. Intended to discredit her efforts, the nickname had only bolstered Annie's resolve. She was soon a force to be reckoned with and an advocate who could not be ignored. Annie's campaign to save the American wild Mustang met its first success in 1955 when the Nevada legislature banned the use of motorized vehicles and airborne herding during roundups. Four years later, Annie won a second apparent victory as Congress passed Public Law 86–234 or what came to be known as the "Wild Horse Annie Law."

Sadly, both the state and federal statutes went widely ignored and unenforced. In the Nevada desert, Mustangs by the thousands were shot from above, tied to truck tires and pursued to exhaustion, and run into death pits. Eyes were shot out, tendons sliced by trip wires, and lungs exploded from overexertion With two laws on the books, Mustangs in Nevada and surrounding states were still being chased, tortured, brutalized, and then slaughtered. Opponents of the Mustang horse rejoiced over Annie's empty victories—Annie saw both as a dry run. The Mustang breed was fading from the American landscape and Annie was just getting started.

By the end of the decade's first year, congressional committees held sixty draft bills that sought to protect the nation's free-roaming wild horses. Many years had passed since Annie's fated encounter with the bloody stock truck, and in the interim she had perfected the art of advocacy, mass appeal, and mass marketing. Made famous with the 1966 publication of Marguerite Henry's book *Mustang: Wild Spirit of the West,* Annie was a hero to school-age children across the country for both her early battles with polio and her Mustang preservation efforts.

With a captive, convincing, and enthusiastic army of soldiers at her beck and call, Annie mustered the ranks and yelled, "Charge!" Thousands upon thousands of letters soon flooded the Washington, D.C., postal system. The nation's greatest nonwartime letter-writing campaign saturated and inundated the Capitol Building and the White House. The American people and the children of America had spoken; the time had come to stop hunting, brutalizing, and murdering America's wild Mustangs.

The American taxpayer and voter had communicated a mandate and on October 4, 1971, Congress responded—forwarding to the White House a unanimously approved bill that spoke to public demand and outrage. Then president Richard Nixon affixed his signature to the Wild Free-Roaming Horses and Burros Act of 1971 and on December 15 the nation finally had a law intended to safeguard the free-roaming wild horse. It had been a long road for advocates such as Wild Horse Annie, Hope Ryden, and the countless others who had dedicated years to the cause. It had been an even longer road for the tens of thousands of Mustangs who had suffered and perished decade after decade.

The wild Mustang that had filled cans of pet food, provided hide and carcass to the captains of industry, and been an unwilling and overmatched target in a cruel, bloodthirsty, and compassionless sport was now safe and protected—or so most thought.

By late 1971, the country had a law that protected the nation's free-roaming wild horses and the Bureau of Land Management and the U.S. Forest Service were charged with enforcing, implementing, and managing its provisions. The Act dictated that:

> . . . *wild free-roaming horses and burros are living symbols of the historic and pioneer spirit of the West; that they contribute to the diversity of life forms within the Nation and enrich the lives of the American people; and that these horses and burros are fast disappearing from the American scene. It is the policy of Congress that wild free-roaming horses and burros shall be protected from capture, branding, harassment, or death; and to accomplish this they are to be considered in the area where presently found, as an integral part of the natural system of the public lands.*[16]

With over 90 percent of the wild horse population roaming on federal rangeland, the lion's share of the work fell to the BLM. Soon, an entire new jargon came to be associated with the wild horse: "Herd Areas (HAs)," "Herd Management Areas (HMAs)," and "Appropriate Management Level (AML)." These terms of art and the accompanying statistics would reveal, in the years that followed, a telling and disturbing story.

Consistent with the '71 Act's directives, wild horses were to be managed at then current population levels. A low wild horse population estimate would guarantee that in the years to come fewer horses would occupy the range. When the BLM projected that 17,300 wild horses roamed federal lands in 1971, the estimate was both unscientific and artificially low. A decade later, a National Academy of Sciences Report concluded: "The 17,000 figure is undoubtedly low to an unknown, but perhaps substantial, degree."[17] The same report further found: "Forage use by wild equids remains a small fraction of the total forage use by domestic animals on western public ranges, regardless of whether the actual number of equids is in accord with the censuses or somewhat higher."[18]

The damage, nevertheless, had long since been done.

The free-roaming Mustang had been deemed "in excess" of its proscribed and accepted population levels and, despite the protections of the '71 Act, the roundups began where they had left off. Horses were surviving on the range at higher than estimated population levels, but those charged with managing the wild herds didn't care. With faulty and misleading statistics as justification, officials once again targeted the American Mustang.

By 1972, critics of the Mustang horse—angered by the passage of the 1971 Act and bolstered by an influx of money and resources—came out swinging for a new round of assault on the free-roaming horse. Once again, their focus was range degradation: the unchecked wild horse population threatened to destroy what little viable grassland remained. The BLM had a solution to the problem: the Adopt-a-Horse-or-Burro Program. For a mere twenty-five dollars, any citizen could own a walking, breathing symbol of the Old West.

In theory, the BLM program seemed a good proposition. Purported excess horses would be removed from the range and sent to loving homes, the range would be saved from the wild horse's allegedly destructive hooves and mouth, and the public at large would be given the opportunity to own a piece of American history. In reality, however, the Adopt-a-Horse-or-Burro Program was anything but ideal and for many of the horses that passed through its gates it was nothing short of a one-way ticket to slaughter.

From its inception, animal welfare organizations such as

the Humane Society of the United States and the American Horse Protection Association warned that the BLM program was poorly managed and incapable of handling the massive influx of horses. Worse yet, the average adopter had never seen, let alone handled, an untamed and untrained wild Mustang. What, the organizations questioned, would happen once newfound adopters discovered that they could not control their new horses? Rather than a solution to the alleged wild horse problem, the BLM program appeared a recipe for disaster.

As the cautionary warnings and concerns went unheeded, the BLM adopted out Mustangs to any and all who petitioned. By 1977, the BLM announced that rangeland conditions were grave, sixty-five thousand wild horses overpopulated the frontier, and drought was imminent. Purportedly lacking sufficient water and forage resources, in just six years the wild horse population had somehow increased by forty-eight thousand head. Either the Mustang was a true survivor, a reproductive machine, the BLM population estimates for 1971 were too low, or the 1977 numbers were too high. It was a flashback to the past and a foretelling of the future, and Mustang advocates again questioned how the wild horse could be living, surviving, and reproducing on a range that allegedly lacked adequate water, shade, and forage.

Questions were plentiful, doubt was abundant, but no answers were forthcoming.

Despite public inquiry and criticism, and with 1,500,000 deer and 250,000 antelope roaming the very same drought-threatened lands, the BLM rounded up 10,000 of the frontier's purported 65,000 wild horses. They were supposed to go to loving, caring homes. They never made it there. Months later while awaiting adoption, 146 Mustangs died and an additional 98 were put down after they froze to the ground—forgotten in a crammed BLM holding pen outside Reno. The following year, a BLM official conceded that 50 percent of the horses funneled through the adoption program ended up at slaughter plants. Several years later, a federal grand jury concluded that 90 percent of the horses adopted out to private owners eventually found their way to slaughterhouses. At least on the range, with allegedly no water and no forage, the Mustang still had a fighting chance.

In theory, the BLM adoption program was an arguably well-intentioned means to preserve an American icon and the Mustang way of life. In practice, however, it was a death sentence for and a surreptitious way to remove the long unwanted and unwelcome wild horse. For years to come, the BLM's Adopt-a-Horse-or-Burro Program would remain terribly mismanaged and utterly broken.

By the mid-1970s, a once wild horse–friendly Congress passed the Federal Land Policy and Management Act of 1976. The Act reclassified 261 million acres of public land for multiple-use management and significantly increased BLM responsibilities. Wild horse, grazing, mineral, timber, hunting, wildlife, and off-road vehicle uses all now fell under the BLM's widened purview. In addition, the Act amended the 1971 law and authorized the use of helicopters and airborne-led roundups. Once again, the Mustang was to be chased, culled, and captured from above. Yet again, the free-roaming horse was in serious peril.

It was a dark day for the American Mustang and the beginning of a new era with new enemies. On paper, wild horse supporters had fought a long and arduous battle with

and defeated, the cattlemen and livestock interests. In reality, however, the 1971 Act was more Band-Aid, more stop-
gap than remedy. New adversaries now targeted the Mustang
horse: off-roaders, hunters and the gun lobby, and the timber and mineral conglomerates. Individually, each of these
adversaries had power, money, and influence. Together, they
created a formidable alliance that had just one goal: to rid
the range of the free-roaming American wild Mustang.

As in the past, opponents of the Mustang horse turned
to their PR spin doctors. The wild horse, they said, was a
feral beast, a foreigner to our native soils, and a threat to in-
digenous wildlife such as the bobcat and the wolf. It was an
illegitimate horse and an interloper, brought to our ranges—
uninvited—by the early Spanish explorers. The glue that held
these various special interests together, the one shared goal,
was their common need for land. The land of the "living
symbols of the historic and pioneer spirit of the West . . ."[19]
The land where the Mustang was to be "protected . . . considered in the area where presently found . . ."[20] Together,
Mustang foes both old and new were primed for the next
wave of battle.

Across the Nevada highlands and dry lands, the free-
roaming Mustang stood little chance against the low-flying,
fast-moving helicopter. Congressional politics and campaign
finance had dealt a serious blow to the cause of the wild horse.
In the year following passage of the Federal Land Policy and
Management Act, Wild Horse Annie, in failing health and
no doubt defeated by recent events, passed away to little men-
tion. Times were dark for the Mustang and they were about
to get darker.

With the start of the Reagan era and the sagebrush

rebellion, less government was better government. As bureaucratic agencies took a less active role, thousands upon thousands of acres of public land were returned to private ownership and the BLM's Adopt-a-Wild-Horse-or-Burro Program faltered. Wild horse adoptions were on a steep decline while ten thousand Mustangs sat captive in overcrowded BLM holding corrals.

Forgotten, ignored, and diseased, many interned horses wasted away; countless others died or were soon to be dead. The iconic, once free and beautiful wild Mustang was rotting away in undersized fenced mud lots ripe with the odor of death. Mud lots where disease, despair, and death were as far as the eye could see.

The BLM needed and soon found a solution for its "excess" horses—the horses removed from the range and housed in its holding facilities. For any party willing to adopt four or more horses, the BLM would waive its $125 per head adoption fee. Those formerly known as "kill buyers" were soon labeled "lot adopters" and business was good, easy, and profitable for these lot adopters. By 1988, a federal appeals court had sided with a lower court's findings that en masse single-party adoptions violated the legislative intent of the 1971 Act and permanently enjoined the practice of lot adoptions. The damage, however, had already been done.

Between the years 1984 and 1987, nearly fifteen thousand Mustangs fell victim to lot adopters and fifteen thousand "living symbols of the historic and pioneer spirit of the West" had met a violent end in slaughterhouses throughout the country. As wild horse advocates and opponents battled in the court of public opinion, the numbers and statistics could not be manipulated or disputed. In the case for the wild horse, the statistics spoke to the facts and the facts spoke to the truth. With regard to the 1980s, the truth was chilling

From 1981 to 1988, 4,350,000 livestock and 2 million deer and elk populated and grazed on 41,500,000 acres of public land. Among the animals that grazed off the land, 68 percent were privately owned stock, 31 percent were game animals, and 1 percent were wild horses. Also present on public land and listed as an endangered species, 50,000 grass-grazing bighorn sheep. Ironically, at 50,000 head the bighorn sheep warranted endangered species protection. At 60,000 head the Mustangs needed to be gathered and relocated.

On the range, the numbers had spoken: the free-roaming Mustang population was statistically insignificant. Still, the wild horse was to blame—and the only animal to be blamed—for range degradation, soil erosion, and any other damage that its critics could muster. At a cost of $100 million to taxpayers spread over ten years, the wild Mustang had been removed from the land that it had inhabited, the range that it had adapted to and survived upon, and the frontier where other species had failed and perished. In the pastures where Mustang bands had once roamed and galloped, grazing allotments were increased, permit fees were paid, and game was hunted. The story of the 1980s was the story of the 1970s and the 1960s: the cattle industry, game interests, and big money controlled.

While the BLM emptied its holding facilities to the lot adopters and readied its mud lots and corrals for an influx of new lifeless, spiritless horses, the National Academy of Science's Committee on Wild, Free-Roaming Horses and Burros issued its Final Report. Commissioned by Congress and comprised of impartial scientists, the committee reported finding "very few (wild horse) areas with heavy vegetation impacts, although we have asked the BLM to show them to us."[21] The facts, the statistics, and now the scientists had exonerated the wild horse. Those fighting to remove the Mustang from the range and the agency charged with its protection merely turned a deaf ear.

As the 1980s drew to a close, over the course of several months five hundred Mustangs in Nevada were methodically harassed, chased, and shot. Nearly forty years since Wild Horse Annie had first encountered a bloodied stock truck on Highway 395 and Mustang blood was still needlessly flowing in the Nevada desert. Though it had escaped the hardships of time and history, the wild horse could not outrun its curse. Death at the hands of man—not nature and not predator—would forever be the Mustang curse.

The decade also began where the 1980s left off, with a scathing report calling into doubt the BLM's ability to properly manage and protect the nation's wild horses. Released in 1990, the General Accountability Office Report to the Secretary of the Interior began with a decades-overdue declaration that debunked the alleged cause and effect association between the wild horse and rangeland degradation. As detailed by the GAO report, "BLM could not provide GAO with any information demonstrating that federal rangeland conditions have significantly improved because of wild horse removals. This lack of impact has occurred largely because BLM has not reduced authorized grazing by domestic live-

In the beginning, each attempt to catch Samson played out like a chess match replete with strategy, tactics, and a great deal of patience.

Burr-removal duty did more to foster our relationship than any tried-and-true training method.

While some of Samson's dark memories would eventually fade away, his scars never would.

Samson loves his apples, but he still chooses when to indulge and when to abstain.

No matter how strong our initial bond, like a magnetized needle facing north, Samson was always drawn to his true direction—west.

The rusted iron gate wouldn't and couldn't withstand Samson the conqueror.

The look in Samson's eye spoke to his fear of, and contempt for, the despised halter.

It was as if Samson was trying to tell me, "You really aren't getting this; me and halters just aren't a good fit."

Horse and horseman join up and, for a brief moment in time, Samson's troubles seemed to fade away.

Just weeks after his first mounting, Samson was a dressage master, blue-ribbon hunter/jumper, and Grand Prix champion all in one. *(Photograph courtesy of Dan Tesar, Dan Tesar Horseshoeing Company)*

The smug, devious, knowing twinkle in Samson's eye kept me coming back for more.

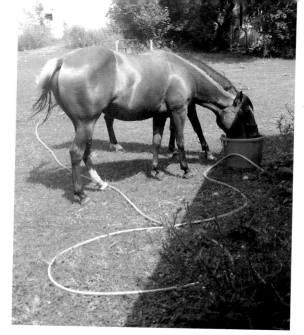

Once upon a time no animal would dare enter Samson's pasture; all of that changed with Valley Girl's arrival.

After more than two years and a great deal of direction from Valley Girl, Studs came to live with the happy couple and the trio formed their own version of *Three's Company*.

Left: Although it took many years, eventually Dan was allowed into Samson's kill zone.

Bottom: Despite his scalping, Ike continues to press his luck eyeing Samson's pasture.

After the incident at the gate and their failed attempt at reconciliation, Samson and Asbestos established a line of demarcation which neither would come to violate.

Whether it is due to his forever wild ways, or his many months of confinement, Samson still refuses to enter any enclosed structure.

The characteristic Roman nose of the Barb horse that Samson was born with, the divot that man gave to him, and a newfound furry coat—all compliments of the harsh Midwest winter and Mother Nature.

On most days Samson resembled a mutt from the pound—a blend of breeds. But on others, he was downright regal.

stock, which because of their vastly larger numbers consume 20 times more forage than wild horses. . . ."[22] Disturbingly, the GAO also found that in areas where wild horses had been removed to protect the soil the BLM had not only failed to decrease livestock numbers but had actually also increased grazing levels.

True to the long-standing claims of wild horse advocates, where Mustangs had been removed cattle were soon found.

The GAO report then took aim at the BLM 1980s roundup of eighty thousand wild horses, stating that, ". . . despite congressional direction, BLM's decisions on how many wild horses to remove from federal rangelands have not been based on direct evidence that existing wild populations exceed what the range can support."[23] Having assailed the BLM for failing to conduct the mandated carrying-capacity studies and range evaluations, the GAO concluded: "Despite the lack of data, BLM has proceeded with horse removals using targets based on perceived population levels dating back to 1971 and/or recommendations from BLM advisory groups comprised largely of livestock permittees."[24] For the Mustang and wild horse advocates, it was vindication. Vindication twenty years in the making and twenty years too late.

Last, the GAO evaluated the BLM Adopt-a-Horse-or-Burro Program and again the picture of a corrupt, mismanaged agency with a hidden agenda came into focus. In its assessment of the practice of lot adoptions, the GAO found that "inhumane treatment and commercial exploitation" ruled the day.[25] The report continued: "BLM did not always comply with its regulations and internal guidelines for approving and monitoring these adoptions. This noncompliance resulted in the inhumane treatment and death of hundreds of horses during the one year probation period when the horses were still owned by the government. Most adopters sold thousands of wild horses to slaughterhouses."[26]

The 1990 GAO report only confirmed what wild horse advocates had been saying for years. Mustangs had been unjustly and illegally removed from the range; federally protected horses had been shipped to slaughter. It was a sad and oft-repeated story. It was the heartbreaking and unfortunate story of a forgotten American icon.

As the twentieth century came to a close, shocking news hit the airwaves: thirty-four Mustangs had been hunted down, mutilated, and shot in Nevada's Virginia Range. It was a gruesome and telling scene: carcasses were strewn across the range, a mare lay dead with her foal still in the womb, legs were broken, lungs collapsed, and one horse had its eye knocked out with a fire extinguisher. The three local men—two of whom were enlisted Marines—charged with the offenses eventually pled out to misdemeanors and received light sentences.

Despite the passage of years and decades, Mustang hunting remained a sick, perverted form of entertainment. To a select few it was a sport; to others it was pest control. Much time had passed, but so little had changed.

Shortly after President George W. Bush took office in 2000, the BLM accelerated its wild horse roundups. Within three short years, Mustang population levels had dropped from 25,000 to 17,900.

By 2004 Mustang advocates were once again clamoring for reform as five Mustangs housed in a BLM holding corral died after suffering from heat exhaustion and dehydration. Left unattended in Nevada's scorching sun with no freshwater source, the horses had been removed from the range due to alleged drought-like conditions. The incident was tragic, avoidable, and quite telling. Wild horses on the range were persevering and surviving; captured Mustangs housed in BLM holding facilities were suffering and dying. The new century was off to a very sad start and the barn walls were about to cave in.

As the final days of 2004 were winding down and as senators finalized their debate over appropriations for the upcoming year, Montana senator Conrad Burns attached a stealth rider to the Fiscal Year 2005 Appropriations Act. The rider amended the 1971 Act and instituted what came to be known as the "three strikes rule"—any wild horse who was ten years of age or older or had been passed over three times for adoption would be eligible for immediate and outright sale. Senators rushing home for the Thanksgiving break passed the Appropriations Act, stealth rider and all, the three strikes rule became law, and the BLM finally had its long-coveted outright sale authority for wild horses.

Nearly twenty years in the making, the assault on the Wild Free-Roaming Horses and Burros Act had come full circle. With the first blow struck in 1976 and at the prompting of various special-interest groups, Congress had dealt the final and fatal blow to a law intended to protect both the free-roaming and captive Mustang. For a three strikes Mustang, the Burns Rider was a death sentence. For wild horse advocates, it was a game changer. Where the gates to former Mustang rangeland remained closed and locked, the gates to the slaughterhouses now opened.

In the weeks following passage of 2004's Burns Rider, buyers descended upon BLM holding facilities and purchased as many three strikes Mustangs as their trailers could carry. Horses who once graced the West's vast ranges, wild Mustangs who had survived Mother Nature's unflinching fury and had escaped the hunt of untold predators, found themselves packed into stock trailers barreling down the interstate to Texas and Illinois and the nation's three remaining slaughterhouses. It was an outcome that officials said would not, could not, occur under the BLM's sale authority guidelines. It was an undignified end for the noble and proud Mustang horse. It was an end not befitting a national treasure.

Antislaughter advocates let out a loud cheer on June 30, 2007, when Cavel International complied with a U.S. District Court Order and shut down operations at its DeKalb, Illinois, slaughterhouse. Congress had defunded horse slaughterhouse inspections, the courts had ordered the USDA to stop inspecting, and the last domestic slaughterhouse was now closed, but that didn't mean the three strikes horses were any safer. Slaughterhouses in Canada and Mexico were still paying by the pound and the Mustang carcass remained a marketable commodity. By late 2007, the Bush era was nearing its end when cattleman and president George W. Bush signed an executive order increasing the number of grazing permits available to livestock interests. It was another year and a different administration, but clout and politics still trumped facts and statistics.

As the first decade of the new millennium neared its end, the stage was set for catastrophe. Public apathy, a push to round up greater numbers of wild horses, and a government agency run amok would equal a disaster in the making. The battle between Samson and I was just getting started, but the war between the BLM and the American wild Mustang was about to claim further mass casualties.

TRIALS, TRIBULATIONS, AND TRAGEDY

A horse is the projection of people's dreams about themselves—strong, powerful, beautiful—and it has the capability of giving us escape from our mundane existence.
—PAM BROWN

In much the same fashion that hardship and cruelty have followed Samson, violence and abuse have dogged the wild Mustang. Just two years after the American public mobilized and Congress passed the Wild Free-Roaming Horses and Burros Act of 1971, sixty of Idaho's last remaining wild horses were chased for forty-five days through the dead of winter, captured, and decimated. Federally protected horses were run off cliffs, legs were broken, hog rings sewn into noses, and carcasses sawed into pieces. Only eleven horses survived, and yet the U.S. Attorney for Idaho declined to press charges. Targeted violence and brutality would continue unabated for years to follow with state and federal officials refusing to prosecute the criminally responsible parties.

Three decades later, in the spring of 2005, three men were arrested for roping and then castrating a wild Mustang stallion. The horse bled to death from his injuries, and the men who used a pocketknife to mutilate him received suspended sentences. Regardless of the year or the decade, it was a far too common story and an all too frequent act. Disinterested legislatures and courts have seen to this fact. Whether by tacit approval or distanced apathy, the message has remained the same: crimes against the unwanted, feral Mustang warrant little concern and even less justice. If history has taught one certainty, it is that the curse of the Mustang has followed Samson and his breed across time and over great distance.

By the second week of December, a fresh coat of snow and frigid temperatures meant that Samson would require his blanket full-time. Weeks of socialization had indicated that he was ready and willing to accept it. But when I knelt down beside him and reached for the surcingles—the straps that would cross beneath his belly and hold the blanket in place—Samson let fly a left hind-leg strike that whizzed past my cheekbone and sliced deep into my neck's right side.

The powerful impact spun me around 180 degrees, leaving me facedown on the ground perpendicular to Samson's body as the pristine white snow turned bloodred. There was no warning, no instigation, no justification, and certainly no explanation.

Through the course of our relationship, acts such as this would remain commonplace. For years to come, unprovoked, unsolicited rage and violence would plague my interactions with Samson. As he lacked malice aforethought, I would come to term these fits "Samson's PTSD moments." Some unknown stimulus triggers a deeply embedded memory and in an instant, in a flash, the chronically abused Mustang—without thinking—erupts. To look upon Samson in the moments following these episodes was to see a horse with glassy, glossed-over eyes, a vacant facial expression, and a complete lack of awareness as to what had just occurred. It was as if he had momentarily blacked out and then regained consciousness. This was the cost of working with a habitually abused animal.

This was the cost of doing business with Samson.

While Samson initially greeted his blanket's permanency with utter disdain, he soon came to realize that it could help him survive the harsh realities of the fast-approaching Midwest winter. The first time that Studs, Ike, and Star saw Samson wearing it, the three entered into a loud and extended chorus of whinnies and nickers. Seemingly berating, deriding, and mocking their most feared neighbor, their cackles announced *wimp, puppy,* and *momma's boy.* Like Joseph with his amazing technicolor dreamcoat, Samson nevertheless held his head high and walked a spirited stride. He now had his first possession, something that he could call his very own.

By the second Sunday of the month, Samson was facing the first of two important tests. The farrier was due out and Samson was to have his first hoof trim free of chemical sedation. Since Amy had unsuccessfully tried her luck with several farriers allegedly well versed with difficult horses, she agreed to give my guy, Dan Tesar, a shot. Dan and I were the same age, had known each other for many years, worked well together, and were good friends. Both professionally and personally, Dan was an anomaly.

On a professional level, Dan knew every inch of a horse's body, inside to outside and then back. With a four-year animal science degree, a farrier certificate, and having grown up with and trained horses, Dan was a walking and talking horse encyclopedia. A journeyman by trade, he had traveled the country both shoeing horses and lecturing on and demonstrating his technique. By forty years of age, he had seen, done, and accomplished it all. When it came to trimming, Dan's angles were right on. When it came to shoeing, Dan was a natural.

Unlike the majority of modern-day farriers who now cold-shoe horses—purchase and install prefabricated and commercially produced stock shoes—Dan hand-builds and forges each and every of his shoes from nothing more than a linear piece of steel. While others are forced to fit a horse's foot to a stock shoe, Dan builds and molds the shoe to fit the hoof. Steel is his medium, horseshoes his artwork, and shoeing his craft.

On a personal level, I found Dan to be one of a dying breed. He took pride in his work, he was unflinchingly honest, his word was his bond, and his bond was as strong as the steel shoes that he built. He would settle for nothing less than perfection for each of his horses and all of his clients. Perhaps the biggest testament to my belief in Dan's abilities came by way of the fact that I employed his services despite the fact that he lived in far northern Wisconsin—more than four and a half hours' driving distance. He was, in my estimation, as good as they came and worth the inherent difficulties associated with having a farrier several hours away.

He was perfect for Samson.

Less than a week earlier, I had finally and successfully lifted and picked out all four of Samson's hooves. It had been a long, violent, and frustrating process. In Samson's mind, his hind legs and especially his hind hooves were a no-fly zone and, like the FAA, he had strictly enforced the no-fly rules. With twelve years to perfect his technique, his hind-leg strikes were both teeth shattering and potentially bone breaking. He was Muhammad Ali and George Foreman all in one. He was a welterweight with a heavyweight's bark and bite.

After weeks of battle, and once Samson had lifted and permitted his hooves to be picked, he—unlike his earlier act of sacrificial defiance—accepted and devoured his peppermint reward. I was now confident that Samson could tolerate his hooves being shaved with the rasp and trimmed with the nippers.

I was not confident that he would tolerate anyone other than me doing it.

Two days prior to the scheduled farrier appointment, I received an urgent e-mail stating that Samson was nursing yet another injury. Studs the paint gelding had ventured too close to the Mustang sentry's fence line and in a fit of anger Samson had teed off on the unforgiving and unyielding steel utility tube gate. Once at the farm, I assessed the injury. With an avulsed hoof wall—a piece left torn and dangling similar to a hangnail—and significant vertical crack to the hoof's "quarter" section, the damage was significant. To make matters worse, the injury was to Samson's left hind hoof—the one that for some unknown reason he guarded with his maximum fervor and wrath.

There was no way around it—I couldn't leave this job to any other. Having never trusted anyone to handle, let alone treat, an injured hoof, Samson was now being asked to let me do both. He was being asked yet again to make a huge, blind leap of faith.

Holding the lead line, the squirrelly Samson, and his hoof while operating the nippers at the same time put my skills to the test. With me bent over in his strike zone and Samson's left leg resting immobilized on my left thigh, both horse and horseman were fully exposed and totally vulnerable. Under Samson's unblinking scrutiny, I grabbed the hoof nippers and wasted no time cutting away the avulsed hoof wall. Next I used the rasp—shaving down all of the sharp edges and evening out the surface of the hoof wall. On the verge of losing it, Samson nevertheless did not lose it. He answered my call to bring his A game and in doing so exercised unflinching trust and tremendous restraint.

Concerned how things would play out during Samson's looming farrier visit, I couldn't help but interject words of instruction with his much-warranted praise. "Way to step it up, buddy," I told my mentally exhausted student. "This is exactly what I need from you when Dan is here."

Two days later with Dan out at the farm the plan was threefold. Part one entailed Dan and me standing in the pasture and casually conversing while I held Samson secured from a distance. The purpose was to demonstrate that much like myself, Dan posed no threat to the ever doubting and threatened Mustang. For phase two, we left Samson in a stall while Dan, standing in the barn aisle in full view, trimmed Studs, Ike, and Star. Though this process of observational or vicarious learning has been rejected by many horse experts, I have successfully employed it countless times throughout the years. While horses lack the ability to replicate a series of observed complex actions, they can take note of pain, threat, discomfort, or ease when watching herd mates.

In this instance, the demonstration that unfolded before Samson's eyes sent what was now a redundant message: that Dan posed no threat and meant no harm. The plan's third component was straightforward: have Dan enter Samson's space and, once the anxious patient relaxed, go to work.

After a few minutes standing beside Samson's right foreleg, Dan had seen enough to formulate the appropriate conclusions. "So," he blurted out with an inquisitive tone, "who messed up this guy?"

"Everyone," I responded. "The better question is who didn't."

"And who," Dan inquired with a grin from ear to ear, "did the hatchet job on Samson's left hind hoof? . . . The poor guy may never walk again."

It was our thing—a way of defusing stress and tension.

After forty-five minutes of Dan whispering reassuringly to Samson, it was time to get the show started. Slowly, Dan bent over, reached down, and lifted the right foreleg. The panicked sound of Samson's hurried and shortened breaths filled the aisle as his eyes nervously darted from Dan to me and then back again to Dan.

"He's hyperventilating," Dan declared as he froze in place. "Do you still want me to continue?"

"Yes," I responded. "This is how he gets."

Dan then placed Samson's right leg between his own, tightened them together like a vice grip, and went to work with the rasp. His fluid and active movements from within Samson's personal space were a first and presented an unquestioned threat to the Mustang's perimeter defenses. It was all so new and all so totally overwhelming. Samson was trying to cope, but it was obvious he was losing this battle as well as his composure. He needed security, reassurance, and a sign that said that everything was going to be all right.

Panic-stricken, he momentarily averted his gaze away

from Dan and turned back toward me. Once again, his eyes spoke. *I am here and consenting to this because of you. I don't know this guy; I only know you. Tell me that this is going to be okay; tell me that I am going to be okay.* Recognizing that Samson was moments away from losing it, I took one step toward his muzzle. Our eyes met for a brief second, and then Samson buried his face deep into my chest. A loud and powerful exhalation eased his taut and constricted muscles from their death grip as Dan, bent over yet fully aware that something had just changed, announced, "Now that's a good boy, Samson."

From that point forward, the afternoon progressed fairly smoothly. At one point while Dan worked on his right hind leg, Samson sent a minor declaration of defiance with a half-hearted kick. Delivered straight back rather than off to the side where Dan stood, the kick was intended more as a statement and less as a strike intended to make contact. Ever consistent and true to himself, Samson sent the identical message when Dan worked on the opposing and guarded left hind hoof. Dan, much like me, was now on notice—Samson was a proud and prideful horse, a horse demanding and commanding of respect.

"This guy's quite the willful horse," Dan proclaimed, "with a sense of humor to boot." *Indeed.*

I steadied my gaze upon Samson and spoke, "Really! Seriously! You are a jerk. The little minis kicked better than you today. For weeks I have been your little human piñata and today you don't even make Dan break a sweat!"

"Oh, he's a cream puff," Dan said. "And I think you, Mitch, I think you're just getting soft in your old age."

If this were any of my other horses, then I would have

been filled with both a sense of pride and one of accomplishment. But this wasn't just another of my many horses. On this day, I was left feeling more like a proud parent than a mere satisfied teacher. It was just one more indication that something was different between this horse and this horseman.

Several years have now passed since Samson's first pedicure, and he still remains anxious and jittery when his hooves are trimmed. Nevertheless, with each of Dan's visits, Samson has assumed the position, as we have come to call it—his face buried in my chest—and stood without incident as his hooves have been nipped and rasped. It is what works for him.

It works for him because on that first afternoon with Dan, with his head buried in my chest, Samson learned something new. He realized that safety and security could help him through a trying and overwhelming experience. He came to recognize that with a little help he could cope rather than fight. That day, Samson discovered self-control, maturity, and inner strength. He also silenced his many critics—the naysayers who had claimed that his legs could not, would not, be handled absent strong chemical sedation. That afternoon, Samson not only silenced his detractors, but he also proved that my belief in him, my conviction that he could and would be rehabilitated and trained, was well founded.

It was the push I needed to keep going.

With his hoof trim a rousing success, I spoke the words that needed to be said before releasing Samson to his pasture: "We are getting there, buddy. One by one, you and I, together, will slay each of your ghosts."

Two days later, I returned for a very rare early-morning

weekday visit. The time had come for the second of Samson's two main benchmarks. As I had requested that he receive a tetanus booster and seasonal vaccinations, my presence was more compulsory than voluntary. In order to avoid any ruffled feathers, I had asked Amy to advise the veterinarian that I would be present and handling Samson so as to ensure everyone's safety.

Once at the farm, I was greeted by the veterinarian's assistant: a short fellow, in his fifties, with what appeared to be an awfully large chip parked on his shoulder. Immediately I had him pegged as one who had spent many years at the track handling and mishandling racehorses owned by others—animals that he could never even aspire to own. I knew his type well, and so did Samson. Resentment and jealousy ruled the assistant's thoughts, and pain and punishment were the only two "skills" in his training repertoire. There was no way this was going to end well.

"So," the assistant declared, "you're the big trainer who is going to both tell and show us how to do our jobs."

Houston, we have a problem.

With far too many similar conversations in my past, I chose the high road, brushed by the little man, and headed into the barn. Once I was inside, the assistant's monologue continued, "It's people like you who end up getting professionals like us injured. I've spent my life working with gigantic hot-blooded, crazed Thoroughbreds. Trust me, I can handle that little horse parked there in that stall with my eyes closed and without even breaking a sweat. No one here needs your help."

While I would never put Samson in harm's way, in this

case he was not the one who was going to be in harm's way. "Be my guest; please, do show me how it's done," I implored the veterinarian's assistant.

Everything from that point forward is more or less a fuzzy, hazy, dusty blur. The assistant opened the stall door. Samson in turn responded with a double-leg hind-end barrage that impacted the door frame and sent wood splinters and the unwelcome intruder flying. The veterinarian's assistant then took off running, jumping onto and then vaulting over the gate that cordoned off the stall area. The entire incident lasted just seconds and was both shockingly violent and exceedingly comical. The brutalized victim and the take-no-prisoners four-legged antagonist were back.

As the dust slowly dissipated, Samson's stall door swung back and forth with no indication of slowing down. It was a scene reminiscent of a Clint Eastwood western: bodies strewn across the saloon floor, the dual doors swinging wildly back and forth as the man with no name stood silent, unmoving, and emotionless. Samson too stood motionless, impassive, and poised for round two.

Lying in the exact spot where he landed after tumbling over the gate, gasping to catch his breath, the assistant just couldn't leave well enough alone, "Okay, Mr. Big Shot, let's see you get within five feet of that stall."

"Turn," I told Samson as I stepped up into the stall. As he spun around and brought his head into my chest, Samson's face came into view and it bore an all-too-familiar expression. As one of five brothers, I knew "the look." When I was growing up, not a month passed when a lawn light or sprinkler head wasn't broken during the throes of some basketball, soccer, football, or wrestling match. In a pretty good month perhaps we shattered a car windshield; in a really great month, a window in the house. We often spent vast amounts of time hashing and rehearsing our explanations: the neighbor's dog broke the sprinkler head while chasing a squirrel; a stone thrown from a passing truck shattered the windshield. Despite all of our efforts, when it came time to tell our father the expression on our faces said that which our mouths could not.

Guilty as charged.

As I looked upon Samson, his expression spoke of guilt. After months together, he knew how I felt about his violent outbursts. He knew that he had broken the rules. I leaned into him and whispered into his left ear. We then exited the stall and seconds later, as I held the lead line, Samson received his shots without incident. Moments later, I released my Mustang pupil to the pasture, with him having passed his exam with flying colors.

"Why do I get the impression that Samson isn't the only one proud of his actions?" Amy declared from several feet behind as I watched Samson gallop through the pasture. "Do you mind telling me what you whispered into his ear?"

Without turning around I answered Amy, "I told him that I was proud of him. I told him that guy got everything he deserved and then some. I told him that he and I were good—there would be no lectures and no punishment today."

This time, the defendant would not be punished for his crime. Both judge and jury ruled that the haunted Mustang's infraction constituted justifiable self-defense.

Over a period of just a few brief days, two distinctively different horsemen had highlighted the difference between good and poor horsemanship. When Dan first saw Samson, he assessed the Mustang's issues and needs and then tailored his actions and behaviors to fit these. Once he decided to approach Samson, he did so with a presence that spoke of quiet confidence and determination. While his mannerisms communicated that he was the boss, his slow, nonthreatening actions simultaneously indicated that he would be both patient and respectful.

The veterinarian's assistant, however, took an entirely different approach. To him, it was just another day and Samson was just another horse. The totality of the assistant's behaviors and mannerisms spoke of threat and intimidation—*comply or I will make you.* Patience and respect were foreign, if not unknown, concepts. Fear was also present and those who are fearful often overcompensate. And when the assistant flung open Samson's stall door, it was obvious that he was more than prepared to dole out pain and punishment.

I saw it, felt it, and knew it, and so did Samson.

Handling and controlling an eleven-hundred-pound animal is no walk in the park. Dictate and manage a horse's movements and actions, do so with a command and control presence, and you will have a horse who trusts and respects you. Abuse that trust and respect, and you will be left with an animal who will put you down and take you out without a moment's hesitation.

Training horses is not unlike constructing a building. Create a strong foundation, and you can build up vertically, one floor on top of the next. Fail to properly complete one floor, and each subsequent and earlier level will come crashing down. Heading into the final days of 2009, Samson's foundational elements—the basic skills required to permit him to move on to more advanced training—were now complete. When Samson first accepted his blanket, he implicitly came to understand that items such as a pad, saddle, and rider would be placed upon his back. Once he yielded and released to pressure, he assented to my control—by bit and otherwise—over his forward, backward, and lateral movements. And when he permitted me to pick up and handle his legs, Samson evinced my dominion and control over his very being.

As winter promptly enveloped the Midwest, I arrived at Amy's farm on December's last Sunday prepared to advance Samson's training. In other words, it was time to build vertically; it was time to construct our building. Weeks prior, I had introduced Samson to my bareback riding pad. Considerably lighter than my forty-five-pound saddle, once affixed with a cinch the pad provided a less threatening, intermediary, and preparatory step to ultimately saddling Samson. Similarly, once Samson had stopped fighting the lead line I introduced a longer twenty-five-foot lounge line.

Needless to say, at both the first and subsequent encounters Samson was less than interested in making new friends. Violence and Samson's rule of three soon followed. Now weeks later, the time had come to fuse together these two core training components: my ability to handle and control Samson from a distance and his ability to move and maintain composure while carrying a saddle-like object atop his back.

With the pad on his back and the cinch tightened, I played the lounge line out several feet and pushed Samson into small circles at a walk. After several minutes, I let out more line and put greater distance between Samson and myself. Though nervous and afraid, Samson kept his violent, explosive twin at bay. Minutes later, I pushed Samson into a slow, prancing trot. He was able to maintain his composure right up until the moment that a gust of wind came off the adjacent barren cornfield and swept between his legs.

With the volatile Mustang now frightened and attached to a longer version of one of his most despised foes—the rope—all bets were off.

Rearing, twisting, and turning in midair like a prized PBR (Professional Bull Riders) bull, Samson was on autopilot—determined to get the pad and cinch off his body or die trying. As he rotated clockwise around my position, concurrently galloping and bucking through the tight confines of the roadside pasture, it was only a matter of time before he ran out of room. I could have sent a ripple wave through or yanked hard on the line, but given Samson's personality either act would have only sent him into the red zone.

Instead, it was time for both horse and trainer to fall back on their many weeks of training. "Easy, eeeeaaasy," I yelled out, "aaaand to a walk!" While many horsemen scoff at the use of verbal commands, I train my horses to recognize and respond to multiple spoken cues. Samson completed one additional complete circle, slowed, and came to a halt.

"Good boy, you are such a good boy," I told my fatigued student as he fought to catch his breath.

"Help me out here, Mitch," Amy blurted out, standing safely behind a huge oak tree. "Last week you gave me a whole safety lecture after I inadvertently coiled Studs' lead line around my hand. I just sat here and watched as you purposely wrapped that lounge line around your right hand while Samson rampaged through the pasture."

Busted, I was totally busted. Amy's observations were correct. I had violated my own rule and deliberately connected Samson and me at the one time when I shouldn't have. As Samson had galloped circles around my position, I noticed that with each rotation he had picked up speed and angled for the perimeter fence's lowest point—the exact spot, in fact, that he had tried to vault after his confrontation with Frank. So after uncovering Samson's escape plan, I did in fact coil the lounge line around my hand. The way I saw it, if Samson was taking off then this time I was going along for the ride.

If a client had deliberately attached him- or herself to an out-of-control horse, I'm sure that I would have blown a gasket raining down criticism. And if some other trainer were to question my actions, then I would no doubt have to agree with the condemnation. But in my mind, the overriding concern was Samson's safety and in this case the ends justified the means. I had attached the lunge line to Samson, pushed him to a walk and then a trot, and placed him in harm's way. Samson had his way of doing things, his code, and I had my own—take responsibility where there was responsibility to be had.

When I coiled the lunge line around my hand, I had no way of knowing whether Samson would vault from the farm with me in tow or respond to my commands and slow to a halt. But I trusted in him and made a leap of faith just as he had with me on many prior occasions. Reckless or not, stupid, or careless, I knew that something about my relationship with Samson was special and I was willing to bet my life on it.

Once Samson appeared less frazzled, I had him complete a clockwise and then counterclockwise circle at a trot. We had to finish the lesson on a positive note and Samson had to learn that violent objection would not release him from his training obligations. I then unclipped the lunge line and headed off to the barn to retrieve an apple. Though the lesson didn't go as planned, I was extremely pleased with the way Samson followed my instruction and recovered from his nearly total meltdown. The day's events had also highlighted the one cardinal rule that every trainer has committed to heart: no matter how much you plan and prepare, "the best laid plans of mice and men often go awry."

In other words, there are no certainties when working with animals.

I entered the barn from a side door as Samson made his way across the pasture. With head up and his walk animated, his body language spoke volumes. *Oh yes, today I earned my apple.* He seemed content and at ease, and I was able to breathe a sigh of relief inasmuch as the day could have ended on a considerably darker note. But then, just as I had let my guard down, I peered down the barn aisle and saw a sight that instantly sent me into panic mode.

Samson was standing by the stalls, his head down, eating hay off the aisle floor. With the outer barn door always left open so that Samson could escape the elements, it wasn't the fact that he was standing in the aisle that raised concern. It was the fact that his head was hanging just below the oversized sharp metal bracket that protruded from the front of his stall—a component of the perimeter defense system that had previously kept the caged Mustang confined. If Samson raised his head, the results would be catastrophic.

I made my way down the aisle to try to ward off the unthinkable. But then, just as I neared the stalls, it happened.

"Oh no," I yelled out, "oh crap!"

The first sound, the result of impact between bone and metal, froze me in my tracks. The second sound, the thud of nearly one thousand pounds crashing down onto the concrete floor, forced me to close my eyes and turned my stomach. I ran down the aisle but could see little through the plumes of hay dust that engulfed the stall area. Before I could get to him, Samson stood up and galloped from the barn.

I located Samson in the roadside pasture's far corner—trembling, violently tossing his head, and kicking at the ground. He was injured and clearly in pain. His body language and posturing were identical to what I had previously observed in the moments following his Frank encounter. Only this time, his message seemed even more emphatic: *Stay the hell away.* As I stopped to look him over, I observed that something else was wrong—gravely wrong. Samson's muscles were bulging out from his neck, saliva was running from his nose, and he was coughing, gagging, and making repeated attempts to swallow.

Samson was in serious distress.

Experience told that I was witnessing an episode of choke—a condition that occurs when food becomes stuck in the esophagus, muscles spasm and tighten, and the horse is unable to clear the obstruction. In this case, I could see the bulge in Samson's neck that identified the spot where the hay sat lodged in his esophagus. While many choke episodes require veterinarian intervention and can be fatal, most horses are able to successfully clear the esophageal obstruction within ten to fifteen minutes. Either way, with daylight fading I knew that I needed to return Samson to the barn and assess his injuries. I also knew that I would be in for a fight.

For his first twelve years, Samson had persevered through everything that life had thrown his way. He had been a fighter and a survivor and a horse who needed no one. Now injured and in distress, Samson needed someone. But needing help and accepting it are two entirely different concepts and this meant that we had a serious problem. Just five days earlier, I had received a 6:00 a.m. emergency call that a horse was down in his stall with signs of colic. Alexandros was his name and he was a big, beautiful, athletic specimen who was also aggressive, stubborn, and at times a bully. Like Samson, he was one of my problem students and, though it had taken a while, he had slowly come to understand that I was the alpha.

When a horse needs to get up, it will rock to get momentum, roll over to get its legs underneath and right itself, throw its weight back on its hind legs, and then use its forelegs to slowly push away from the ground and rise up. "Cast" in his stall—stuck against the wall and unable to stand up— Alexandros could do none of these. He was scared, in pain, and kicking violently at those trying to save him. So after an hour of fighting to get their horse up, his owners called for my help. When I arrived at the barn, I walked into the stall, worked a line under his down side, folded it across his exposed side, and pulled him away from the wall. I then shouted, "Get up; get up now!" Mustering what little reserves he had left, Alexandros instinctively complied.

That was the nature of my relationship with Alexandros; I did not have this with Samson. The habituation, redundancy, and training benchmarks—none of it mattered now.

What would happen in the next several minutes would be the true test of my progress with Samson.

Determined not to return to the scene of his injury, Samson locked his knees and hocks and went rigid. Recognizing that we could not afford an hour-long standoff, I instantly announced my intentions, "You and I are going into that barn under civil terms or with you kicking and screaming. Either way, we're going."

Back in the barn, under the glare of the overhead lighting, I first examined and then, in the hope of dislodging the impacted material, massaged the area of Samson's neck that held the tennis ball–sized clump of hay. Throughout this process, Samson continued to cough, sneeze, and violently shake his head. The head tossing told me that I needed to redirect my attention back to his head.

Peering at her injured Mustang from several feet away, and in a tone that curdled my blood, Amy screamed, "Oh my god, he scalped himself—there's blood everywhere!"

Due to the fading daylight outside and the choke episode, I had yet to even look upon Samson's forehead. Shockingly, Amy's observation was correct—a large section of Samson's forehead, just above the right eye, was gone. It was a bloody wound, a considerable trauma, and an injury that needed immediate attention. Over the years, I have seen and treated dozens of traumatic, often critical, injuries and illnesses, but what I saw right then hit me in a way I was not accustomed to.

I tried to brush Samson's forelock aside to examine the wound, but several attempted head butts and foreleg strikes said, *Don't even think about it.* Up until this moment, I thought I had seen and experienced the best, or worst, of Samson's anger, violence, and defense. I was wrong. Weakened, vulnerable, and exposed, Samson was battling pain and discomfort from two different sources, and the last thing he wanted was me in his face. As his behavior turned increasingly threatening and he slowly started to implode, his fear, pain, and distrust seemed to fuse together.

First he reared up. Then his rearing turned to bucking; bucking turned into kicking. In just seconds, we had hurricane and tropical depression Samson. There was little I could do but try to hold him still and talk him down. And then, after a couple of minutes, Samson's meltdown suddenly stopped with the immediacy with which it began. Once again, he had that dazed, blank, PTSD look that said that he had been gone for a while and had just returned. As he slowly came back, he stared into my eyes with a look that said, *I get it; I need your help with this one.*

It was my signal to get to work.

When I put the surgical gloves on, like Superman with kryptonite, Samson shook and shuddered. Standing in front of the injured Mustang, I held a syringe filled with Betadine in one hand and a large gauze pad in the other. Irrigating the wound with my right hand while covering his eye with my left would leave me totally exposed to a head butt, bite, or anything else Samson could throw my way.

There was little I could do to protect myself but remind him of our agreement, "You and I still have a binding contract. I trust you, and you trust me. I have yet to lead you astray and today will be no different."

Once the look in Samson's eyes signaled recognition, I gave the "lower" command. The Mustang dropped his head to my waist and I started irrigating the wound. Next came the numbing antibiotic ointment that would protect the wound and promote healing. Stitches weren't really necessary, so Mother Nature would be left to run her course while I monitored for signs of infection and other complications.

With gravity, saliva, and a gentle massage having dislodged the ball of hay from his esophagus, I tried to walk Samson back to his stall, but he simply wouldn't budge. He was staring into my eyes, looking for my attention, determined not to move. Once I acknowledged his gaze, Samson ever so slowly closed and then opened his eyelids. For most, this minor act wouldn't have said much; for Samson, it said everything. For me, it meant the world.

Thank you.

"Yes," I told him, "you are welcome, old boy."

Patient and doctor retired for the evening. The day had seen a tragic accident and a true exhibition of trust. Horse and horseman had cast aside their fears, doubts, and reservations and each believed in the other. It was a day that I, and I hope Samson, will never forget. In the months that followed, not a week passed without Samson suffering some form of injury. When he charged the three crazed dogs who teased him from the safe side of the fence, he lacerated his chest. When he chased the chickens, ducks, and geese from his pasture, the barbed-wire fence sliced and diced. Plainly put, this was Samson. He would not be mocked and he would not be chided. Nonetheless, this battle-scarred gladiator slept easy, for he knew that he had his own on-call, 24/7 trauma nurse.

I returned the following day, Monday, the twenty-eighth day of December, to find wound and patient doing fine. Seconds after my arrival, Amy got right up in my face. "You

said back in October that we would assess things by the end
of the year. I need to know that Samson is going to be
mounted and ridden in order for him to stay. I want him to
be like a normal horse—something good has to come out
of this crazy life of mine."

In that instant, I understood the true nature of the relationship between Samson and Amy. I recognized that Amy
did indeed have a vested interest in her Mustang's successes
and failures. After her recent bout with illness, the failed relationship, the change of career, her move to the country,
and all the ensuing chaos, Amy was left questioning her life
and her fate. Samson's mounting could right Amy's derailed
train, validate her life-changing decisions, and make it all
worth it. Whether or not I liked it, Amy's and Samson's fates
were inextricably intertwined.

Up until that moment, there had been no manual that
instructed that I continue Samson's training. In just a few
short months, Samson had made great strides. He had given
and received trust and respect and somewhat consensually
assented to my control, care, and custody. Nonetheless, violent outbursts were weekly, if not daily. At times, Samson's
lapses were the result of his untold demons, ghosts, and his
engrained fear of man. In other instances, his fits were the
actions of a twelve-year-old horse rebuffing and rejecting my
ever-increasing control.

If I was to continue Samson's training, if the intent was
to saddle break this Mustang, then my degree of control and
his corresponding ability to assent would have to exponentially increase. And as my grip over Samson tightened, both
the unpredictable victim and the willful aged Mustang would
respond in kind with greater bark and greater bite. Yes, I

believed that saddle breaking Samson would provide an authorized outlet for his great stores of energy, keep him stimulated, and improve his self-image. But conversely, I had to consider my health and safety and the overall cost of making such a commitment.

Taking Samson to the next training level would no doubt invite a huge struggle and an epic battle. As I looked upon this impressive warrior and his freshly scabbed wound, as I considered our fates, in Nevada Samson's brothers, sisters, and cousins—still free and still wild—were engaged in their very own colossal struggle and epic battle. For on this very day, the BLM started the Calico Mountains winter roundup.

Over the objections of Mustang advocacy and animal welfare organizations, the BLM was moving forward with its ill-advised and potentially catastrophic helicopter-led rundown of some twenty-seven hundred wild Mustangs—nearly 90 percent of Nevada's Calico Mountains wild horse population. Court actions seeking injunctions had been filed and lost. The BLM was set and determined. Winter conditions or not, Mustangs would be chased, culled, and captured. My hope for Samson was that he could be bit and saddle broke, mounted, and ridden. But more important, my hope was that he could, once and for all, shed his past's many demons and ghosts. The very same ghosts and demons, in fact, that now had the Calico Mountains Mustangs in their sights.

In the weeks that followed, Samson and his Nevada cousins would be concurrently engaged in all-out warfare. He would fight to maintain his independence and autonomy; they would fight for their lives. Both would struggle to maintain and preserve their wild ways. Sadly, for Samson's herd mates, it was a struggle with a predetermined outcome. The

Calico Mountains roundup would cost dozens their lives and go down as the deadliest BLM operation in decades. The horse that had survived the horrors of the Early and Middle Ages, withstood the charge of the cavalry, battled the captains of industry, and outlasted Mustang Fever was now engaged in a battle that it could not and would not win.

No longer affiliated with the therapy center, I should have had more time, more freedom, to get to everything on my plate. But as Samson's instruction had progressed, as his skills had advanced, this perpetually doubting and distrusting horse needed more of my time and a great deal more of my patience. Having worked with horses across Illinois, Indiana, and Wisconsin, I understood the concept of sacrifice and commitment. But whether I realized it or not, my Samson Experience was swallowing me whole and would come at a cost.

I really had no choice in the matter. To say no to Amy would damn Samson and seal his fate.

Horse and horseman stared hard into each other's eyes. "He'll be broke and mounted by spring, or not at all."

Samson's clock was ticking.

9

DETERMINED FOUR-LEGGED CAPTIVES

*A horse gallops with its lungs, perseveres with its heart,
and wins with its character.*

—FEDERICO TESIO

When the BLM announced that it planned to move forward with the Calico Mountains winter roundup, twenty-seven hundred wild Mustangs living on 550,000 acres in five Herd Management Areas instantly became targets for the low-flying BLM contractor's helicopters. It was a new year but still the same old story: horses were being removed for their own protection and horses were being relocated to prevent rangeland degradation. The decision was especially surprising given the sworn testimony by a local BLM wild horse expert two years earlier that ". . . there's significantly more animals out there than what we thought were, so I would have expected the monitoring data to show higher levels of use than what I collected. And I guess I'm learning it's a big country, animals move."[27] With 180 acres of rangeland previously available to each free-roaming horse, life would drastically change for the Calico Mustangs. Chased, harassed, and then interned, the Calico wild horses who survived the fated winter roundup would soon be relocated to holding facilities with a mere seven hundred square feet per animal.

As the new year started, Samson the formerly wild, maladjusted Mustang had claimed yet another casualty. Only this victim hadn't been charged and run off from deep within the pasture, hadn't been mercilessly kicked, and hadn't been bodychecked to the ground. This casualty had never even crossed paths with the unruly Mustang.

Samson's latest victim was in fact my girlfriend, Jamie.

Weeks earlier, I had told Jamie of my intention to move out to the suburbs after eighteen years living in downtown Chicago. The weekday commute back into the city would be nowhere near as time-consuming as the countless hours I had spent driving to and from the numerous horse farms that dotted the outlying counties. Jamie and I had been dating for only about nine months, so I didn't think it necessary or appropriate to seek her approval. Her response was brief and to the point: "It isn't my business; do whatever works for you and your horses."

I couldn't tell if her statement signaled hurt, anger, indifference, or a combination of the three. Perhaps if she was a horse, I would have been able to decipher what it meant; perhaps not. Either way, in the three weeks since we more or less had had nothing to do with each other.

And then, on New Year's Eve, as Chicago's lakefront fireworks display heralded the start of 2010, as the reds, blues, and greens exploded above our heads, our relationship imploded. Jamie was angered by my refusal to take a trip out of town and leave Samson, and her feelings of rejection boiled over. My recent actions had been thoughtless and my priorities had been skewed—the sentiments that seemed to sum up her feelings.

"You care more about that horse than you do about me," Jamie declared in summary.

While I certainly tried to understand Jamie's position, the smirk on my face said that I could not. Since rejoining with Samson, I had indeed bent over backward to cater to everyone's needs—friends, family, legal clientele, horse clients, and my significant other. Ironically, the one person's needs—the only person's needs—that had been neglected were my own. Unable to devote any more time and any more effort and clearly earning failing marks in the boyfriend department, I suggested that Jamie search elsewhere for the one man who could satisfy her needs and her wants.

As Samson learned to walk under lead, Jamie simply walked.

I probably should have been upset by this unfortunate start to the new year. With my fortieth birthday just weeks away, still unmarried and childless, still wanting marriage and children, I was once again a jockey with no horse, a horse with no jockey. Perhaps I should have blamed Samson for suddenly overly complicating my life and ruining what may have been a promising relationship. Maybe it was time to grow up—to hunker down as a lawyer and stop my crusade to rescue, rehabilitate, and fix every broken horse who came my way.

The problem, however, was that I wasn't devastated, I didn't blame Samson for my romantic failings, and I didn't immerse myself in my legal work. In truth, if Jamie were "the one" then she would have understood, if not admired, my work with Samson. While she by no means had to share my passion, she at a minimum had to respect it. And if she truly had feelings for me, then Jamie would have suspended her needs for more than just a brief few weeks and sacrificed for me in the same vein as I had sacrificed for Samson.

I was alone again, but this time I had Samson and he had me.

The following day, my arrival at the farm brought a troubling and bizarre sight. As I pulled up the driveway, two of the property's resident canines were running wildly and barking vociferously as the third, Cosmo the horse-Lab, sat wedged between the barn's two large sliding doors. With his head sticking out and the rest of his body stuck on the other side of the doors, Cosmo was yelping for his life and in one heck of a fix. I jumped out of my truck and immediately headed toward the trapped canine, but my rescue mission was abruptly aborted as the black mutt—the dog who shunned all human contact—stepped in my path and took up a definitive defensive position.

Oh no, you don't.

With Cosmo frazzled, frightened, exhausted, and left unable to defend himself, the mutt was prepared to do it for him. Like two gunfighters squaring off in a Sergio Leone spaghetti western, human and human hater squared off and stared each other down. Then, the oldest dog of the pack— the plump shepherd mix I affectionately labeled "Jenny Craig"—appeared at my side and diffused the tense standoff.

Moments later, the black mutt wearily and slowly came to my side. In one halting and hesitant movement, she rubbed against my left leg and looked up to me with heavy, doubting eyes. *Please, I know he isn't the smartest, but can't you help my friend?* I bent down and lowered my hand to pet her, but the mutt cowered, dropped her head, and seemingly braced for a beating. She, like every other animal at the farm, was an outcast, a victim, a reject.

"Yes, I can take care of this. Let's go rescue that dumb lug," I said aloud as I gently rubbed the black mutt's forehead.

Once free, Cosmo instantly became my new best friend. A quick phone call to Amy disclosed that all three dogs had been deliberately locked in the barn's second story due to the unlawful actions of just one. With three open and ongoing homicide investigations—two chickens and one duck—Cosmo was the prime suspect and apparently the farm's other aspiring Hannibal Lecter. Spotted with feathers lodged between his teeth and sporting a sudden disinterest in his kibble rations, he was in fact the only suspect.

Having been previously charged and arraigned, Cosmo was ordered to house arrest and denied the freedom to roam the property when no one was home. Guilty by association, Jenny Craig and the mutt were ordered to share his sentence and keep him company. Once the trio had hatched their escape plan, they somehow managed to open the door that led to the second story, and travel down the rotting stairs to the main floor. There the two coconspirators were able to slip through the gap between the outer doors while Cosmo, apparently failing to take into account his considerable size difference over his cohorts, had become stuck. I couldn't help but think he was about as dim as they came.

At Amy's direction, I let the two mostly innocent escapees roam free and returned Cosmo to the second floor of the barn, where, in a scene straight out of *CSI,* I tried to re-create the canine gang's escape from Alcatraz. As I stood staring at the seemingly unmovable, now-closed fifty-pound sliding door, Cosmo attempted a second prison break. Using a combination of physics, leverage, and brute force, he was able to pry the door open while I stood admiring his mix of brawn and brains. Suddenly I wasn't so convinced that he was the dumb lug I had believed him to be. Realizing that he would quickly escape once I exited, I piled up four tractor tires in front of the door as Cosmo stared dejectedly at the unmovable mass.

"That's why you're man's best friend and not the other way around. We have the superior intellect," I proudly announced to the canine criminal.

Or maybe not—standing in the dark, basking in all my glory, I quickly happened upon a troubling discovery. Cosmo and I were now cellmates. I knew that there was a hay chute and ladder in the far corner, but I also knew that there were a dozen or so gaping holes in the floor that I would have to traverse in the dark. As I contemplated my predicament, Cosmo rubbed up against my leg and barked.

Swallowing my pride, I sought out the only available help: "Between the two of us, you are clearly the brains, so what do you think?"

Seemingly fully comprehending my interrogatory, Cosmo leaned into my hand, and I grabbed his collar. And then, like a guide dog leading his master, he led me around each and every hole and over to the hay chute and ladder. I sat down and heaped praise upon my canine savior only to have him disappear into the darkness. He returned moments later, first dropping into my lap a bowl filled with dog food, then gingerly setting down a bowl of water and, last, several chew toys.

Woof, woof, woof. *Eat up; drink up; what is mine is yours; we are now brothers.*

"No thanks," I responded to my gracious host. "I already had lunch and prison rations have never been to my liking."

After fifteen minutes playing with my newfound blood brother, I made my way over to the hay chute and ladder. As I was about to disappear through the opening, Cosmo, apparently under the belief that we were now inseparable, decided to hitch a ride. When he placed his right paw upon my right shoulder and affixed his left to the corresponding side, I was nothing but impressed with his deductive reasoning powers. Looking up at Cosmo, I realized that this horse–Lab mixed-breed former stray, a canine I once believed to be little more than dim and dense, was no doubt a superdog. He could, in my estimation, run circles around both Underdog and Pavlov's mutt.

It was an important reminder that looks can be deceiving and assumptions can be dangerous.

Hanging from the ladder, I gazed up at the hitcher as he rained a thick wax of drool down onto my face. "No way, buddy, you've got a hearing date and a jury trial ahead of you. I can't be the arbiter of your fate or a co-conspirator."

Having examined the evidence against the accused canine and concluded that he was no doubt a carnivore, I handed up to Cosmo a piece of teriyaki beef jerky, which he instantly devoured. I then offered some culinary advice to my new friend: "Next time, when you go after the chickens and ducks, make sure they are first cooked; it makes for a much better meal." I retreated down the ladder, stepped onto the concrete floor, and provided one last piece of parting advice as Cosmo's head dangled precariously through the hole: "And one more thing Mr. Defendant, as a lawyer I would strongly counsel that from now on, you dispose of all incriminating evidence after the commission of the crime."

To this day, the untouchable black mutt greets my weekly arrival and allows me to pet her; Cosmo the superdog and I remain the best of friends.

When I ventured out to catch Samson, he was nowhere to be found. Now in our fourth month working together, not a week had passed without my having to drudge to the property's far northwest corner to capture this homesick, homeless horse. This day would be no different.

After several minutes, I located my pupil, standing in his usual spot in the far corner of the pasture. The sight of him instantly numbed whatever pain I felt from my recent breakup with Jamie.

As I approached from the rear, Samson stood peering out across the endless acres of farmland—staring aimlessly and endlessly at the miles of rolling and dipping hills in the distance. Every few seconds, he would glance back over his right shoulder, note my nearing proximity, and then promptly return his gaze to the vast, open, and inviting landscape that unfolded just beyond the electric line.

Samson was ever so close but still so far from liberty, freedom, and the vast frontier. Week after week this scene replayed itself and week after week it broke my heart. It was as if a force was calling to or pulling at Samson. Like Greek sailors transfixed by the Sirens' song, this once wild and free Mustang would not, could not, turn away. And while Samson longed for and cherished the safety and safe harbor of his far-off homeland, at that very moment Nevada's ranges were anything but safe and secure for the free-roaming wild Mustang.

Thousands of miles away from Samson's safe Midwest confines, wild horses in northwestern Nevada were being chased, culled, and captured. They were also dying. Deaths were inevitable, according to the BLM. Elderly and infirm horses, those allegedly weakened by purported poor range conditions, would face an uphill battle for their survival. Just days into the roundup, one death, however, caught the immediate attention of humane observers. This loss of life didn't involve an elderly or infirm horse. In this instance, after days of horror, trauma, pain, and suffering, a nine-month-old foal's life was prematurely cut short.

The foal's tragic story began on January 2 when it, along with its dam and herd, was chased by helicopter for up to fourteen miles across the craggy, jagged Calico terrain. Young and weak, the foal had no choice but to keep up with its mother; to fall behind meant a certain and lonely death. Once it had been captured by BLM wranglers, the foal was segregated, examined, and identified as sickly. For several days it languished, until it was no longer able to stand under its own weight. After a subsequent medical exam yielded the conclusion that two of the foal's hooves had completely sloughed off, the young horse was put down. The BLM identified the cause of death as hoof trauma from roundup operations.

With this young foal denied the opportunity to roam wild and free as an adult horse, its story was both tragic and telling. Neither elderly nor infirm, the neophyte Mustang quite literally had its hooves run off. For many involved in the roundups, the death was little more than the cost of doing business. Young or old, sick or healthy, some loss of life was inevitable—they would say. "The range cannot support our nation's wild herds" is what the brochures and press releases would read.

But this young foal didn't fall to dehydration, starvation, heat exposure, or the frontier's dangerous predators. Removed from the range allegedly for its own good and for its own protection, this horse—like countless prior and many since—fell to the helicopter's rotor blades, the wranglers' rope, and the BLM's policies. And while most paid little heed to this story, the foal's sad and painful end was much more than just a single loss of life. It was a sign, an omen, and a warning.

In the weeks to follow, tragedy would once again descend upon the wild horse. Herded into muddy, cramped corrals, overheated and exhausted, adult horses would falter, mares would miscarry, allegedly protected wild horses would perish, and an entire generation of young and unborn Calico Mustangs would meet the same tragic fate as the nine-month-old foal.

This probably could have been—should have been—Samson's story. But he was a fighter and a survivor—a proud and true wild American Mustang. Whereas luck and fate shunned the young foal, both had granted Samson a reprieve. This unruly, cantankerous Mustang was destined for bigger and better things. Like the great biblical figure, Samson the combative, beaten-down wild horse was fated to deliver his kind from hardship, oppression, and tragedy.

By midmonth, winter's frigid chill held rural McHenry County in its vice-like grip. Samson and I pushed forward.

On his good days, Samson was focused and engaged. But on his bad days, the still-wild-at-heart Mustang remained as unpredictable as Plains weather. Working with Samson was a process. A process that required patience, time, and a thorough understanding of this horse's many ghosts and demons. Deciphering and distinguishing Samson the terrified victim from Samson the willful wild horse was taking my training skills to a whole new level.

The objective for the month was to increase Samson's maneuverability while figuratively tightening the reins on my challenging student. I could achieve the latter by managing and directing Samson's forward, backward, and lateral movements. Once again, my ability to instruct Samson when and where to move was imperative and essential. The first advanced skills that my bipolar pupil needed to tackle were the turn on the forehand and the pivot on the hindquarters.

A turn on the forehand requires that a horse's hind legs arc around its forelegs—which remain more or less stationary. In order to complete the maneuver, the horse must first adduct, step one hind leg in front of the stationary opposite, and then abduct, reach outward and away from its body with the previously planted hind leg. Similar to the turn on the forehand, the pivot on the hindquarters directs the horse to move a foreleg out sideways away from its body and then continue the motion as the front legs arc around the hind legs, which are lifted and then planted down in place.

In effect, during both maneuvers the horse is using two of its legs to walk a circle around the other two mostly stationary limbs. If turning on the forehand, the horse's body is rotating around the forelegs. When pivoting on the haunches, it is circling around the two hind legs. In both instances, the horse's learned ability to move away from the application of pressure initiates each lateral movement.

Teaching Samson to rotate laterally required that he and I get up close and personal. Though horse and trainer were no doubt intimately acquainted by this point, this nevertheless remained a very hard pill for the ever-solitary Samson to swallow. If asking him to turn on the forehand, I was required to stand back by Samson's rump—within his kick radius—and use my fist to gently apply pressure against his side until he rotated his hind end out and away. When directing a pivot on the hindquarters, I stood just off Samson's shoulder—well within his head-butt zone—pressing against his neck and face until he yielded and rotated in the opposite direction.

Having me in his personal space, applying pressure and making a mockery of his defensive perimeter, was simply a fact of life that Samson would have to accept. Though he was not happy about it, Samson's abstention from violence indicated that he had begrudgingly accepted this reality. When, however, I stood back at a distance and gently tapped him with a long riding crop in lieu of my hand, Samson fiercely declared that he had seen and tolerated enough.

Samson the warrior was primed for a return engagement.

My time with Samson had already revealed that he had a long history with the riding crop. Perhaps it too closely resembled the cattle prod—an oft-used tool of BLM wranglers. Or maybe a riding crop had been employed in one of his many beat-downs. Either way, I had long since known that this horse had drawn a line in the pasture and, as far as he was concerned, no one or no thing was going to cross it. Like a torpedo snaking, veering, and jerking to find its target, his hind-leg strikes ensured that the crop would not come into contact with his body. With Samson consciously and deliberately protecting his ever-so-guarded hindquarters at one end and his head at the other, I simply could not win.

Samson was once again defending himself from a long-despised enemy. The list only continued to grow: the helicopter, rope, halter, and now riding crop. This Mustang was truly battle tested.

As in our previous encounters, Samson's reactions were rote, responsive, defensive, and learned. Call his actions what you will—obstructive, unacceptable, or dilatory—but the one thing they were not was malicious. More important, these actions were not directed at me and accordingly could not be taken personally. In one moment, Samson would forcefully strike at the crop. Seconds later, he would stand idle as I pressed my fist into his flank and initiated a pivot. This horse's list of enemies was no doubt lengthy, but unlike all those who had come before me, thankfully, my name was nowhere to be found. If I wanted to fix Samson's issues, then I would have to employ a measured combination of both praise and punishment.

In instances such as this, the greatest error that owners make is their steadfast refusal to permit their horse to make mistakes. Horses learn by trial and error. As the alpha leader, an owner's acceptance or rejection of a specific action in turn dictates a horse's continued and subsequent behaviors. Time, patience, and instruction, on the one hand, will lead to a vast array of desired, appropriate responses. Yelling, hitting, and pain, on the other hand, will only shake to the core an animal who by its very nature is already doubting, insecure, herd oriented, and in need of constant reassurance and instruction.

Punishment for Samson, like all of my horses, often took the form of physical exertion. Compliance meant rest and leisure; obstruction meant work and exercise. Tight circles at a trot is or rather was one such example of an excellent method of punishment until Samson and I crossed paths. With his body moving in circles and his eyes fixed on mine, this unabashedly direct Mustang frequently mocked this oft-applied mandated punishment. Each time I sent him off, I felt as if I could read his thoughts.

Hey, buddy, seriously? Running me, for real? I've spent my life running. Have that friend of yours fit me with a good pair of running shoes and I could run the Boston Marathon. I would have thought you knew better!

In order to properly execute both the turn on the forehand and the pivot on the hindquarters, Samson would have to accept the crop's touch and yield to its pressure. Ever the difficult yet deductive student, one afternoon after he had completed a compulsory punitive time-out, Samson arrived at what he believed was a fair and equitable solution to both of our problems. As I started to raise the crop from my side, and with it still several feet from his body, Samson promptly shifted his weight, moved his legs, and first executed a turn on the forehand, followed by a pivot on the hindquarters. Both were perfect.

Look at me, his smug look said. *I can do this without that thing even touching me.* Like a parent who hides a smile and laughter following a child's hilarious yet inappropriate comment, I too masked my amusement.

Eventually, Samson came to realize that despite his long and unfortunate history with the riding crop and cattle prod, in my hands no such instrument would bring him harm. It was once again a decision, a realization, premised upon our mutual trust and the bond first forged in a darkened, damp stall months earlier. Incidents such as this soon led me to the realization that over time I had come to respect and admire Samson's proud and prideful ways. This was a courageous animal—a solitary figure willing to cast aside deep, scarring memories and start anew. Always true to himself and his ways, he didn't snuggle up for treats, didn't aim to please his two-legged captors, and didn't feign interest or dedication. If you wanted Samson's attention and respect, then you had to earn it.

Horse and trainer were working together, and in Samson's mind that was all that needed to be said to express his feelings.

Samson's ways had also kept this horse alive, and fed him hope when there was no hope to be found. After fifteen years, I was once again challenged and inspired. I was falling back in love with my first love. Yet I was terrified of failing this horse and consumed with the potential consequences. And while Samson's strong character and resolve were no doubt admirable, he was not the only one of his kind to possess these qualities.

As Samson gazed out across the rural midwestern frozen tundra, the one thing that his gaze couldn't detect, but the one thing that humane observers' cameras could, was the life-or-death struggles of a similarly willful, proud, and prideful wild Mustang stallion. Determined resolve and the yearning for freedom and liberty, it turns out, were traits not remotely exclusive to my combative student. These were breed-wide traits and characteristics, and in the Calico Mountains Complex they were on full display.

Out West, a descendant of Samson's old Nevada herd decided he had had enough of his cramped BLM corral. With cameras rolling, the captured wild stallion, whom Mustang advocates dubbed "Freedom," leapt the corral railing, burst through barbed wire, and galloped back to the Nevada mountains. Though contractors chased him with horses and dogs, the wounded stallion escaped.

Samson and Freedom, his stallion compatriot thousands of miles away, had two things in common: they were both proud and determined, and they were both separated from their kind—they were both alone.

Despite all of our progress, Samson and Amy remained estranged. So the following week, I decided to take the initiative and force the issue—urging Amy to lift and pick out Samson's hooves. But after she lifted and picked just one hoof, Amy announced, "No more." When she was asked to brush Samson's back, she completed one stroke and promptly departed. Notwithstanding her indifference, Amy continued to insist that we advance Samson's training. While her fear of the once-lawless Mustang was certainly justified, it was now clear that Amy would not play an active role in Samson's rehabilitation. He was, for her, a symbol more than a project.

Having observed Samson at his worst, and fully aware that his anger could reach its flash point in mere seconds,

Amy was scared to death of Samson. The last place that she wanted to be was underneath Samson; the last place he wanted to be was anywhere near Amy. And though she didn't recognize it at the time and while it was by no means deliberate or conscious, Amy's fear had already doomed her relationship with Samson.

As a species of prey and flight, horses are governed by an overriding concern for safety and security. If equines had a motto, it would be "live to run another day." When a horse detects a threat or senses fear in a nearby animal or human, it is going to do whatever it can to get away, and get away fast. And while some level of apprehension will always be present when working with large animals, the introduction of a terrified handler to a horse who by its nature is already prone to flight would be analogous to pouring gasoline on a raging fire.

Once it is sensed by horses, fear is like a cancer. It grows, spreads, and dominates the equine mind. Horses are, in my estimation, walking, breathing fear detectors. They sense it, smell it, hear it, and react to it.

It is the one certain impediment to harmonious relations between horse and horseman.

Fear is the single most determinative factor that explains why a horse will act calm and compliant with one handler and moments later, with another, turn skittish and combative. Group-oriented by virtue of nature and nurture, horses crave the safety and security provided by the herd. As such, they are followers—not individuals. A horse will follow and submit to a strong herd leader who exudes authority, strength, and confidence. If led by a weak, indecisive alpha, that very same horse will lose its sense of security, confidence, and overall sense of direction. Doubt soon evolves into fear, which in short order gives rise to insecurity. Once consumed by fear and insecurity, a horse becomes an eleven-hundred-pound mass of unchecked emotions, reverts to instinct, and takes to immediate flight.

Like fear, an absence of patience can be equally destructive to the horse–human relationship. Time and patience are with little doubt the most significant yet most overlooked factors when properly training any horse. With both, you can cure nearly any vice, any evil. Without either, you can just as easily ruin a good horse as push a troubled one over the edge.

Required when both initially bonding with a horse and then again once skills are introduced and taught, time and patience are required at all times, with all horses. Fail to properly take the time to establish a relationship with your horse and you will never reach the skills development phase. Establish the proper bond with your horse but fail to initially break down skills to the most basic components and you will have a mount lacking in both ability and execution.

Combined, these tenets form my first rule of horsemanship: fear begets insecurity; impatience breeds failure. Just as a herd-bound horse looks to a lead stallion or alpha mare for strength and security, a domesticated horse expects its handler to be both strong and confident. If strength and confidence are absent, then a willing horse promptly turns unwilling, afraid, and insecure. If fearful, a handler must slow down the process and compartmentalize his or her actions. With time and patience, fear will decrease and confidence will increase. Act like you're in charge, behave like you know what you are doing, and a horse will follow your lead. Alternatively, let fear govern and control your actions, fail to take baby steps, and a calm horse turns punchy; an amped-up horse turns to fear-driven flight or fight.

Fear, it turns out, begets insecurity in both humans and horses.

Consumed with justified fear, Amy had found it difficult to look beyond Samson's storied past deeds. As I deliberated on the problem, I was reminded of a horse who lived, ironically, just a few miles down the road from Amy's farm. A three-year-old Thoroughbred racetrack reject, Sky's first home following her retirement was with a farmer and his young daughter. No different from any other track-trained horse, Sky was large and aggressive and knew a great deal about "go" and very little about "whoa." Since a child was involved, this story's ending was a foregone conclusion. Children take to hobbies the way they grow in and out of their clothes. One month it's a great fit; the next month it's a hand-me-down.

Horses, needless to say, are not hand-me-downs and are not easily discarded.

After several failed attempts to teach Sky the most basic of skills, the farmer quickly realized that he had bitten off far more than he could chew. Even for a skilled trainer, a track horse can be quite the challenge. As the days turned to weeks, the family's collective need for instant gratification—the need to have a horse who could be immediately saddled, mounted, and ridden—led to a chilling effect for this beautiful hot-blooded horse specimen. In no time, Sky went from a prized purchase to a mistake—a regret.

Soon, Sky was relegated to a sad and solitary existence in a mud lot. Fed just enough to keep her alive, and with no exercise, she bore little resemblance to the shiny-coated, proud, and athletically gifted horse who had stepped from the trailer months before. At some point, the neighbors intervened and, after some convincing, Sky's owners agreed to transfer her title to an interested couple.

A proud and commanding horse, Sky had understandably grown resentful and standoffish. After several failed attempts to catch and load Sky for the trip to her new home, I was called out to get the job done. Once Sky was successfully delivered to her new owners, I walked her out to a large grass pasture, dropped two flakes of hay at her side, rubbed her neck, and exited the enclosure. I then urged Sky's owners to move slowly and cautiously with their new horse; acceptance and interaction would come in time. Having observed that malnourishment had made Sky deeply food aggressive and protective, I implored both to throw Sky's hay rations over the fence and avoid, at least for the time being, any approach with food in hand. I then said my good-byes and departed with a sense that Sky was off to a fresh start.

Days later, I received a phone call advising that Sky was once again in need of a new home. When I inquired as to why, I was informed that Sky had allegedly attacked one of her owners. In the back of my mind, I already had a pretty good idea of what had transpired. The following weekend, I made the two-hour drive out to Sky's new home. Upon my arrival, I immediately jumped the fence, walked out to, and greeted Sky. She slowly advanced on my position and snugged up against my shoulder. There was no hint of malice, aggression, or threat and I was now certain of what had gone down days before.

Moments later, the husband and wife duo appeared. For several minutes, I listened intently as they used terms such as "mean," "crazed," and "violent" to describe their recent four-legged acquisition. While their loaded adjectives painted a troubling picture, neither could provide a single fact that could account for their ill will toward Sky. I pressed harder and eventually the duo's female half buckled. As she explained it, Sky had approached her husband, postured on him, and then attempted to grab two flakes of hay from him as he entered her pasture. When he dropped the hay and swung his arms at her, Sky responded with a halfhearted kick, which, by the wife's own admission, was not intended to make contact.

That was literally the entire story.

I turned and looked at the husband and then waited for it. "It is totally ridiculous that we put ourselves out for this horse and I'm not even able to walk hay out there," he angrily explained. "You spent two hours with her, dumped hay at her feet, petted her on the neck, and walked away without so much as a hiccup on her part. How long do I have to wait to receive that same treatment? I gave her food and shelter and so far I have nothing to show for it."

And there it was.

Sky and Samson had much more in common than just their close geographic proximity. Both Thoroughbreds and Mustangs seem to generate a great deal of interest, excitement, and prestige when first rescued, adopted, or purchased. The fact that they suddenly own a Thoroughbred or Mustang seems to infuse some owners with an air of horsemanship excellence—a sense that they have taken on and conquered the toughest of breeds. But after the novelty gives way to fear, impatience, and eventual imprudence, more often than with other types of horses the Mustang and the Thoroughbred are back on the truck and headed for auction or, worse yet, slaughter.

When I first met the couple who took Sky in, it was patently obvious that both husband and wife were mortally terrified of their imposing, powerful horse. With Sky anxious and standoffish from months of abuse and neglect, this was the last thing that she needed and she promptly fed off their fear. Further compounding the problem, Sky's owners threw caution and patience to the wind and forced compliance and acceptance upon a horse who was not yet ready to comply or accept. While the farmer had attempted to sprint through the training process, Sky's new owners had sought to bypass the natural bonding process that would have permitted them, in short order, to establish a trusting and healthy relationship with their horse.

Both practices were fatally flawed and certain to fail.

Where haste and impatience take the place of time and patience, steps in the natural order of instruction, learning, and bonding are invariably passed over, if not entirely omitted. Sky's confrontation with her owner demonstrates that impatience not only breeds failure but can just as easily lead to rash decisions and careless actions. When you are working around horses, there are no do-overs. There are no second chances. Imprudent behavior can maim, injure, or kill. Having witnessed countless accidents and injuries over the years caused by impatient owners looking for instant results, I can state with absolute certainty that there are no shortcuts when working and training horses.

Sky's short saga did in fact conclude in a happy ending.

With my two subsequent visits and a newfound understanding of their animal, Sky's owners came to realize the critical role that fear and patience can play when forging a meaningful and lasting bond between horse and human. In turn, and in mere days, Sky came to accept her new owners on her terms and under her own volition. Together thereafter, Sky and her owners enjoyed a contented and lasting relationship.

My continued hope was that the same would be true for Samson and Amy. Nevertheless, if Amy could not learn to look past Samson's previous misdeeds, if she could not cast aside her fears and learn to take baby steps, then this Mustang's future would remain cast in doubt.

As January's cold, dark days dwindled, thousands of miles away the BLM made a surprising announcement. After receiving thousands of protest e-mails from Mustang advocates, the BLM decided to postpone the roundup of two hundred wild horses living on 225,000 acres in Utah's Confusion Mountains. The proposed roundup would have left fewer than one hundred horses—a population far below the required minimum threshold to ensure biological diversity and sustain the herd's continued viability. The Utah horses had received a suspended sentence; there would be no such reprieve for the Calico Mustangs.

Low-flying helicopters were strafing and chasing the Calico herd and Mustangs were dying. And as the month came to a close, disturbing news leaked from the BLM Nevada holding facilities: captured adult horses were dying in large numbers; in utero Mustang foals were being stillborn. In just a matter of days, the numbers would tell two chilling stories. The first would be of formerly wild and free Mustangs taking their last breaths caged and penned. The second, even more disturbing story would be that an entire generation of Mustangs would never have the opportunity to take their first breaths.

High in the Nevada mountains, roundup observers reported a strange sight: a lone, lame Mustang stallion stalking and observing a BLM trap site and its caged prisoners. It was Freedom, the combative escaped Mustang stallion searching for his herd. Injured, he was now an easy target for his many two- and four-legged predators. His future was most certainly in doubt.

On the wintry Illinois dairy farm, Samson stood at the edge of his pasture, staring, as he always did, west. The solitary Mustang still sought his herd, still saw himself as an unwilling captive, and still longed for a home. Samson and his wild Mustang cousin now shared another commonality: their futures, their fates, remained uncertain.

10

THE ENEMY AT THE GATE

If three people say you are an ass, put on a bridle.
—SPANISH PROVERB

As the fated Calico winter roundup entered its second month, a flurry of disturbing new reports quickly awoke the American public's ire. Under intense public scrutiny and criticism, Department of the Interior chief Ken Salazar turned to the *Los Angeles Times* to justify and explain the BLM's actions. Writing as a guest columnist, Salazar declared that Mustang lands were sensitive and sparse, that wild horses had damaged ecosystems, and that the herds were at risk of starvation. It was a tale repeated many times over many years.

Near fifty years earlier, when the BLM tried to remove the historically significant Pryor Mountains Mustangs—the blue roans, red roans, duns, grullos, and palominos—the story was nearly identical. An untouched, untainted direct link to the Spanish Mustang and the Conquistador horse, Montana's Pryor horses were allegedly starving, dying, and destroying the terrain. When television news correspondent and journalist Hope Ryden aired her documentary on July

11, 1968, images of healthy, well-adjusted horses were beamed into living rooms across the country. The cat was out of the bag. The horse had escaped the barn. The undernourished, starving Mustang was nowhere to be seen.

Now decades later, images captured in the Calico Mountains told the very same story. While many years had passed, the horse that had discovered, built, and symbiotically survived on the western frontier was still the enemy.

February's first days were dark, frigid, and wet. Most owners stopped working their horses during the cold months, so winter was the one time of the year when I could work on and refine my riding skills. This season, however, Samson's schooling needs changed all of that. As both humans and animals alike battled winter's doldrums, with the aid of a sidepull and a patient instructor, Samson the quick study started to flex at the poll, bend at the neck, and yield to pressure applied via the reins. Closely resembling a rope halter, the sidepull—with stainless-steel rein rings attached to both the left and right cheek—reinforces the concept of the yield to pressure. It provides a way to teach a horse to yield to eventual bit pressure without having to actually engage a bit and harm the horse's mouth. Initially fixed and rigid, a horse who flexes and bends becomes responsive, fluid, mobile, and at one with the rider's hands.

Slowly but surely, Samson's previously strung-out posture—his outline—took on a new appearance. With longitudinal flexion he brought his hind legs under his body, rounded his back, and extended his neck higher and straighter. Physics and anatomy were now working in Samson's favor; his power and strength were harnessed, and like a compressed spring he was ready to launch. When he ever so slightly turned his head to the side and released to the rein's pull, Samson simultaneously flexed at the poll, back, and lumbar spine. Lateral flexion was taking over and this horse was learning how to bend.

Samson the once wild, undisciplined, disjointed, and uncollected Mustang was starting to look like a supple horse.

A supple horse freely and easily shifts its balance between forward, backward, and lateral motion. With Samson's movements now appearing fluid, the time was ripe for him to learn how to back up. In nature, horses seldom move in reverse. For this reason, many horsemen consider the rein-back an unnatural and difficult gait—refusing to teach it on account of their horses' strong initial adverse reactions. Still others teach the rein-back, only to subsequently employ it solely as punishment for a horse's ill behaviors. I, however, have always subscribed to the belief that when directed to do so a horse should freely and effortlessly move in reverse. If introduced and taught properly, the rein-back should be natural, fluid, and nonstressful.

Just as a car that won't travel in reverse is missing 50 percent of its capabilities, a horse who won't back up is stuck in gear.

When the time came to teach Samson the rein-back, he seemingly lost all faith and confidence in my abilities. For the first time, the student doubted his teacher. *No,* Samson's expression would say, *I really don't think you want me to do that—I just think you're confused right now.* Backing up exposed Samson to danger, and while he could no doubt inflict grave injury with his hind legs and hindquarters, he preferred to face all known threats head-on. There he could employ the rear, head-butt, and foreleg strikes and skin-shredding bites that were the tools of his trade. In Samson's mind, moving in reverse both exposed him to unknown threats and neutralized his potent weapons arsenal. Needless to say, throughout the course of his rein-back schooling Samson the warrior remained steadfast in his belief that I was a teacher working off a faulty lesson plan.

Days later, after watching one of our sessions, Lisa made some observations that were spot-on: "Wow, that's a great rein-back, but I don't know that I've ever seen a horse quite that pissed off about having to do it." In the absence of a kick, bite, or head butt, Samson's hard stare and irritated facial expression communicated all that he wanted said. Disgruntled or not, Samson had executed as he was taught, and that was enough for me.

February's first Sunday brought what was to be a principal step in transforming this once-lawless Mustang into a saddle-broke horse. With the first signs of collection, flexion, and bending, Samson was ready for the bridle and bit. In light of his terribly sensitive ears, the choice of headstall—the western version of the English-style bridle—mandated great care, thought, and deliberation. Requiring that I push Samson's damaged ear through a small, oval opening, the slot ear headstall was thus less than optimal. The browband headstall, on the other hand, would bring little interference to Samson's ears and proved to be the tack of choice for this baggage-laden Mustang. Having worked with his ears for many weeks, I had anticipated that placing and removing the headstall would ignite Samson's anger and defense. But since Samson had no such dark history with the bit, I hoped for a smooth and peaceful first encounter.

Despite my hopes, once again this horse's strong dislike

for being controlled by anyone or anything quickly trampled my desire for a combat-free introduction.

As expected, Samson flew into a rage when the headstall crossed over his ears. Once it was fitted to his head and the bit was in his mouth, Samson's eyelids narrowed, his gaze turned cold, his respirations increased, and his spine turned rigid. He was primed for battle. He had searched and perused our contract, its many addendums, riders, and subsequent attachments, and found no reference to an unyielding stainless-steel mouthpiece and restrictive headstall and my total dominion over his movement and his very being. Samson wanted to renegotiate our agreement, but for this horse renegotiation did not include casual and friendly interaction and compromise.

Similar to many of my two-legged attorney counterparts, Samson sought to renegotiate with a mix of threat, force, and intimidation. He threw his head hard to the right and then the left, tossed it high in the air, and then down between his forelegs. He repeatedly and forcefully smashed his right foreleg into the hard soil and rocked back and forth like a mechanical bull. Whereas in our previous skirmishes Samson had waged war against a host of ghosts, demons, and painful memories, on this occasion he battled a new and foreign enemy.

Though the bit was unknown to him, a wealth of experience had taught this horse to assume it was a tool of domination. Samson's abusive past wasn't responsible for this impressive display of defiance—this was Samson the willful, domineering wild Mustang. This was the aging warrior warhorse who refused to be controlled.

Deciphering when Samson's violent reactions were borne

out of his dark formative experiences and when they derived from a set-in-his-ways alpha horse continued to be a constant and ever-evolving challenge. Reacting to and showing the proper level of restraint and knowing when to apply the appropriate amount of discipline was both frustrating and complicated. And as we figured it all out, I became a more adept horseman and Samson became a more controlled and less of a controlling horse.

The following week Samson took his fight to a whole new level. He pitched, rocked, and violently tossed his head like a dog with a new chew toy. The fury and the sheer power of his struggles sent Samson's body crashing down to the ground, coming to rest on its right side. No matter how hard he tried, Samson could not dislodge the bit and the headstall. Defeat was inevitable. Vanquished in battle but not in spirit, from that moment forward Samson grudgingly accepted both the bit and headstall. Nevertheless, more than a year would pass before this emotionally scarred horse would comfortably accept the headstall's placement and removal and the corresponding contact with his damaged ears.

In more ways than one, it was a special occasion. Samson's first encounter with the bit and bridle had passed without injury to horse or trainer. He deserved a special reward, and because it was my fortieth birthday he was to receive quite the treat. Since I had no way of knowing the actual day that he was born, I had already decided that the two of us would share my birthday. Apples, maple syrup, and peppermints were had by all. And though the last thing that Samson needed was a sugar high, I took great pleasure in watching this once perpetually stoic horse devour his birthday surprise.

As Samson relished his hyperglycemic treat, the Calico Mustangs likewise received a gift of sorts. Just outside of Gerlach, Nevada, the BLM declared an end to its Calico Mountains Complex gather. Contractors had removed 1,922 horses—fewer than the 2,700 predicted and targeted— and claims that the ubiquitous wild Mustang had overpopulated the Calico range were cast in doubt. Concurrent with the Calico gather's conclusion, the BLM also announced the postponement of the Eagle Herd Management Area roundup.

Covering more acreage than the state of Rhode Island and with twenty-seven hundred cattle grazing unhindered, the Eagle Herd Management Area and its wild horses had been in the crosshairs ever since the BLM announced its intention to drop the wild horse population to fewer than one hundred Mustangs. With Utah's Confusion Mountains roundup similarly deferred one month prior, there was newfound hope that the BLM had discovered the error of its ways. Where Mustang welfare advocates should have been pleased, they were instead gravely concerned. Something had rattled the BLM's cage.

In short order, animal welfare organizations would discover that shocking fatality statistics, and not their advocacy efforts, had stalled the winter roundups.

Processing my own sugar high, I cut through the barn on the way back to my truck. There I discovered Felicity—the feral, tail-less, human-hating resident barn cat. Like all of the farm's four-legged inhabitants, she too was an unwanted societal outcast. Curled into a tight ball in her small nylon cat house, fast asleep atop a leftover sheet of fiberglass insulation,

Felicity was oblivious and impervious to winter's chill. Though Amy and Lisa possessed the best of intentions when they carpeted Felicity's dwelling, the glass fiber reinforced insulation was terribly hazardous to the resident feline's eyes and throat.

On the spot, I renamed the purring and contented cat. From that moment forward, she was Asbestos. Feeling like the Grinch who stole Christmas, I pulled Asbestos from her one-bedroom apartment and promptly discarded the sheet of insulation.

Staring up at me from her now-frigid abode, Asbestos' eyes remained fixed on my torso. Having removed her one source of both warmth and contentment, I was certain she was mapping the best route to strike at and tear out my heart. In an instant, she sprang from the ground, flew past my insulated Carhartt jacket's partially open zipper, snaked through my down vest, and came to rest between my insulated button-down shirt and my long underwear top. I had ravaged her home and Asbestos clearly believed that I owed her.

I was now Samson's teacher, Cosmo's best friend, and Asbestos' furnace.

In that instant, months of prolonged predatory stares, guttural hisses, and fluffed tails were erased. Up until that moment, the tail-less cat had been the one farm animal who had rejected my overtures. She detested Samson and he despised her. By implication, I too was the enemy. But now all of that would change. For many weeks to follow and until spring's first thaw, Asbestos the tail-less feral barn cat would make her weekly leap of faith—each time landing successfully between my warm and inviting winter layers.

Like Samson, Cosmo the standoffish black mutt, and me,

Asbestos and I had forged an odd and strange relationship. In no time, she would come to be a loyal companion and my always present shadow. I had no way of knowing that in a few weeks Asbestos would attempt a similar armistice with Samson that would nearly cost me my life.

Entering the barn at the most inopportune of moments, Amy stopped dead in her tracks as she observed two pointy ears protruding from my many layers of clothing.

"What the hell is it with you and these animals?" she blurted out. "Next you'll have the skunk that lives under the porch taking naps in your truck. Lisa is up in the house and we have a cake. You're invited—that mangy fur ball is not."

Many years ago, I learned that it was best to interact with my horse-owning clientele in the same fashion as my legal clients—keep things on a strictly professional basis. Go in, get the job done, and get out. Whenever I deviated from this model, clients would start treating me like a friend, ask for favors, or fail to pay for services rendered. This instance would be no different. Once I was inside Amy's residence, the distanced business cordiality that had governed each of our prior dealings promptly flew out the aging home's rickety front door.

"So," Amy shouted out in a tone that indicated that a gut shot was on its way, "you're forty years old and you've got nothing to show for yourself. No wife, no kids, no family. Don't you think your mother is fairly disappointed in you? If you don't get your act together, you are going to be all alone, just like Samson!"

When I was working as an attorney in a high-rise office, more often than not personal boundaries were respected and lines were not crossed. Yet whenever I entered the home of one of my horse-owning clients the opposite was almost always the case. I knew better than to follow Amy into the house, and though I assumed that she was simply poking fun, I was prepared to make a hasty retreat. I finished my piece of cake, thanked my hosts, and headed straight for the door.

But Amy was not finished.

Standing strategically behind her younger sister, Amy continued, "Though you would never care to admit it, you are more similar than dissimilar to Samson. I can see why you two are getting along so famously."

The tone of Amy's voice combined with a quick glimpse over my shoulder at her facial expression told me that her words were not intended in jest. An undercurrent of resentment had rippled through her statements and the impeaching tone had not escaped me. This wasn't the first time that my ability to bond with a client's horse had caused problems. But this was my job; I had nearly twenty years of experience that had instructed what and what not to do.

If I had met Samson at the beginning of my career, I wouldn't have survived the encounter. Years of experience from working hardcase horses had kept me safe, and through no fault of her own Amy lacked this knowledge. Still, none of that mattered now. Where Amy had failed to bond with Samson, I had succeeded. It was now clear that Amy's combined growing frustration over Samson's slow progress and her inability to bond with him had infected our relationship. She was becoming increasingly impatient and she wanted to see her Mustang mounted and ridden.

Amy needed to know that some good had come out of a

life—her life—that had been turned on its head. This was as much about Amy as it was about Samson.

Driving home via the twisting, fog-enveloped rural roads, I mulled over Amy's comments. Long since comfortable in my own skin, at forty years old I knew who and what I was. I was an educated, honest, and hardworking adult—most certainly not a disappointment to anyone. While true love and a lifetime partner had to date escaped my grasp, I still believed that both were out there waiting for me.

Dedicated to my clients' interests, I was a zealous and sincere legal advocate. Perhaps I could have been or should have been a more successful attorney. With many battles fought and won, however, I had my share of victories that brought pride and accomplishment. Yet my true source of pride, my one constant source of happiness, was the dozens upon dozens of horses I had saved from a bullet backyard backhoe burial. My work with troubled horses had made a difference; my efforts had saved lives.

My first equine encounter occurred at the ripe age of seven years old. Horses had been trucked into my summer day camp and all campers were to receive rides. By day's end, the only children who had yet to ride were the youngest and they were loud, wound up, and wild. They were also incessantly teasing and picking on a sole, solitary horse who stood tied in the pen's far corner. His name was Comanche, a name and a horse that I will never forget. Comanche was an old, ragged horse—he had seen better days and he had more than paid his dues. Disregarding warnings to stay clear of the cantankerous senior citizen, I discreetly shuffled down to where the lone horse stood, stuck my hand into the pen, and gently petted Comanche's face.

"You must know something that the other kids don't," the wrangler declared from inside the pen, "because everyone else thinks he's a grumpy and sour old fella."

"No," I responded, "he just doesn't like being made fun of and laughed at. He's just misunderstood."

I was the only camper who rode Comanche that afternoon. For that retirement-ready horse, I was nothing more than one of the many bratty little kids who had been thrown atop his aged and worn-out back. For me, the encounter was pivotal and the lesson learned formative. Though young and naïve, I looked at and then through Comanche. I didn't see what others saw; I saw a horse with feelings, emotions, and a soul. I discovered that appearances can be deceiving and I learned to stop, look, and observe rather than assume.

Comanche was truly the first of the many similarly misunderstood horses I have encountered since. To this very day, the teachings of that summer afternoon still resonate when I tell young riders, "Never assume and never presume: never assume a horse is bad; never presume a horse won't hurt you." It is a golden rule that reminds riders to both show respect and exercise caution around horses. A rule borne out of a random encounter between a horse who had seen a great deal and a future horseman who had yet to see anything.

It was a rule I carried with me through each and every of my dealings with Samson.

With thirty minutes of driving down and an additional thirty to go until I reached my new home in Chicago's northwest suburbs, I considered Amy's statement that Samson and I were more similar than dissimilar. This was a horse who had first endured the harsh realities of the wild only to subsequently suffer through the cold brutality of the domestic world. A strong personality and willful ways had helped him persevere where others had fallen. Samson knew how to fight and he knew how to survive. He also knew how to forgive and forget. This Mustang had more than proven his mettle.

Regardless of how Amy had intended her comments, she couldn't have paid me a higher compliment.

Hearing what I believed to be a reference to wild horses on the radio, I turned up the volume and listened intently: between the gather sight and holding facilities, a total of thirty-seven culled Calico Mustangs had perished. Shockingly, an additional thirty mares had miscarried and thirty unborn foals had forever been lost. Outraged by the tragic loss of life, Wayne Pacelle, president and CEO of the Humane Society of the United States, lambasted the BLM, "It's shameful. It's totally inconsistent with the proper and humane management of these populations, and it's happening at a time when the program is so severely broken, and they've lost the trust of the American people in handling their responsibilities."[28]

Whether well-intentioned or motivated by politics and profit, the Calico roundup had become a deadly debacle.

In the weeks that followed, more foals would be aborted and more detained Mustangs would fall. There was little I could do to stop the carnage in Nevada, but there was a great deal I could do for my misunderstood Mustang pupil. As winter's chill retreated, Samson's training advanced. Slowly, he learned to be steered and controlled from the ground. When he walked, halted, and turned in response to my cues, he was as one with the bit, bridle, and reins. When he reacted to my verbal direction, he was a swaggering student.

But when Ike the miniature horse snuck under a downed

fence board, through a partially ajar gate, and into Samson's pasture to feast on his grass, he was judge, jury, and executioner. Borders had been crossed, territories violated, and forage stores consumed. Goldilocks merely had to face three bears; poor Ike had to face an enraged, authoritarian dictator. The fight was over before it even started.

With Ike's mane detached from his neck, Samson the Indian warrior warhorse had quite literally scalped the considerably smaller interloper. Amy was enraged, and she wanted Samson gone. The Mustang's only defense was that he knew no better; it was his way, the way of the wild. Fortunately for the accused, he had a seasoned litigator who argued his case.

"You can't blame him," I declared in summation. "He saw a threat to his territory, to his authority, and he dealt with it the only way he knew how."

While the injury would no doubt freeze a passerby in her tracks, the actual wound was mostly superficial—it looked worse than it was. With no other bite or kick wounds, this had been Ike's lucky day. As I cleaned and treated the wound, Samson the sentry stood at the gate guarding against a repeat incursion. His hard, unflinching gaze remained fixed and focused on Ike. There was no air of victory, no sign of remorse. Rules had been broken and punishment was exacted. For Samson, it was that cut-and-dry.

Frazzled and dazed, Ike refused to glance back at the stoic Mustang.

As I discarded my blood-laden surgical gloves into a plastic bag, my mind drifted to the day's news: pursued across the rocky Nevada terrain days earlier, a second Calico foal had sloughed its hooves and been put down. I looked back over to my little friend and spoke, "You got lucky today, Ikey—you're alive. With Samson, there are no second chances, so let's not have a repeat of this incident." And with that in mind, I grabbed a hammer and nails and went to work on the fence that separated the enforcer from the enforced.

Days later, with Dan back at the farm, we were just about to finish trimming the last hoof when Samson erupted.

"Holy Jesus!" Dan exclaimed as he ran toward the fence. "What the hell was that?"

Realizing that I had failed to educate Dan on the over-flying airborne threat, I kept my explanation short and sweet: "Basically, if you're near Samson and a helicopter flies overhead again, just get as far away as fast as you can."

So much and yet so little had changed for this terminally haunted horse.

Now in our fifth month of training, with lead line in hand I had managed, controlled, and taught my pupil the ways and skills of a domesticated horse. We were now just days away from working with the saddle pad and saddle, which in turn meant that I would require the use of both hands. In other words, I needed Samson to stand tied. He had already learned to hold his stand and yield to pressure, so theoretically this shouldn't have been a problem. But this was Samson—nothing ever came easy or simple with this horse.

This was the one lesson I had pretty much dreaded.

Training horses to stand tied and not fight is a service I have provided untold times to countless clients. When taught properly, it is a skill that reinforces patience, obedience, and respect. If it is taught improperly, the results can be catastrophic for both horse and handler. As I devised a lesson plan, my concern remained focused on Samson's tendency to patiently wait several sessions before he violently rejected any new stimulus. Nearly half a year working with this problem Mustang, and Samson's rule of three lived on. It was a game, a strategy, and disobedience all rolled into one. But a tantrum while being held by lead line was one thing; an explosion while tied was an entirely different story.

In this instance, the source of my trepidation was the reality that I had nothing to tie Samson to. No hitching post, no large tree, and no fence post secure enough. I was left with no option but to tie Samson to an old, rusted, ramshackle iron farm gate, which was part of the pasture perimeter fence.

The skies darkened, the lightning and thunder started up, and the horsemanship gods turned over in their graves; I was about to violate a cardinal rule and tie a horse to a large, movable object.

During our first stand-tied lessons, I simply looped the rope around the gate's crossbar, thus allowing Samson some latitude to move, wiggle, and figure things out. The concept was rudimentary: once he had learned that he could not pull away or get away, Samson would release to the rope's mild pressure and stand tied. With a lengthy list of ways in which a stand-tied lesson can go bad, my knife was out, unfolded, and ready to sever the rope. But because I still held the lead line in my hand, Samson remained somewhat composed and fairly compliant.

This was, simply put, the hallmark of our relationship— for this doubting and combative horse, I was both a calming agent and authoritative figure. While Samson had yet to explode, the honeymoon between this stern, determined warrior and the unyielding gate that sought to limit and control his actions was about to come to a crashing end.

The following week, using a quick-release knot, I secured Samson to the gate and moved away. At first, he seemed unfazed. But as his gaze fixed on and then followed the twisting and snaking lead line to its very end, as he realized that I no longer held it in my hand, Samson's mood promptly shifted. The planets realigned, his gaze hardened, and time slowed. Before my eyes, Samson metamorphosed. Only in this instance, he didn't outright explode; calculating and deliberate, Samson had a plan.

Raising his head high, Samson gradually pulled at the rope. Slowly, he lowered his head in increments, gently tugging at each level before slightly dropping his head down to the next. He was probing for something. Like a woodpecker digging for a soft spot, Samson was searching for a flaw, a weakness. And then, with Samson's head nearly down between his legs, the iron gate cried uncle and emitted an ever-so-faint creak.

Bingo. Samson had found that which he sought.

His eyes fixed on mine, his head static and unmoving, Samson's gaze and body language spoke: *I have achieved success and soon victory.* Foolishly, I thought some admonishing words might deter the pending calamity, "Now listen, I am not amused by your—" I was too late; Samson had discovered leverage. Mustering all of his strength and power and with his head and neck locked and braced, Samson shot into reverse as the iron gate, like an accordion, collapsed in on itself. As if there had ever been any doubt, Samson was once again victorious.

Though not especially pleased with my pupil's actions, I couldn't help but admire his power, strength, and intelligence. My facial expression evidenced firm disapproval, while my eyes held a slight twinkle. As I looked upon Samson, in his eyes I noted that very same twinkle.

Having defeated yet another enemy, Samson had made his point and thereafter stood tied like a well-trained horse. Several months passed without incident. And then, one afternoon in late spring, I arrived at the farm, caught, and then tied Samson. Since our first stand-tied lessons, I had made a habit and practice of using a knotted lead line to secure the gate to the adjoining fence post. I had little trust in the gate's chain, so the tied line provided a simple, safe, and secure backup system. Ten minutes into this lesson, however, I realized that I had forgotten the rope in my truck.

I'm only going to have Samson tied for a few minutes, I told myself. *He's a pro at this; there shouldn't be a problem.*

Call it laziness or call it complacency. Call it what you will, but by virtue of a truly unforeseen set of events it was a mistake that would cost me dearly.

Bent over and picking out his left hind hoof, I felt Samson's muscles contract and his limbs stiffen. A jerk, ripple, and then shock wave traveled from horse to handler. Something was very wrong. Looking back between my legs, I observed a shocking and disturbing sight. With only her bottom half-visible and standing upright on her hind legs, Asbestos was directly underneath Samson. An easy target for his spine-shattering foreleg strikes and flesh-lacerating bites, she was in Samson's kill zone.

Since the day that she first jumped into my jacket, Asbestos and I had enjoyed a blossoming friendship. Each week, she would come outside, lie down, and observe every session without fail. If I meowed three times, she meowed three times; if I responded with seven, she answered in kind. With him tied and involuntarily subject to each and every conversation, Mr. Intolerant's eyes darted back and forth from feline to trainer.

Samson's expression said it all: *My god! Will you two just shut up already!*

Apparently under the belief that it was time to let bygones be bygones, on this day Asbestos had extended an olive branch to her mutually detesting equine neighbor. Given Samson's strong dislike of every animal who roamed the farm, when I first peered through my legs and saw the feline upright I was certain that the carnivorous Mustang held Asbestos' tiny head in his mouth. Mortified and horrified, upon second glance I quickly realized that Asbestos was kneading and licking Samson's chest.

A touching and moving scene, it was nonetheless a critical misjudgment of a horse who knew little of peace offerings, friendship, and intimacy.

Nearly instantly the chain and all hell broke loose. Moving as one, where Samson went the gate followed. Impact was inevitable. Hopelessly and haplessly stuck in an inverted v–like space where the gate's opposite end sat hinged to the fence, I helplessly watched as the two-hundred-pound iron predator swung around and closed in on its prey. Just moments before the collision, I observed Samson's right hind leg kicked out, braced, and primed to take the brunt of the impact.

My mind raced, calculated, and then considered the options. With an unhealed separated left shoulder incurred months earlier when a wash rack water hose blew, sending a thirteen-hundred-pound elephant-sized horse barreling into my torso, intervention on my part would no doubt prove costly. If I didn't intervene, a fractured equid cannon bone, splint bone, long or short pastern, or any combination thereof was a certainty. There would be no tomorrow for my Mustang pupil.

Moments before impact between gate and horse, like a swimmer leaving the starting block I shot forward into nothing but air. Calling upon my experiences years earlier as a running back, I tucked my chin into my chest, pulled my right shoulder in, kicked my waist out to the left, and led with my left shoulder. I was going to throw the block of my life.

Everything went to black.

I regained consciousness to Samson's moist muzzle in my face and his deep, dark eyes staring down at me. The gate had completely swung back on itself, and now horse and horseman were trapped in this inverted v–like space. Though my brain was just rebooting, the minimal cognitive abilities I possessed told me that I was in grave danger. Looking up upon Samson, I was now the one within his kill zone.

This was the one place I knew never to venture—a blind spot where Samson's innate and instinctive defensive systems would kick in and he would trample and shred any and all trespassers.

The left side of my body not responding and with nowhere to crawl, I looked up at the bug-eyed, panting Mustang. To my surprise, Samson stared back at me with a calming, relaxed gaze. *No worries! Take your time; catch your breath; get your wits about you. I owe you this one.* For sure, Samson and Asbestos both owed me. Weeks would pass before Samson would again comfortably stand tied, but with Asbestos, the troubled Mustang, and me each owning a portion of the blame, we, like every other time, worked through it.

As February's days dwindled, Samson and I were nearly ready to enter our next phase of training. In preparation, I placed my saddle atop a stand in the corncrib pasture's far corner. Once I had caught Samson in the south pasture, I walked him through the gate that led into the crib pasture as he performed his ritualized, mandatory visual security sweep for predators, dangers, and abnormalities. Within seconds, his posture tightened, his head raised, his neck cocked, and his nostrils flared. At thirty yards' distance, Samson had zeroed in on an intruder, anomaly, and threat to his well-being.

Showcasing his tremendous visual capabilities, Samson had located a target that in his mind posed imminent danger and certain harm. Though he was a warrior's warrior, Samson's abusive past —his many battles and victories fought against those who had sought to beat him down— had come at a deep and profound cost. He was now a battle-tested, shell-shocked warrior who saw anything and everything new as a tool of pain and punishment. Terrified and poised for battle, Samson refused to enter the corncrib pasture.

At that moment, and though we were so close to achieving our goal, I knew we had a long journey ahead of us.

This reaction to the saddle, in addition to Samson's near catastrophe with Asbestos and the gate, highlights the difficulties and hazards associated with training and handling any large animal. While the many inherent risks and dangers cannot be eliminated, when working with horses there are ways to safely minimize one's exposure to both threat and injury. With this in mind, my second rule of horsemanship postulates and reminds owners to always remember where a horse comes from and to never forget how a horse moves, sees, thinks, and reacts.

More often than not, horse owners err by attributing complex human thoughts, cognitive processes, and emotions to their four-legged companions. Lacking a brain that permits multilayer thought processes and deductive reasoning, horses are driven more by primal, instinctive motivators than emotion. Whether a best friend, investment, or aid in work, the horse is still an animal and must always be treated and handled as such.

In order to understand how a horse learns, a true horseman must first grasp how his steed thinks, perceives, and comprehends. Unlike its equid counterpart, the human brain is dedicated mostly to the cerebrum and thought, memory, association, and conscious decision making. Conversely, the horse brain is predominantly comprised of cerebellum, which manages gross muscle coordination, movement, and control. In other words, humans think, horses act. Where a person first evaluates a threat, a horse runs from it. As the horse is an animal of prey and creature of flight, it stands to reason that natural selection and evolution have gifted the horse with the resources required to survive and flourish in the inhospitable wild.

While the equine mind is designed primarily to learn and remember items of biological significance, particularly safe and hostile locales, food, water, and forage locations, it can, nevertheless, grasp and digest extensive information when it is presented in the proper manner. With many different techniques available to teach Samson various skills and modify certain of his behaviors, I employed a combination of each and every method to help my pupil weather the learning process.

At the most rudimentary level, habituation teaches a horse to accept a stimulus through repeated or prolonged exposure. Such desensitization can occur through approach and retreat training—applying a stimulus and then removing it before the horse reacts negatively. Alternatively, flooding maintains and sustains a stimulus until the point at which a horse no longer reacts with an undesirable, adverse response. Many trainers will similarly rely upon classical conditioning, made famous by Pavlov and his dog, teaching their horse to create associations between unrelated stimuli. In effect, the horse learns to relate a cue or signal with a subsequent and otherwise-unrelated event and response.

So, a horse who has been turned out in a pasture that abuts a heavily traveled road will eventually be habituated to cars and motorcycles. The animal who accepts its winter blanket after weeks of being exposed to it has been desensitized to the otherwise-scary object. And the horse who is told the word "trot" each time it is simultaneously tapped with a crop and transitioned from a walk to a trot will quickly associate the word with the acceleration of its gait.

Operant conditioning, otherwise known as trial-and-error learning, is a third method of instruction, which when employed helps a horse create a link between a behavior and a resulting positive or negative consequence. Once applied repeatedly and consistently, trial-and-error training directs a horse to modify its behavior based upon the either positive or negative consequences to its original actions. When a trainer is working with conditioning methods and techniques, positive reinforcement is often used to compel a desired behavior's repeated repetition. In contrast, negative reinforcement is applied up until the moment that a sought-after action first occurs, at which time it is removed in reward for compliance.

The rider, for example, who applies leg pressure to his or her horse to direct it to speed up and then instantly releases the leg aid once there is compliance is employing operant conditioning and negative reinforcement. Similarly, these same methods explain why a previously unwilling horse will load onto a trailer once its owner retrieves a lunge whip. And last, the horse who lifts its leg and immediately receives a treat has learned, through positive reinforcement, the benefits to continually repeating this act.

From our first encounter to the present day, Samson, like every horse I have worked with, has been trained via a combination of habituation, classical, and operant conditioning. Whether I was approaching Samson in his stall or in the pasture, leaving a cooling blanket sitting on a fence, placing and removing the halter, or handling his legs and hooves, each and every corresponding method of instruction has had its time and place. In each instance that these methods were applied, Samson came to grasp, understand, and apply skills that he previously could not comprehend and had vehemently rejected. Violence and excessive punishment, techniques mistakenly employed and applied over the years to modify this horse's behaviors and conduct, were not now and had never been necessary to mold this wild Mustang into a domesticated companion and partner.

While many owners understand the various ways in which horses can learn and apply skills, most lack a true appreciation of the manner in which their mounts see and perceive the outside world. Time after time, I have stood by and watched as owners have punished horses for hesitating before entering a stall or momentarily balking before loading onto a trailer. Likewise, I have observed in horror as many a rider has disciplined his or her horse for lowering a head when walking into a puddle or stepping onto a bridge, or for suddenly raising its head to look upon a potential threat far off in the distance.

Because it is an animal of prey, natural selection and evolution have furnished the horse with an eye that is the largest of any land mammal and a visual cortex that handles one-third of all sensory input transmitted to the equine brain. With a field of vision consisting of a 340-degree arc around its body, horses can track movement and detect predators like no other. Gifted with this tremendous visual acuity, they view the outside world through a combination of monocular and binocular vision. Whereas humans solely possess binocular vision, retinal cells called cones permit a horse to simultaneously view and process independent images from both the left and right eye. A second set of cones enhances a horse's vision and affords binocular vision for a very limited arcing span of 55 to 65 degrees directly in front of the horse. With a significant number of rods—cells in the retina responsible for night vision—horses also possesses excellent vision during the evening hours.

By virtue of its numerous evolutionary-directed ocular enhancements, a horse can detect and flee from nearly any impending threat. Notwithstanding these heightened and acute visual capabilities, a horse's visual spectrum contains several gaps and weak points. All horses, for example, have blind spots in front of the muzzle, behind the rump, and along the sides. A horse will accordingly step to the side to see what is behind it and back up and lower its head to see what sits in front.

As horses primarily rely upon their monocular vision, they in turn lack good depth perception. Accordingly, a horse will lower its head to judge closer distances and raise it to evaluate objects at greater distance. When alternating between monocular and binocular viewing, a horse will experience brief blurred vision. While horses see better in low light than humans and cats, their eyes have a harder time shifting from light to dark environs and will require several seconds to make the adjustment. And with a nearly complete circular field of vision, a horse will often freeze or spook when confronted with even the slightest movement or activity from within its realm.

With even a minor appreciation of how horses view and perceive the world around them, horse owners can come to understand their animals' actions and help each develop confidence and security in an otherwise-threat-charged world. The owner who, for example, permits a horse to stand for several moments before entering a darkened stall or trailer might discover that the horse will no longer object to entry. A horse who is permitted to lower its head to evaluate a puddle or bridge may very well enter or cross each with ease. And if afforded several momentary seconds to track, locate, and identify any sudden movement from within its vicinity, a horse will promptly transition from an animal of threat detection and defense to a trusty trail companion.

The understood horse is a happy, willing, and compliant horse.

While Samson remained terrified of the saddle and petrified in his tracks, thousands of miles away the Calico

Mustangs—torn from their herds and their lands—likewise stood scared stiff in holding corrals and pens. New environs, unfamiliar horses from different herds comingled and fighting to establish authority, a changed diet, and the ever-present stench of death had them panicked and agitated. With fifty-three Mustangs now lost at the holding facilities and an additional thirty-five unborn foals delivered stillborn, these Mustangs had every right to be nervous, doubting, and afraid. The tragic and continual loss of life required explanations, but none were forthcoming.

Unabated, Mustangs—adult and unborn—would continue to perish.

As I was a nondrinker and one never interested in the party scene, my birthday had come and gone without much fanfare. Most would probably say I was boring, but my birthdays were anything but. My twenty-fifth birthday was spent hanging off a mountain at fourteen thousand feet; my thirtieth, sledding across the Arctic Circle in subzero temperatures. Fearful that time apart would cause my Mustang pupil to recoil, grow distant, and retreat back into his shell, this year I had failed to plan a big fortieth-birthday adventure.

But now I was faced with a terribly difficult decision. Recognizing that I had deferred my celebratory vacation, two of my brothers had given me a gift—one was going skiing in Jackson Hole with his family; if I chose to join them, my airfare would be covered.

My concerns with regard to Samson were twofold. First, just weeks away from mounting, a potential skiing injury and subsequent break in training would not only set back our accomplishments but most likely undo all that had been taught and learned. Second, I would be away for ten days.

Numerous previous experiences had instructed that three days of separation between Samson and me would cause minor issues; five days or more would produce the old fear-riddled, doubting, untrusting enemy combatant. I knew that each day that we were apart would amount to weeks in Samson's mind. The longer I was away, the greater the likelihood that Samson's old persona would once again take hold only to possibly never retreat.

Everyone I consulted declared that my theory was ridiculous. "You have spent months with this horse," they would say. "He will pick up right where you left off." But I knew Samson; I knew that he was different. Having gone years without a day, let alone a week, off, I decided it was time for a vacation. A break and time away would do me good. My heart told me that our bond was strong enough to survive my absence; my gut counseled that Samson would not let me back in once I returned.

I should have listened to my gut.

11

ALONE AGAIN AND SOLITARY

A colt you may break,
but an old horse you never can.

—FRENCH PROVERB

With the BLM's Calico Mountains Complex roundup concluded hundreds of horses short of its original goal, critics promptly assailed the agency for both overstating wild horse population estimates and overdramatizing purported Mustang-induced rangeland degradation. These criticisms were nothing new; they were in fact over half a century in the making.

Decades earlier, while in attendance at a June 6, 1952, Virginia City BLM permit hearing, Wild Horse Annie's husband, rancher Charlie Johnston, sardonically heralded the BLM's facts, processes, and methodologies, "I was most impressed by the BLM's statistics and I'd sure as hell like to have the secret to making stock multiply the way they said the Mustangs did: one hundred this year, 200 the next, 400 the next, and so on! Yes sir, I'd sure like to know the secret."[29]

Nearly sixty years later, the Calico roundup had exposed

still-faulty BLM population estimates and the arguable existence of a still-present hidden agenda. The new information was welcomed and disseminated, but like everything else in life, the good news came at a cost: mature and yet-to-be-born Mustang lives. Mustangs were suffering and dying so that the flawed and faulty system designed to protect them could be exposed.

As I arrived at the farm for March's first visit, I was greeted not by my equine student but, rather, by an old nemesis. Opening the doors that led into the barn, I nearly became the farm's second gelded resident. Springing forth from the darkness, the young goat who had ravaged my truck and her two pointy horns ran through my legs and then down the driveway—nearly taking my reproductive capabilities along for the ride. If I didn't know any better, I would have thought that she had been lying in wait.

Ike, Cosmo, the black mutt, and Asbestos were my best buddies, but the goats, geese, roosters, and chickens remained my sworn enemies.

February's dark and cold days now passed, Mother Nature was providing early signs that winter was preparing to make its exit. If I had believed, if I had hoped, that winter's deep accumulating snowfall would be present for and soften my numerous and soon to be certain involuntary exits from atop Samson's back, I had definitely miscalculated. Still many weeks away from mounting Samson, I now knew that there would be no soft snow cover to ease my pain. First things first, however, Samson needed to learn to be responsive to the bit and then accept his saddle pads.

Whereas many trainers, will first mount a horse and then subsequently teach it to turn and maneuver, I choose to instill each of these skills through groundwork introduced prior to the first mounting. If the horse won't yield to the bit, won't stop or turn, then I won't saddle it. In effect, the first mounting is the final layer of a multilayer cake, the final act of a multiple-act play. Mounting a horse says that I have taught the animal all that it needs to know to perform under saddle—the animal understands my expectations and knows what needs to be done. Once again, the informed horse is an educated, understanding, and capable horse. For Samson, this meant that he had to learn how to yield to the bit's direction—the time had come to long-line Samson.

Long-lining teaches a horse to respond to and then move as one with the bit. When one long-lines a horse, driving lines are attached to the bit rings on each side of the animal's mouth and its movements and direction of travel are controlled by a handler standing several yards behind. Over time and with practice, the horse learns to expect, interpret, and then respond to rein and bit cues. The horse learns to be controlled.

Long-lining for Samson would mean that I dictated when, where, and how he walked. Voluntarily or involuntarily, he would have to surrender control and lose what little independence and autonomy he still held on to. It also meant that both sides of his mouth would be attached to twenty-five feet of his greatest enemy—the rope. Making matters worse, I would be standing far behind his rump and manipulating him via two lines attached to his mouth. Two of Samson's worst fears were about to become a fixture of his training regimen and there was no way he was going to succumb to this willingly.

Working with an array of horses over the course of many

years, I learned a long time ago that no two are ever the same. Thus, I pride myself on being flexible when breaking, instructing, and training. While the skills I teach are almost always the same, the manner and speed in which I present each is always different. The horse, the pupil, dictates when and how I present each new element of a training program. With Samson, this meant that my training motto of flexibility quickly gave rise to a new term of art: "compromise." While many, if not most, trainers would undoubtedly criticize this concept, for Samson and me it worked.

After great thought and deliberation, the art of compromise led me to the conclusion that long-lining Samson would only retard our accomplishments. It would take weeks of hassle, if not violence, before Samson would even consider the idea of accepting, being attached to, and then being controlled by the driving lines. The benefits didn't remotely outweigh the costs. And so, I decided to basically short-line Samson. I would attach a set of reins and operate them while standing at his side.

It took very little time and even less effort for Samson to make his decision. Short-lining it was. Compromise had prevented one less battle and saved horse and horseman from a great deal of aggravation. Call it cheating, cutting corners, or a failure to assert myself, but I called it simply smart.

In Samson's space—that's where I spent most of my time throughout our subsequent sessions. And though like everything else it took a great deal of time and a great deal more patience, Samson came to release into the bit, flex at the poll, and bend at the neck. He learned to steer and he learned how to be controlled. And oddly enough, he seemed okay with that. Horse and bit were one; horse and horseman were soon to be one.

We were inching ever closer to our ultimate goal.

The following week, Samson and I entered the final phase of his training: socialization to the pads and saddle. With his first saddling just weeks away, Samson needed to recognize that the saddle posed little threat and no chance of physical harm. Each session, we moved closer to the innocuous saddle parked in the pasture's far corner. Ever astute and always processing, the closer we moved to the saddle, the more I was certain that this horse knew what was coming—that he and the saddle were about to forge an intimate relationship. It was during these brief little strolls toward the saddle that Samson the battle-hardened warrior started strategizing and planning his final stand.

Before Samson could take the saddle, he had to accept the saddle pads. With my nervous pupil tied to the gate, I first rubbed him with my waffled neoprene nonslip pad liner. Dark black and apparently quite ominous, the pad liner sent Samson's perimeter defenses to high alert. Refusing any hint of contact with the liner, Samson kicked his hindquarters out and he danced in place—he did whatever it took to avoid physical contact with this new threat. Though quite the line dancer, standing tied Samson had nowhere to go.

Next came the saddle pad. Samson's short back and boney and still-undernourished frame made him a perfect candidate for my extrathick, durable, contoured canvas pad. It was my best pad, and up until this point I had taken great care to ensure that it stayed that way. And while this prized pad had valiantly survived many an unbroken horse, Samson had identified it as a threat and he now had it in his sights.

It never stood a chance.

The canvas pad survived two of its first encounters with Samson, but by the following week when the rule of three kicked in, my prized possession took one hell of a beating. With both liner and pad resting atop his back, Samson made it clear that like his biblical namesake, he would not go quietly. He collapsed his front end, raised his hindquarters, and released a single powerful buck. The pad and liner were ejected high into the air and then tumbled to the ground beneath Samson the conqueror. A dust cloud encircled the crime scene as my four-legged warrior took a long pause to stare into my eyes.

Did you see that? his gaze said. *Now watch this!*

Like the swinging pendulum of a grandfather clock, Samson rocked back and forth. Using alternating fore- and hind-leg strikes, he mercilessly unloaded on the pad and liner as if he were a fighter pummeling a cornered opponent. When the bell sounded and the round ended, Samson stepped to his right, gazed back across his left shoulder, looked down, and eyed the defeated pad, liner, and saddle—*now that is how it's done.*

At that very moment, I was anything but pleased with my pupil. My $30 pad liner was shredded; my $120 canvas pad, though not destroyed, was no longer prized and no longer pristine. I was now concerned for my saddle—it had survived many a crazed steed, none of which was the likes of this horse. If our experience with the pad and liner was any indicator, Samson's eventual saddling was doomed and destined to fail.

Looking upon Samson, I realized that the old-time saying of the range that described the Mustang horse "once a wild one always a wild one"[30] fit Samson to a T. His eyes alert and alive, his body pulsating with adrenaline, his posture upright and proud, Samson lived for battle and warfare. Once he was victorious, victory for this horse was like a drug. It empowered him, energized him, and sent him into the stratosphere. The range, the herd, nature, nurture, and the wild had hardwired this animal and nothing was going to change that. Under lead, under control of the bit, and soon to be broke, Samson was anything but a domesticated horse.

At that moment, I made a change in course. When speaking of my work with Samson, I no longer stated that I was in the process of breaking him. It was a concession that Samson did not know of, but it was a concession that he had earned. Though he had at times tried my patience, he had now earned and he now deserved my admiration and my respect. No one was going to break this horse; that much was clear.

As Samson struggled to stay true to his character and identity, his formerly free-roaming and now-captive cousins struggled to survive in the BLM's Nevada holding facilities. While the month had started with a long-awaited court ruling that BLM cattle-grazing allotments had been improperly issued in an area of Arizona known as the Byner Complex, by mid-March the Calico Mustang death toll had passed into triple digits with sixty-nine deceased at holding facilities and thirty-nine aborted foals. Both animal welfare advocates and BLM spokespersons cited hyperlipemia, a disease associated with pregnancy, stress, or transportation, as the cause of many of the deaths. Mustang advocates focused their attention on roundup-induced stress, combined with the feeding of rich hay to desert horses that had evolved to survive on sparse rations. The BLM countered that the Calico Mustangs had arrived at the holding facilities already suffering from starvation and on death's doorstep.

Photographs and videos taken by humane observers told a contrary story.

Despite the tragic and increasing loss of life, and while ostensibly disregarding the growing public furor, the BLM declared the Nevada roundup a success: "The Calico gather wasn't ill fated. It was conducted in a professional and humane manner and achieved the goal of bringing an overpopulation of wild horses in the Calico Complex within established appropriate management levels."[31] With nineteen hundred fewer horses on the range and with nearly seven hundred thousand dollars in its coffers, both the BLM and the contractor that had handled the Calico operation stuck to their guns and heralded the roundup as a huge success. They were the only ones to do so.

"Listen here, buddy, you need to take it easy the next week." I told Samson as I said my prevacation good-byes. "No epic battles with your three cousins, the dogs, the geese, chickens, and goats. Stay away from that damn fence. You've earned a vacation; catch up on your sleep; take in the warm spring breezes; just please take it easy for the next ten days."

It was mid-March, and I was ready for my much-needed vacation. Amy and I had not spoken since the birthday incident and my batteries needed a recharge. Her inability to connect with Samson was no longer my problem or my concern—she wanted her horse fixed and she didn't care how I went about it. Now my only focus was on him and his saddling, but I was finding it hard to leave. Feeling torn and doubting my decision to take a break, I abruptly turned and walked away.

As I was seated in my truck backing down the driveway, the sight of Samson standing uncharacteristically static and unmoving halted my hurried departure. Normally when I released Samson at the end of each training session, in an act of measured defiance he would instantly bolt from my presence. On this occasion, he hadn't moved an inch. As one who has oft cautioned clients to refrain from attributing human feelings and thoughts to their horses, I understood that Samson could not have comprehended my parting words. Nonetheless, I was concerned that he had detected my heavy words and heavy heart.

I jumped out of my truck, vaulted the perimeter fence, and ran back across the pasture to Samson. Before I could reach him, he took the initiative and came trotting up to me. It was the first and for that matter the only time that this has ever occurred. What for most horses would be a normal, everyday occurrence was for this horse a truly telling act, a statement, and a cry for reassurance. As I stood next to him, Samson buried his face in my chest.

As I had spent the vast majority of my time split between dealing with Samson the aged and set-in-his-ways warrior and Samson the terminally haunted and abused victim, this was one of the few instances where I interacted with Samson the horse. Never needing anyone and never having anyone to need, Samson now stood seemingly alarmed and gravely concerned that he was losing the one and the only thing he had going for him—a friend. Needy, worried, and altogether vulnerable, Samson had exposed himself. These moments were few and far between, but these moments more than made up for Samson's endless hours of doubt and fear-fueled standoffishness, his stubborn and willful noncompliance, his violent PTSD fits, and his oft-combative ways. And while these moments were fleeting, each provided the little that I needed to continue.

Leaning into Samson's left ear, I whispered, "I'm going, but I'm not leaving—that I promise."

Sadly, my words would not matter.

The following morning, I had one last stop to make—a bandage check—before heading off to Wyoming. Just a block shy of my client's house, I found myself behind a row of cars stopped at a railroad crossing. The gates up and the red lights not flashing, I was perplexed as to why traffic was at a complete standstill. After I observed several motorists standing out in the pouring rain snapping photos and taking videos, I knew that something was amiss. Stretching my head out the window, I was shocked by the chaotic scene that unfolded before my eyes.

"If you're calling about the four horses that have been galloping through the streets for the last fifteen minutes, we're trying to get our people there as soon as possible," the 911 dispatcher advised.

"I'm going to try and catch them, so please have the officers silence their sirens," I responded.

Four horses were pacing back and forth at the railroad crossing, lathered in sweat, pumped with adrenaline, and searching for a way across. After running wildly for fifteen minutes, they were, at that very moment, unapproachable.

I had spent countless hours at this very spot—teaching clients' horses to gather their courage and walk across peacefully. My experiences instructed that this group would not attempt such a crossing. As I gazed out the window, I observed a Good Samaritan approaching the horses with cupped hand, as if carrying a handful of grain.

"You don't want to do that!" I shouted from five cars back.

A bullying gelding swung his rump around and sent her tumbling onto the pavement. Winded but unscathed, she jumped to her feet and ran back to her car. A situation like this could get even a trained professional killed—she was lucky to have escaped with her life. As the group collectively squealed and madly raced from one side of the road to the other, I surveyed the scene.

The area's busiest four-way intersection was three hundred yards back in the direction that the horses had started. Cars would be whizzing through at 50 miles per hour; tragedy, both human and equine, would be a certainty. If the horses started back that way, I would have to stop and then catch them before they made it anywhere near there. But these horses weren't wearing halters—stopping them would be hard enough, catching each next to impossible. Two of the horses seemed to be following the lead of the lone mare. She would be my primary target. *Catch her and they will follow,* I told myself. The brash gelding—riled and clearly looking for his next victim—would be left to last.

"So you're just going to stand there and not do a thing!" a voice yelled out from the direction of the tracks.

Momentarily turning away from the crazed band of equines, I quickly recognized my client's neighbor, who was standing some twenty feet from the horses with her hands parked on her hips. It was easy to recall why I had declined her many previous attempts to hire me. With a disapproving look, she turned and headed on a direct intercept course for the one horse I knew not to approach. *Thank you very much,* I thought to myself. *Now we'll have a chase.*

Wasting no time, the riled gelding shot forward, racing down the open southbound lane at an all-out gallop. The three others followed closely behind. I jumped into my truck, did a U-turn, floored the accelerator, and took off in pursuit. Over the course of the last fifteen years, I have been called out to numerous equine-involved incidents. These have included capturing horses who had dumped their riders and wouldn't be caught, horses who had escaped their pasture, and, sadly, trailer accidents. But on this day, as the horses galloped down the highway, darted in and out of oncoming traffic, and neared the busy intersection, I had simply and fortuitously happened upon the scene.

The horse gods were shining on this band of marauding equines.

Flashing my headlights and with hazards blinking, I sped south in the northbound lanes. Oncoming traffic could see the horses and was pulling onto the shoulder out of my way. The horses were closing in on the intersection and I was running out of roadway. For a moment, I thought all hope was lost. But then I remembered that there was an emergency access driveway that fed into the adjacent forest preserve. I had used it in the past when called out to assist in the capture of runaway horses. We would pass by it just before reaching the intersection—it was our last and only hope.

I gunned my truck and sped ahead of the group. I shot just past the driveway, slammed on the brakes, and left my truck parked diagonally across the roadway. I now had a choke point to funnel the horses up the driveway. All that was left to do was to get out on the roadway and force the horses to take the hard right turn onto the emergency driveway. With the horses galloping at close to 30 miles per hour, if they failed to make the turn and ran into me I would be finished. Giving this fact little thought, I hastily grabbed a lead line from inside my truck, took a deep breath, stepped out onto the roadway, and started swinging my arms and twirling the lead line in the air.

"*Whoa* there, honey. *W-h-o-o-a-a!*" I yelled out as I focused my stare on the mare.

She collapsed her hind end and dug her hind hooves into the pavement. The two horses following closely behind followed suit. The three were trying to stop, but due to the rain-slickened pavement, it didn't look like they were going to make it. *Way to go, Mitch, you didn't take into account the rain,* were the words bouncing around in my head.

The three horses came to a sliding stop less than two feet from sending me to my maker.

The crazed gelding, the troublemaker of the bunch, flew past at full speed—just grazing my arm in the process. I wasn't worried about him; I knew he would double back and come looking for his herd. Without wasting any time, I reached into my truck and pulled out several lead lines and halters. I quickly looped a lead line around the mare's neck and then did the same with her two fellow escapees. Just as I had the third horse secured with a line around his neck, the obstructive gelding returned and forced his way right into the middle of the herd.

"Oh no," I told him. "I know better than to try this with

you. You just hang out here with your buddies, catch your breath, calm down, and then we'll give you and the lead line a try."

"That's ridiculous," a man in five-hundred-dollar riding boots and breeches cried out as he exited his car. "Hand me that lead line and I'll catch her."

With several horse-boarding establishments located nearby, I knew that it was only a matter of time before reinforcements would arrive. Before I could even correct his mischaracterization of the horse's sex, the man in the ironed, spotless riding outfit brusquely stepped up toward the horses and sent the gelding galloping back down the roadway. This in turn sent the three remaining horses into a frenzy. They reared up on their hind legs and wildly punched their forelimbs into the air. They spun, they kicked, and they bit. Their target was of course the one person holding them.

Me.

A crowd of local horse enthusiasts quickly gathered and offered up suggestions on how to catch the runaway gelding. "You should throw grain all over the road," one suggested. "Walk up to him with a bag of peppermints," another interjected. A third recommended that we all speak in hushed, welcoming tones and the horse would come seek us out. An older gentleman, decked out with cowboy hat and boots, disagreed with all three pundits: "I'll rope him and tie him to the front of my truck. Trust me; he won't be getting away from that."

I had had enough. Officers from several law enforcement agencies were now on scene, and I turned to the one who knew me and laid out the plan, "If we can find three people to briefly hold each of these horses, then I can catch the lone dissenter. And I don't need or want any of these here horse experts helping me out."

To my amazement, not a one of the four alleged horse experts volunteered to hold the unruly escapees. Instead, three strangers—all animal lovers but none of whom had any experience handling horses—stepped up and did the duty. Over the course of the next fifteen minutes, I approached on and then retreated from the combative gelding as he ran wildly through the forest preserve. I knew that he wanted to be with his herd, and he knew that I would not permit this until he assented to being caught. When he finally turned, faced me, and dropped his head, our battle of wills and wits had come to an end.

Just as I was putting a halter on the now-compliant gelding, the urban myth of the unwanted, abandoned Mustang entered the equation. "Do you know what these are?" a well-known local horsewoman asked the crowd. "These are BLM Mustangs; they are being bought at auction and dumped by owners who don't want them. This has been happening all across the country; this is what happens when you shut down all of the slaughterhouses."

Most in the horse world have heard these stories, all derived from the myth of the unwanted horse. Mustangs were being abandoned at highway rest stops, dumped at unoccupied farms, and in this instance left right in the middle of the road. Fabricated by critics of the wild Mustang and by horse slaughter advocates, the stories were fiction, but misinformation in the wrong hands can be a dangerous thing. Ironically, in this case the four runaway horses were anything but unwanted abandoned Mustangs. They were in fact four prized, pampered, and very valuable polo ponies.

Later that day, after receiving a phone call from the owner, I visited the farm where all four horses lived. Grazing in their pasture, these were not the horses I had chased and captured hours earlier. Three of the four were calm, content, and excessively friendly. The obstinate gelding, he was still rambunctious and borderline obnoxious—it was just his way.

"The gate was off one of its hinges; they just pushed it down and took off," the owner explained. She then continued, "I don't know how you knew it, but the mare is definitely the leader of the pack. And as for my trouble child, he has never been caught without a full bucket of grain, so you'll have to teach me your secret."

Fortunately for all involved, he was just my type.

Hours later, in the skies above the continental United States, I pondered the day's events and I thought about my wayward Mustang all alone in his pasture. Unlike the polo ponies, he was a horse who could have been—maybe even may have been—abandoned. For the better part of his life, Samson had lacked purpose, control, and someone to care for him. He was anything but wanted. Nevertheless, he and the polo ponies shared something in common. All had crossed my path by way of a chance encounter. And all, I wanted to believe, were now the better for it.

Exhausted, I closed my eyes and tried to drift off. Riddled with guilt, feeling as if I had abandoned Samson, I couldn't fall asleep.

Eleven days later, I returned to the farm fully intact, refreshed, anxious, and nervous as to what I might find. As I inched my truck alongside the perimeter fence, I looked out across the corncrib pasture and instantly recognized that trouble lay ahead. Seconds after Samson and I locked gazes, my problem student launched himself forward like the Road-runner, bolted through the gate leading into the south pasture, and disappeared in a plume of dust. My gut had it right; my heart had it wrong.

While at that moment I understood that my absence had created a problem, I had no idea of what I was in for. In just eleven short days, Samson had fully retreated into the dark, solitary abyss that had been his home, shelter, and world for so many years. Feeling abandoned and yet again unwanted, he had returned to the one place where he couldn't be hurt and the one place that no others could venture. The place where he needed no one and there was no one to need. On this day, as I attempted to rescue Samson from this abyss, I would learn firsthand the power, determination, and destructive capabilities of a wounded horse who believed he was better off all on his own.

I located Samson in the pasture's far southwest corner, hidden among the trees and dense brush. His eyes were filled with disdain and distrust. He had ignored his better judgment, surrendered his will, and lent me his heart and I had abandoned him. I hadn't pummeled him with whips or two-by-fours, but I was no better than all the others who had hurt this horse. The trust we had worked so hard to build was gone.

At ten yards and closing, I halted my approach, immediately recognizing the signs of an animal in fear for his life and poised to attack. This was not the horse who had accepted the lead line's control, the bridle and bit's domination, and the saddle pad and liner's unyielding presence. Rather, this was the fear-riddled, perpetually doubting, defensive beast that I first encountered months earlier in a locked stall. The old Samson was back.

"Hey, buddy," I calmly addressed him, "obviously our little break didn't suit you. But keep in mind, you and I still have a binding contract."

I took one step closer to Samson. Flatly rejecting my overture, he exited his protected spot and galloped diagonally across the pasture to the far opposite corner. For the next hour, I slowly approached on, and then retreated from, Samson. Each time I neared, he would dart off. The south pasture was the length and width of a football field, so Samson knew that he had the upper hand. Looking back, I wish that I had videoed the events of this day so that those more qualified than myself could observe and analyze his actions. Five months of bonding, interacting, and training had been wiped clean in a matter of days. Fifteen years of working with damaged horses and this was indeed a first.

I had already learned a great deal from this troubled animal, and on this day school was in session.

Despite his apprehension, Samson had yet to charge on me. This told me that somewhere, deep down, he knew that I meant him no harm. Since our first meeting, I had been the anomaly, the only one who hadn't tried to hurt him. But now, due to our time and distance apart, I was clumped back in with the masses—the many who had mistreated and abused this horse. Samson's perpetual fear and doubt of the two-legged predator had been renewed, and though his heart longed for my attention his brain yet again instructed skepticism and defense.

An hour and a half into the ordeal, Samson and I were standing in the crib pasture just inches apart. As with our very first encounters, the left side of his body was foreclosed to my approach. Moving at a snail's pace, I clipped on to

Samson's halter. Consumed with fear and doubt, he launched himself into the stratosphere, and my shoulder followed. As I crumpled to the ground in agony grasping my dislocated shoulder, Samson stood over me. For the first time, I saw remorse in him.

In my head, I heard the sound of waves crashing against the beach—advancing, then retreating, advancing and retreating.

This incident, combined with the story of the four runaway polo ponies, together demonstrate that whether trained or not, in motion or standing static, horses, like any animal, can be dangerous and highly unpredictable. The trick, the key, to managing, training, and maintaining a harmonious relationship with any horse is set forth in my third, and most important, rule of horsemanship: a horseman must always keep and maintain a command and control presence. Put another way, when things go south, you must always be in command, even when you're not in control.

As herd-bound, insecure animals, horses are driven by a fear complex that instructs and mandates flight. Behave like you can control any situation, confront rather than shy away from a problem, exude the confidence of a herd's lead stallion or alpha mare, and you can limit, if not curtail, a horse's innate desire to flee. Your confidence becomes your horse's confidence. When a horse challenges with its behavior, stay with it, don't run, don't hide, and don't act threatened. If your horse becomes frightened, then convince it that there's nothing to fear. A measured combination of compassion, understanding, respect, and a firm command and control presence will curtail even the most wayward steed.

Command and control also dictates that each and every

horseperson manage and keep in check his or her own emotions. On countless occasions, I have observed insecure riders out on trail, horsemen hesitant to vault over a jump or apprehensive to load their horse onto a trailer, and owners taking out their bad day on their four-legged companion. In these situations, a horse both absorbs and feeds off its handler's thoughts, emotions, and doubts. A blowup is no longer a possibility but, rather, a certainty.

If you are insecure on trail, ride instead in an enclosed arena. If a jump is too high, then lower it. If afraid to load your horse, then don't transport. When in a foul mood, don't go picking a fight with an animal who can dispatch you with one strike. While there is no place for any of the three, in my opinion ego, fear, and anger account for a good 90 percent of all horse-related incidents.

As I like to tell my clients, "Before you ask a horse to be at peace with you, you must be at peace with yourself."

The final week of March, I tripled my sessions with Samson. It was the only thing I could do to regain lost ground and rebuild the trust that had been lost. As I was already backlogged at work, the hole I dug for myself quickly collapsed into a bottomless void. Again all questioned my commitment to Samson. And again I pressed on. Slowly but surely, starting from scratch, student and teacher rebuilt their bonds and rehashed each and every previously introduced skill. If patience was a virtue, then I must have been Job.

As the week came to an end, I received word that Samson had a deep, penetrating wound to his right cheek. A neighbor who owned horses had visited the farm to try to assess the injury, but Samson charged on him before he ever made it over the fence. When I arrived and treated the laceration, it was, when compared to Samson's first facial injury, a study in contrasts. He stood calmly, lowered his head, and immediately submitted to treatment. I was pleased but starting to see the writing on the barn wall. Samson was still wild-at-heart, still distrusting of all humans, and it was starting to look like Samson was a one-person horse.

Samson's wound was serious, but he would survive. In Nevada, as the death toll continued to rise, the same could not be said for many of the Calico Mustangs. With the Calico story permeating national headlines, the untimely winter roundup was a debacle and a PR nightmare. Mustang opponents and horse slaughter advocates had the solution: reintroduce horse slaughter and reopen the slaughterhouses across the nation.

Back in Illinois, a state representative renewed a resolution calling for the reversal of the state's ban on horse slaughter. The unwanted horse, defined by the American Association of Equine Practitioners as horses who are feral and unadoptable, geriatric, incurably lame, have behavior problems, are dangerous, or horses who fail to meet owner's expectations because of cost, color, or temperament, was now the root of all evils. Slaughter proponents argued that the forty thousand Mustangs in BLM holding facilities, the recently culled Calico horses, and the nation's countless unwanted domesticated horses could be dispatched in short order once the slaughterhouses reopened. Like my work with Samson, Mustang preservation efforts advanced and then retreated. Protected or not, the wild Mustang remained chronically and habitually threatened.

Out at the farm for the month's final session, I realized that if any horse fit the bill, fit the very definition of unwanted, it had been this Mustang. Despite this fact, as the day's lesson concluded Samson walked up to and then calmly circled the saddle. Horse slaughter advocates, wild horse haters, and their alleged experts had it all wrong. All horses have worth and even the most unwanted horse will find someone who wants him.

Heading into April, we were now ready to enter the final phase of training: placing the saddle on and then mounting Samson. This damaged horse was ever so close to disproving his many critics—those who had labeled him unwanted, worthless, and less than worthy of the cost of a bullet. I expected that the final month of Samson's training would be ripe with conflict, willful objection, and violence. What I didn't expect, what I couldn't have foreseen, was that a new arrival at the farm would cause Samson to reject my teachings, my plans, and my friendship.

Just shy of reaching our ultimate goal, I would be forced to reconsider my plans to mount and ride Samson. I would have to consider abandoning him.

12

BATTLE!

*A horse can lend its rider the speed and strength
he or she lacks, but the rider who is wise remembers
it is no more than a loan.*

—PAM BROWN

hrough time and across great distance, derogatory labels have followed the wild Mustang as it has grazed America's grasslands, roamed its immense basins, and galloped across its vast mountain ranges. The wild horse of the 1920s was the evil destroyer of the range. The Mustang of the 1950s was an inbred mongrel. Throughout the 1980s, the free-roaming wild horse was an interloper and feral pest. And as horses in the dozens perished in the days following the winter of 2010 Calico roundup, the ill-fated Mustangs were deemed by many as "unwanted" and the "cockroaches of the West."

Back in the Midwest, Samson and I were primed to enter the final phase of his training. We were ever so closer to erasing the hateful and negative terms that, much like chronic abuse and the Samson Rules, had dogged this horse for the last seven years of his sad and painful life. We were inching ever so closer to rewriting Samson's history.

My arrival at the farm for April's first visit signaled that the time had come to saddle my headstrong pupil. With saddle and stand parked just feet away from the tied Mustang, he wasn't agitated and he wasn't simmering. Calm, cool, stoic, and collected, he seemed to know what was coming. Since the moment he had been introduced to the saddle, as we had made concentric circles and moved closer to this new foe Samson had been planning and strategizing.

He was prepared for battle.

As I picked the forty-five-pound saddle up from the stand, Samson's respirations increased, his neck turned erect, and his frame went rigid. I stood alongside Samson's right side— his comfortable side—and the saddle rested on my left forearm as the Mustang, suddenly consumed with fear, appeared primed to explode. I remained in that position for an additional twenty minutes until his panic subsided. Then, ever so slowly and gradually, using my right hand I raised the right stirrup and rubbed his shoulder blade, girth area, barrel, and flank.

Three massive vibrations traveled through Samson as if he had been shocked with a defibrillator. Nonetheless, the gate remained on its hinges and Samson's hooves remained on the ground. I then repeated the entire exercise from his guarded left side, and though Samson forcefully objected, in short time he relented.

"Well," I commented to my attentive pupil, "I am surprised and impressed by your newfound restraint and control. Perhaps this won't be so bad after all."

Who was I kidding?

Seizing the moment, I decided to charge forward. With saddle in hand, I slowly approached his left side. Standing tied to the gate, Samson flexed, braced, glanced back over his left shoulder, and shot a hard stare my way. His focused, calculating gaze left me immediately concerned. Confident, even a little smug, Samson was lying in wait.

I lifted the saddle high above his back and then started to lower it down. It was just inches from touchdown when Samson calmly and coolly crossed and then uncrossed his hind legs. Next he kicked his hind end out to the right and executed a nearly perfect turn on the forehand. He had rotated completely to his right and I was left holding the saddle above nothing but air.

After a third failed attempt to lower the saddle onto his back, I glanced over at the Mustang. Nearly instantly I recognized the not so subtle twinkle in his eye that had become a fixture of our training sessions. Samson didn't need to possess the ability to speak for me to know his thoughts: *Hey, genius, you taught me this! What did you expect?* While I understood that at that moment Samson stood terrified of the saddle, I also recognized that he was determined to make me earn this one.

Through the course of our relationship, this has remained the one defining characteristic of our relations—Samson has never made anything easy and has made a point of consistently and constantly challenging me and my abilities. Though most trainers would find this behavior unacceptable, I have valued and indeed cherished this Mustang's ways, for they taught that a good horseman never stops questioning his methods, improving his skills, and learning new ways.

Once Samson grew tired of toying with me and held his stand, I gently placed the saddle atop his back. Then, after several minutes passed, I removed the saddle before he chose to forcibly eject it. Though I had neither attached nor tightened the cinch, Samson was now a saddled horse. As I looked upon him, I expected the vanquished warrior to appear defeated and downtrodden. But to my surprise, the surly Mustang refused to lower his head in shame.

Samson now held a secret—a potent weapon to add to his vast arsenal. The Mustang warhorse who had once fought battles with a scorched-earth policy had versed himself in the subtleties of guerilla warfare. He was now, for the first time in his life, both an explosive and violent warrior and a stealth and covert combatant. I had, no doubt, created a monster.

By the weekend, Samson had amassed his observations and intel and was prepared to engage his rule of three. This time, he would not disappoint. As Samson stood tied to the gate, I scooped Asbestos up from her comfortable spot in the grass just feet away and deposited her nearly ten yards from what I anticipated would be our battle's epicenter. My calculations and estimations were, needless to say, way off.

Moments later, as I placed the saddle atop his back, Samson exploded with a single buck that appeared powerful enough to shatter the saddle's internal frame—the saddle tree. To this day, the sight of my saddle vaulting through the air like a ballistic missile on a straight trajectory toward Asbestos remains a troubling memory. Seconds before becoming a former inhabitant of the farm, Asbestos sprang from her spot in the grass as the saddle crashed to the ground with a resounding thud. Given the mutual disdain between horse and feline, I couldn't help but think that Samson's plan had worked to perfection.

Over the course of the next hour, my frequent-flyer saddle covered all the points of the map—taking flight to the east, west, north, and south. Repeatedly placing the saddle atop Samson, I stood witness to a buck fest with Samson the star and my saddle the hapless victim. And as the minutes ticked by, I realized that this abused and terribly damaged horse and the aged, prideful, and willful Mustang, when combined, presented a formidable and daunting challenge to the successful completion of this project. I didn't need to be a genius to understand that in a few short weeks I would be the projectile being catapulted from Samson's back. Yes, the troubled Mustang had let me in, but his dark past had kept him ever doubting and distrusting. Despite the fact that I had forged an unbreakable bond with my student, I was going to have to earn—through blood, sweat, and probably some tears—the right to mount Samson.

In Nevada, the tears of humane observers and the blood and sweat of interned Mustangs were clear signs that the Calico carnage had yet to slow. With 125 Mustangs deceased, and bolstered by the ongoing debate over the alleged "unwanted" horse, wild horse critics and slaughter advocates redirected their efforts, appealing to individual state legislators to authorize and reinstitute horse slaughter. Stealing a page from the Mustanger PR spin book of the 1950s, slaughter proponents counseled that horse slaughter would bring wealth and jobs to their constituents and simultaneously rid their communities of the feral and wild pest of the West. In Samson's home state of Illinois, where efforts to reintroduce horse slaughter remained strong, the state senate president assured horse welfare organizations that the proposed bill to reopen the shuttered slaughterhouses would not make it to the senate floor. The words were reassuring but, in the big picture, provided little comfort.

For the captured Calico Mustangs and their then forty thousand cousins detained throughout the country, so little had changed. Targeted on the range for acts of senseless violence, they were equally at peril in the BLM short- and long-term holding facilities. There was no safe harbor for this nation's wild horses. Their survival, their future, remained in doubt.

Thousands of miles away in McHenry County, having witnessed Samson's exhibition of defiance, I harbored my own doubts as to whether this wild horse could be mounted and ridden.

The first time I saw the pair, they were standing in the pasture, just inches apart. Samson was smitten with his new mare and he was a changed horse. His eyes were no longer warm; his posturing announced that my approach would be met with bloodshed. With his mare in tow, he had been transported back to the Nevada mountains and his wild ways. Samson the alpha Mustang stallion would not be separated from his newfound harem of one.

I was shocked and dismayed that Amy had brought a mare to the farm just as we were nearing our ultimate goal. Though her intentions were good, everything, all that Samson had learned and all that we had accomplished, was now at risk.

The newest addition to Amy and Lisa's game preserve had

arrived as a board horse just two days prior. Because Samson had previously shown some distanced tolerance for a mare temporarily housed at the farm the year prior, the sisters had permitted the two to become pasture mates. Samson, to my amazement, was instantly taken and smitten. As I looked out upon the courting duo, the mare caught sight of my gaze and instantly ran over. She was a large horse, substantially taller, wider, and thicker than Samson. Her appearance indicated that she was young; her behavior suggested she lacked schooling and training. Once at the fence, she was overtly sociable, engaging, and animated.

She was the antithesis of Samson.

Borrowing a title from a movie of my youth and by virtue of her bubbly personality and dirty-blond coloring, I named the mare Valley Girl. As I talked to and petted her, Samson slammed his right foreleg into the ground, squealed high-pitched wails, and shot me daggers. The totality of his mannerisms and appearance spoke of contempt, disdain, and threat. His message was clear: stay away from Valley Girl.

As I passed through the gate that led from the crib to the south pasture, Samson—amped up and agitated—nervously circled his newfound love interest. Feeding off of his negative energy, Valley Girl immediately erupted into an explosive rage. Running, bucking, and squealing, she bolted to the pasture's far corner with Samson close behind. Now I had a very serious problem—two horses who refused to be separated.

As if things weren't bad enough, seconds later the skies opened up unleashing a drenching downpour. With the sun still shining, it was a strange sight, an omen, and a sign that nothing on this day would go as planned.

I spent the next hour trying to segregate the two lovers. The south pasture was the length and width of a football field, so it was a losing proposition. Samson, for his part, abstained from direct threat and violence—merely seeking flight with each of my many approaches. He knew better. Untrained and immature, Valley Girl, on the other hand, did not. She kicked out at me, charged on my position, and tried to run me down. Knowing better than to turn my back on Samson, between the two explosive equines I was outmanned, outgunned, and overpowered. I felt like a carved wooden horse bolted to a merry-go-round—left rotating in a continuous 360-degree arc but going nowhere.

Eventually, I was able to chase Samson into the crib pasture. Just as I closed the gate, Valley Girl rammed it at a full gallop. She was left dazed, confused, and on the ground but no worse for the wear. As I waited for her to get back to her feet, a strange sensation warned that danger was near. I rotated around to find Samson rapidly approaching on my position. At three feet away, he halted, raised his head, and looked down on me.

It was his one last and final warning: *Move away from the gate, or I will move you.*

Nose to muzzle, we squared off on each other. The look in Samson's eyes said that he would not succumb willingly. My gaze, my body language, said that he had no say in the matter. The encounter was just getting started and it was to be the greatest battle of our relationship.

Free of anger and impatience, I turned the training clock back and sought to move and keep Samson moving until he evinced some form of compliance. Stocked full of pure rage and contempt, the Mustang wanted no part of the pressure/

release-of-pressure game. He knew my strategy, and experience had taught him how to avoid it. He ran.

Like a still-free Mustang galloping across the open desert, he was wild, untamed, and uncatchable. Undaunted by the close confines of the crib pasture, Samson's stampeding hooves shredded the moist soil—blanketing his underside with layer upon layer of wet, adhering mud. Seeking shelter behind the corncrib and out of sight, he would await my approach and then promptly scurry around the building to the opposite side. Round and round we went: clockwise, counterclockwise, and then back again. Repeatedly and endlessly we played this game of cat and mouse. Each time that I moved him away from the structure, he would eventually find his way back.

Like hamsters on a wheel, we circled, and circled, and circled.

A second hour passed and I was no closer to catching my determined and disobedient student. When he needed to catch his breath, he would run to the pasture's far corner, slow his respirations, and rest while I slowly drudged through the muddy, quicksand-like pasture. There was no doubt in my mind—Samson had played this game before. As I was dressed for what had been forecasted as a sunny day, the elements and the horse were taking a toll on me. With the downpour showing no sign of subsiding and Samson no closer to surrender, the law of diminishing returns counseled that it was time to step back and regroup. In fifteen years of working with difficult horses, I had never failed to catch a horse. In fifteen years, I had never been so humbled.

On this day, Samson was the victor, I was the vanquished.

When I opened the gate separating the crib and south

pastures, Valley Girl flew past at a full gallop and promptly rejoined her new mate with a chorus of celebratory nickers and neighs. Drenched to the bone, spent and defeated, I retreated back over the perimeter fence. Samson no longer needed me. Worse yet, he no longer wanted me. My prized pupil had disregarded my teachings and rejected my friendship. It was the lowest point of my career. I only wanted what was best for Samson, and it seemed that was Valley Girl. I was not going to force anything on him; I was not going to repeat the mistakes of those who had come before me. Leaning against the pasture fence, I said what I believed was my final good-bye.

Standing there in the pouring rain, I hit rock bottom.

As he neared the fence, Samson's nostrils shot steam into the air. His customary victory swagger was missing; the twinkle in his eye, absent. He looked upon me in a way that I had never seen. *You left just when you were becoming interesting,* were the words that I imputed to his piercing gaze. I interrupted my good-byes to gaze upon the animal who had become so much more than just a student and a troubled horse. He was now a friend, my friend, and I stopped to consider his perspective.

Samson's herd, his ways, his entire existence had all long since been lost. The moment that he was mounted, he would lose the little remaining autonomy he had left. To make matters worse, I was trying to separate him from his mare—a piece of his past he had only recently recaptured. Samson needed me to understand who he was, what he was, and where he had come from. This wasn't about me; this was about Samson.

"I promise," I yelled out, "that you will be mounted with

the respect which you are due. I promise to respect your relationship with Valley Girl!"

Samson had reminded me of what mattered and what was important. "I will be back, and we will finish this," were the words I spoke as Samson stared into my eyes from just inches away.

Driving home, I replayed each and every of my visits with Samson. My rationale for training this Mustang had been and remained simple: to give Samson purpose, to instill him with a sense of worth and value, and to ultimately improve and make his life better. Training Samson had never been about me, it had always been about him, and it had to remain that way. My desires, my ego, could not and would not factor into my decision to mount and ride this horse. If Valley Girl provided Samson with true happiness, if he no longer needed or desired my schooling, my direction, and my friendship, then I would step aside and remove myself from the equation.

I decided that I would clear my schedule for the following day, return to the farm, and objectively assess Samson's mannerisms, expressions, and actions. If I observed contempt, disdain, and anger, then I would call an end to Samson's training. Ironically, we were so close and yet further than we had ever been from achieving our final goal of rewriting Samson's story. But happiness was what I wanted for this Mustang, happiness is what he deserved, and happiness is what he would get.

Twenty-four hours later, with battle lines drawn, Samson, Valley Girl, and I reengaged. After forty minutes, I was able to cull Samson into the crib pasture. Thirty minutes later, I had him caught and under lead. Though Samson put up a fierce fight, there was no sign of the prior day's contempt, disdain, or anger. It was all I needed to move forward.

Walking Samson to the gate where I would tie him, I realized that the lead line connected to his halter was not the one that I had been using since our first encounter. This lead line had a steel rope clamp affixed to it; my other line was hardware free. The steel clamp could prove to be quite dangerous in the event of a blowup, but I had left my other lead line with a client who was learning to tie his horse. *No big deal,* I told myself, *what could happen?* Once again, it was a grave miscalculation.

Just as I finished tying Samson to the gate, a loud crash sent me reeling around. Turning toward the gate that separated the crib and south pastures, I observed Valley Girl crumpled on the ground, unmoving. Unable to control her separation anxiety, she had, once again, rammed the gate at full speed. Instantly I went into emergency mode as my brain instructed that Samson was at that moment my overriding concern. Whirling back around to him, I instantly recognized that I was too late.

Though present and accounted for in physical form, the Mustang was no longer in control of his actions and reactions. Valley Girl was down; the collision had flipped his switch. Twisting, turning, wrenching, and pulling, Samson was a tied, rampaging beast. Out of the corner of my right eye, I noticed something hurdling toward my face and instinctively, reflexively, threw my right hand in its path. In a true exhibition of the power of *Equuus caballus,* Samson's rage had literally pried apart the closed end of the rope clamp—releasing the lead line and catapulting the steel clamp like a bullet from a gun.

As I looked down at my right index finger, the sight of exposed bone and profuse bleeding, combined with nearly immediate nausea, told me that my finger was broken. With Valley Girl still down, Samson ramped up by her side, and my finger mangled, I had to gather my thoughts and triage the injuries. Wrapping my finger in a bandana, I grabbed my backup lead line and caught and then retied Samson. Next I ran to the gate and helped Valley Girl to her feet. I then returned to Samson and confirmed that he was injury free.

It could have been worse, I thought to myself. *At least a helicopter didn't fly overhead.*

Despite Valley Girl's momentary lapse of judgment and my broken finger, I chose to push forward and end the day on a positive note. I placed my saddle on Samson's back and attached, then tightened and tied the cinch. While Samson's animated response communicated that he was less than pleased with this development, there was no sign of contempt, disdain, or anger. All I saw was Samson merely being Samson.

As I watched Samson and his mare affectionately reunite, I realized that what was already destined to be the most challenging mounting of my career had just become that much more difficult and perilous. An unanticipated arrival, an unexpected love interest, had literally and figuratively rocked my and Samson's world. *How,* I questioned myself, *am I going to mount this Mustang with that lawless, insecure, immature hussy rampaging about?* While Valley Girl had turned my world upside down, I nonetheless recognized that she had righted Samson's. And so, I welcomed her arrival and, like everything else in this crazy relationship, decided that we would simply deal with it.

Ironically, in time Valley Girl would be the best thing that ever happened to Samson.

The following week, I implemented a plan designed to remedy the latest challenge to my abilities—Samson's separation anxiety–riddled girlfriend. Repeatedly, I removed Samson from the pasture, kept him apart from Valley Girl for increasing increments of time, and then returned him before the young mare would explode. The strategy was simple: to teach the insecure Valley Girl that no matter what, Samson would always return to her. Once she made it through an entire hour without a meltdown, Valley Girl received the ultimate reward, the icing on the cake—she received an apple. A quick study, Valley Girl promptly figured out my reward system, and her youthful and immature separation-related antics quickly subsided.

As the young mare dealt with her insecurities, Samson was learning to accept my body weight. Placing my foot in the left stirrup, I pulled myself up, straightened my body, and leaned hard against the saddle. The stirrup, the saddle, and Samson were now holding my 175 pounds. The first few times I did this, the frightened Mustang kicked out at me with his left hind leg. The next dozen, he tried to run out from under me.

I could have parked Samson face-first in front of a wall in order to obstruct his attempts at flight, but inasmuch as his actions were inevitable, I decided to cut to the chase: openly invite and then address the problem. Working from within the vast and open south pasture, with me standing up in both the left and right stirrup, Samson was provided every opportunity to bolt. And this horse repeatedly seized the moment. Time after time, he would charge off; I would jump off and double him back into a tight circle. Over the next several weeks, I saddled Samson, walked him through the pastures, and stood up on his left and then his right side.

We had nothing but time.

By the second week of May, Samson's fear had started to recede and the willful, calculating aged Mustang warrior soon replaced the doubting, insecure horse. When I arrived at the farm late in the day on May 14, one quick glance out at Samson told me that the warm spring day had him primed for battle. Once he was saddled, we walked through the crib and south pastures as Samson raced to get away, bucked, and reared up. He simply couldn't stand still. This horse was truly feeling his oats. Over the next hour, Samson uncharacteristically expended huge stores of energy both celebrating spring's arrival and doing battle with the saddle.

"Well, you are certainly all horse today," I told Samson. "I know this probably isn't the day to do this, but hey, if you're pumped then I'm pumped. So, let's do this."

Without hesitating, I grabbed the reins and Samson's mane in my left hand and the cantle in my right, placed my left foot in the stirrup, threw my right leg over his back, and sat atop the Mustang. He stood silent, unmoving, and tense. To be honest, I think he was shocked by the immediacy of it all. I leaned forward to rub the right side of his neck, but a quick head toss advised that this was no time for comfort, praise, or affection. Samson was thinking, digesting, and in-putting and he wanted to be left alone. Using a trick of the trade, I released a loud sigh in the hopes that Samson would follow suit and release his tension. He didn't. Yes, Samson was frightened, but he was also clearly annoyed and agitated.

"Oh, come on, old man, get over it." I told him in a comforting yet mocking tone. "You damn well knew this was coming. This is a good thing. I am truly proud of you, ole boy, and you in turn should be proud of yourself."

Refusing to flinch, twitch, or move, Samson remained stoic, impassive, and focused. His head was cocked slightly to the right, just enough so that he could see me with his right eye. He had the look of a boxer who had lost the bout but didn't want to leave the ring. This fighter wasn't quite sure if he should concede the victory or stand and fight. Samson was one proud horse and I tried my best to understand his wash of emotions.

"Okay, buddy, I get where you are coming from." I told him. "But where others have been broken, you, my friend, have your spirit intact. So *walk up* for me and we'll call it a day."

Samson lurched forward. He understood the command but was simply too scared to fully execute it. So we waited: waited for Samson to muster his courage, waited for him to get his legs underneath him, and waited for this Mustang to take the biggest steps of his life. And then, with a human being planted on his back, Samson the wild Mustang warhorse took two steps forward, back into history. Instantly my nervous energy converted into beaming pride.

My dismount, as expected, sent Samson into a tiff, but we had plenty of time to work out the kinks. On this truly special and momentous day, Samson had earned his apple and maple syrup. But when presented with his favorite treat, he narrowed his gaze, curled his upper lip, and contemptuously turned away. You had to love this horse and how he stayed true to his ways, true to his self. This was Samson, the unbroken, true wild American Mustang.

I placed the treat in the grass and released Samson. He walked over to it, lowered his head, glanced at me for several moments, and then devoured his most prized reward.

"You did good today, old man; you did good." I told him as I exited the pasture.

Amy received the good news via e-mail.

Days later, Samson's second mounting went off without incident. He walked when prompted, circled when directed, and held his stand when told to do so. All was right with the world. That is, all was right up until Samson's third mounting. On this day, even an uneducated observer could have deduced that Samson was prepared for battle. His gaze was fixed, cold, and unyielding. His respirations were long and deep; his muscles, taut and constricted.

Samson the warrior was back in the house.

For the first several minutes of the ride, all went as planned. And then, after we walked to the south pasture's far fence line, we turned back to nothing but vast open space. Gazing out at the pasture that unfolded before him, Samson promptly realized that he had a runway, room to take me for a ride, and an opportunity to put me in my place. For a split second, my mount turned and looked back at me over his right shoulder.

Buckle up; the ride is about to start.

Once his head returned to the vertical position, he exploded. Like a dolphin arcing out of and then back into the water, Samson leapt forward, crowhopping across the pasture. I applied leg pressure to his abdomen and tried to push him forward into a normal gait. Samson slammed on the brakes, lowered his head, and unleashed a flurry of spine-jarring bucks. He was a professional bucking horse, a champion PBR bull, and a wild Mustang all packaged into one. My back—its two herniated and one bulged disk—took the full impact of each powerful jolt.

Jerking up on the reins, I raised Samson's head, pulling him out of bucking position. Again I applied leg pressure to get him moving forward; Samson responded by bursting into an all-out gallop. Bounding toward the pasture's north perimeter and Valley Girl—our one vociferous and visibly upset spectator—horse and rider were headed for a serious collision with the unyielding, razor-sharp barbed-wire fence. Using my right hand, I yanked hard on the right rein and doubled Samson back. The hard tug on his mouth in turn sent Samson into a wild and crazed buck fest. Before I even knew it, he had put twenty-two continuous bucks into me.

Once again, I applied leg pressure to push Samson out of his static, bucking position. He in turn erupted into a wild brakeless gallop. With no end in sight to Samson's madness and once we had exceeded the safety parameters of my "twenty-buck rule," my inner voice instructed that it was time to say *arrivederci* and emergency dismount this horse. I kicked my feet out of the stirrups, pressed both hands against the saddle pommel, pushed hard, and ejected myself backward off of Samson.

Still holding the reins in my left hand, I landed off to the side of Samson's left hind leg. He made no effort to fight, flee, or kick. Concerned that an equipment issue may have caused his meltdown, I checked the saddle, pads, and cinch. It was a hollow, pointless gesture—deep down I knew exactly what had caused this eruption. Samson's rule of three lived. Invigorated by his actions, Samson's heart was pumping double time, his eyes were crystal clear, and his body was pulsating with kinetic energy. He was alive and basking in the thrill of victory.

I too was alive and ever thankful for being in one piece. Nonetheless, my forty-year-old body had taken a massive and jarring beating. I remounted and rode Samson for forty-five minutes—his animated act of defiance having bought him a serious workout. For his part, Samson didn't really seem to care how long the ride lasted. He lived for battle; he lived for this. Seeking to accentuate the positive, I told myself that I had experienced and survived the best of Samson's worst. I convinced myself that Samson had expressed his feelings, excised his demons, and we could now move forward.

I was, yet again, so wrong.

Days later when I jumped on Samson's back, horse and rider never made it out of mounting position. Sitting atop the Mustang, I leaned down to my right, grabbed the stirrup, and pushed my foot in. Then, while still bent over, I realized that Samson's head was cocked to the right and he was looking at me with that evil right eye of his. He looked down at the stirrup, and then up to me, down at the stirrup, and then back up at me. The gleam in his eye was unmistakable. *Are you all set? Comfy? Good!*

"Oh crap!" I exclaimed. From a complete standstill, Samson unloaded.

As I had survived many a bucking horse, my experiences had instructed that the biggest and strongest horses are not the horses who inflict the most damage. The smart horses,

the ones who throw a buck into you when you are swinging your right leg over the saddle and mounting, or pulling
it back across the saddle when dismounting, are in fact the
most dangerous. They know to strike when you are exposed,
defenseless, and vulnerable. Samson, however, was an equal-
opportunity combatant. He believed that warfare should take
place on a level playing field, and thus he waited until I had
brought my leg over his back and placed my foot in the stirrup and was seated.

It really didn't matter, for I never stood a chance.

In less than a second, Samson hammered me with the
three most powerful, violent, and painful bucks of my career. He launched me like a drunken rodeo clown high into
the stratosphere and terminal velocity brought me crashing
back down into the hard soil. Facedown in the mud, I was
thoroughly dazed and certain that some part of my body was
no longer where it belonged. Tilting my head up, I looked
over at Samson, standing just yards away.

Without blinking, he stared at me long and hard. His expression bore no signs of contempt, anger, remorse, or de-
light. In that moment, I realized that Samson's explosive
demonstration was intended not as an act of war but, rather,
as the communication of a message: *Never forget who and what
I am.* In twenty years of riding horses, I had been involuntarily ejected on only three occasions. I had never been ex-
pelled in three bucks. It was a truly humbling experience
and a message I have never forgotten.

The following week, midride, Samson again flew into a
buck fest. Only this time, I knew how he moved, how he
pitched, angled, and maneuvered. And though it took
twenty-five bucks and a total disregard of my "twenty-buck

rule," I rode him out. Both Samson and I had each relished a victory and each wallowed in a defeat. Something happened to us both on those rides: a mutual understanding of sorts. Two aging warriors had squared off and engaged in battle. There was no winner and there was no loser. There was only mutual respect, mutual admiration, and mutual friendship. There was only a horse and a horseman.

In the western part of the United States, the captured Calico Mustangs were still dying. Together, these horses along with those still free and their forty thousand cousins held in BLM holding facilities were known by labels other than "historically significant," "majestic," "wild," and "free-roaming." Sadly, the Mustang horse long heralded for its speed, endurance, adaptability, and fortitude was still feral, still unwanted, still the curse of the range, and still the cockroach of the West. To many, it remained an inbred mongrel and vermin-like beast.

Back in McHenry County, Illinois, one Mustang had rewritten his life story and in the process cast aside his hateful labels. This Mustang was no longer worthless, no longer hopeless, no longer without purpose, and no longer unwanted. He was no longer untrainable, unmountable, and unridable. If Samson could rewrite his history, then I held out hope that the once prized and celebrated and now-forgotten American wild Mustang could rewrite its history.

Amy's formerly lawless, maladjusted Mustang was now whole again. Only time would tell if his rehabilitation would be her redemption.

Samson was under saddle. He was not, however, broken.

The term was not fitting for this horse. Though he had been trained, mounted, and ridden, a part of Samson would forever roam the western frontier as a true wild American Mustang. A part of Samson would forever be wild and free as nature had intended him to be.

13

A HORSE AT HOME,
A HORSE FOR THE AGES

A Hibernian sage once wrote that there are three things
which a man never forgets: the girl of his early youth,
a devoted teacher, and a great horse.

—C. J. J. MULLEN

While the BLM's Calico gather operations concluded in early February 2010, in the weeks and then months that followed interned wild Mustangs continued to perish. By May, with 39 unborn horses aborted and a total of 134 lives lost, the current and future generation of free-roaming Calico Mustangs had been decimated. With a total of 126 horses lost in gather operations for all of 2008, the ill-advised and deadly Calico operation signaled that mismanagement, reckless indifference, and negligence still permeated the BLM Wild Horse and Burro Program. And in the same vein that unspeakable horrors brought newfound protection for the wild horse in 1971, by midsummer of 2010 the Calico winter tragedy—the unnecessary and avoidable loss of life—would compel a reversal in BLM policy.

As the circular story of the wild Mustang continued to redundantly rotate, under unrelenting public and congressional pressure, scrutiny, and criticism, change was coming. For the American wild horse, death would again pave the road to salvation.

In the weeks following his first mounting, Samson worked hard to come to terms with his new reality. He was domesticated, but he was no Mr. Ed—having a person seated on his back remained a tough pill for this Mustang to swallow. This was a horse who was used to going it all on his own; he didn't need or want a passenger along for the ride. Making matters worse, I wasn't just a passenger; I was the driver.

Despite Samson's resentment, violence remained absent during this period. We had been there and done that, and now the only elixir for Samson's ills was a combination of my time, patience, and understanding. Having long counseled clients, "shaky rider, shaky horse, scared rider, crazy horse," I knew in this case Samson needed my A game. The goal of course was to build Samson's confidence, to give him direction, purpose, and an outlet for his tremendous stores of pent-up energy.

Yet, as his first month under saddle neared its end, the horse I sat atop was anything but confident, comfortable, or content. I questioned whether Samson was too old, too damaged, and too far gone to be ridden.

And then one afternoon, I trotted Samson along the fence line where the two minis and Studs stood grazing. Normally, they would hurl mocking nickers and insulting neighs from the safety of their adjoining pasture. Now, gazing out at Samson as if he were royalty traversing Westminster Abbey's central aisle, they were quiet, deferential. In an instant my mount's sluggish, disjointed gait turned animated and collected. His stride covered feet rather than just inches and his hanging head shot up to the vertical position.

Samson held his head high and strutted like a Triple Crown winner.

"Praise the tall, but saddle the small," was the Mexican proverb I whispered into Samson's ear. This wild-at-heart Mustang had come full circle and was now all horse.

It was time for me to say good-bye. Samson had been trained, mounted, and ridden—my services were no longer needed; my duties, now complete. Carrying baggage from my recent past, with the wound of the Quarter Horse sold out from under me still fresh, I feared that Samson would be sent away. His continued presence, I figured, would only elicit bad memories. But then, one afternoon, Amy and I passed on the driveway and my concerns were laid to rest.

"It's a beautiful thing," she started, without making eye contact, "seeing him with a saddle and rider on his back. I can't imagine that he belongs anywhere else but here."

Amy had observed her new and improved, somewhat composed Mustang model and declared that he could stay. And I had observed that she seemed happier, at ease, and at peace with herself, her decisions, and her fate. Samson's rehabilitation had been Amy's validation. She was now accepting of her choices, her decisions, and her new life. Both rescuer and horse now had purpose; both were now whole again. And together, both had a new start.

Amy and Samson were no longer stuck together. They now belonged together. Samson's training was complete; he would have a home, if he wanted it. But I had yet to leave. For some reason, I couldn't say good-bye.

As Samson and I turned the corner in McHenry County, thousands of miles away in Denver the BLM was gearing up for its mid-June 2010 Wild Horse Workshop. Seeking to stem the fervor over the Calico tragedy, just days before the start of the workshop the BLM issued what many called a historic press release. "It's a new day, and we need a fresh look at the Wild Horse and Burro Program," announced BLM director Bob Abbey.[32] Outlining a "new strategy," Abbey declared that the BLM would no longer permit the outright sale without limitation of excess Mustangs and the euthanasia of otherwise-healthy excess horses.

Other options that the BLM would be weighing would include the potential reintroduction of wild horses into areas where they no longer existed, the increased use of fertility controls, the establishment of preserves for unadoptable horses, the designation of selected herds as "treasured," and the use of science and research to help manage the nation's wild horses. In Abbey's own words, "As part of this effort, we want all those with an interest in wild horses and burros and their public lands to consider our initial ideas and offer their own."[33] Built upon the corpses of deceased Calico Mustangs, the BLM pronouncements were grand, and wild horse advocates could only hope that this time the promises would amount to more than mere PR jargon.

Days later, Samson and I once again joined up for a ride in the corncrib pasture. Only on this day, the absence of suitable and safe training environs; an overly flirtatious mare; the fury of an overtly jealous former stallion; and the return of an old enemy would nearly take my life. I always knew that the corncrib pasture's dangerous terrain would cost me, and on this day it was time to pay the piper. Samson's celebration of the BLM pronouncement would put me on the ground and under his hooves.

It was a summer afternoon like any other. As Samson and I executed figure eights in the corncrib pasture, Studs and Valley Girl quietly and discreetly rendezvoused at the fence separating the south and north pastures. After several moments of mutual petting and grooming, the mare's hushed nickers quickly yielded to high-pitched wails as Studs planted numerous love bites across her topside. With his back to the escalating commotion and his direction of travel under my control, Samson could do little but slowly simmer. But once we reached the fence line and turned back, he caught a glimpse of the nefarious couple entangled in what he most certainly envisioned as an elicit and scandalous affair. In mere seconds my calm and humble mount transformed into a violent, possessive wild stallion.

In other words, all hell broke loose.

Before I had time to react, horse and rider were bounding at an all-out gallop toward the surreptitious lovers. Directly in our path sat the aged but still patently effective barbed-wire fence. Determined and now completely consumed by the primal emotions that had ruled his prior life, Samson gave little thought and paid even less attention to the pending impact. As we closed the distance to the fence line, I, however, remained transfixed on the barrier's rusted and jagged barbs. Pulling hard on the right rein, I doubled Samson back, applied leg pressure, and pushed my jealous steed to the opposite side of the pasture.

Turning Samson so that he faced the flirting couple, I was not only my pupil's trainer but also his marriage counselor, "Look, what they're doing is natural for your kind. You have nothing to worry about, ole boy." For a moment, it seemed as though Samson accepted my trite explanation of what was for him a capital offense. And then, after Samson looked back to me, then across to his mare, and back to me again, for the second time all hell broke loose.

Interchangeably running and bucking, Samson was determined to make it over or through the barbed-wire fence. Just several yards shy of impact, I yanked hard on the reins and pulled Samson into a sliding stop. I then took a pause to gather my thoughts, take a deep breath, and assess the situation. We were standing amid the corncrib pasture's western perimeter replete with low-hanging branches, roots protruding from the ground like trip wires, and a randomly poured, menacingly threatening concrete pad. This was no place for horse and horseman to duke it out.

Okay, I told myself, *you've got this under control: just diffuse the situation.* If the incident had ended at that very moment, Samson and I would have walked away none the worse for the wear. But the horse gods had different plans for me.

Off in the distance, I heard the all-too-familiar sound of a low-flying, fast-approaching helicopter. "Oh, come on! You have got to be kidding me," I blurted out. Before I could even act, Samson reacted. In one explosive motion, he leapt from the grass directly onto the concrete pad. There, standing static, he repeatedly bounced off of the hard surface like an Olympic gymnast vaulting from the springboard. *One, two, three, four, five,* I counted in my head the continuous, jarring bucks.

Samson the professional bucking horse/PBR bull was out of retirement and back in the arena.

Gravely concerned that Samson was going to tip over backward, throw me down onto the concrete, and land on top of me, I decided to emergency dismount. I glanced over to the right, but twenty feet of concrete advised against such a move. Off to my left, the soft soil was only three feet away, so left it was. This time I wasn't going off the backside. This time I was going to leap off and just pray that I cleared the concrete.

I landed in the soil just inches from the concrete pad with a loud thud and a judge's score of a perfect 10. As I congratulated myself on the nearly flawless dismount and started to rise up to my hands and knees, the helicopter flew directly over our heads. Unable to contain and harness his fear, Samson leapt to his left. Without even knowing it, he smashed me back down into the ground and ran me over like a steamroller moving across blacktop.

In the moments that followed, I tried to inventory the damage. My greatest concern was for my head, neck, and spine. A shredded T-shirt and blood flowing from four distinct locations on my back told me that Samson had trampled me with all four hooves. The fact that I could move my hands, arms, legs, and feet said that he had miraculously missed my spinal cord. More concerned with Samson's well-being than my own injuries, I promptly shifted my gaze over to my Mustang pupil standing several feet off to the left. Manic breathing, pulsating nostrils, and an expression that said, *My god, what have I done? I just killed my one and only friend,* convinced me that he could not account for his actions. It was yet another of his many PTSD fits.

"Do you see this?" I said to Samson as I peeled back what

remained of my T-shirt and flashed the four bloody, freshly minted full-size hoofprints. "This is why they say jealousy is the root of all evils. I hope you learned a lesson today."

With another of my nine lives expended, I felt blessed and fortunate to be alive. As for Samson, with the day's events fueled by a strange confluence of circumstances I didn't feel that discipline was necessary or appropriate. In the weeks that followed, on the days that Valley Girl and Studs met up at the gate and the other days when the trauma transport chopper cut across the sky Samson behaved under saddle and once again proved that he could distinguish right from wrong and learn from his mistakes.

Like Achilles with his heel, like the biblical Samson and his golden locks, this Mustang had exposed a weakness. Only his weakness wasn't a physical deformity or a deity-gifted aberration. Samson's weakness was his innate, instinctive need for a herd and a mate. Samson's weakness was his mare, Valley Girl.

And as for the airborne mechanical beast that first tore this Mustang from his herd, his land, and his home, when not under saddle Samson has never failed to express his hatred and disdain for this long-despised enemy. While Samson held a tenuous détente with the rope, halter, and riding crop, his long-standing battles with the helicopter would continue. It was fitting that Samson was unable to quash his contempt for the low-flying threat, for every heroic tale needs its evil foil and every superhero needs his archnemesis.

Perhaps Samson's exhibition that summer afternoon represented a celebratory act of the BLM's recent purported change in course. Or, more likely, his animated actions were a warning, a call to arms to all wild horse advocates to stay the course and to never forget that in years prior similar promises and assurances had been cast and then cast aside. If the latter, then Samson was both a wild-at-heart Mustang and a soothsayer. For in the months to come, the BLM's activities would constitute anything but a new strategy and a new start when it came to managing the nation's wild Mustangs.

In the weeks following the BLM's pronouncements, the policies and practices of the agency charged with managing this nation's Mustangs fell far short of matching its director's grand declarations. In California, for example, 1,855 wild horses—nearly 80 percent of the area's horse population—living on 789,852 acres were targeted for capture and collection. With four times more cattle than horses authorized in the Twin Peaks Herd Management Area, northeastern California would be left with little more than 500 wild horses. Miles away in northwestern Colorado, a small band of isolated free-roaming horses known as the West Douglas wild horse herd was targeted for complete elimination.

Back in Nevada, the BLM showed no sign of learning from its mistakes. In Ely, 55,000 acres of the Moriah Herd Area were scheduled to be zeroed out. Just to the north in the Tuscarora region of Elko County, faced with an alleged water shortage "emergency," three herds, over fourteen hundred horses, living on 455,000 acres stood in the BLM's sights. Where four thousand cattle were permitted to graze in the Tuscarora Herd Management Area, no more than five hundred Mustangs would remain. It was a roundup scheduled for the season's hottest, most unforgiving days, and it was an undertaking destined to become the next Calico.

By mid-July, twelve Tuscarora Mustangs had perished

from dehydration and roundup-related activities. Immediately the ASPCA, the Animal Welfare Institute, and the American Wild Horse Preservation Campaign expressed outrage. The Humane Society of the United States, through its president, Wayne Pacelle, joined in the chorus of criticism: "Methods for capturing, handling and transporting wild horses during gathers are centered, more often than not, on a bureaucratic timeline and agency convenience rather than animal welfare. We urge the agency to place an immediate moratorium on all gather and removal operations until the BLM develops and is prepared to implement a new wild horse management strategy."[34]

Bowing to public scrutiny and criticism and seeking to avoid a repeat of the Calico debacle, on July 15 the BLM temporarily suspended its Tuscarora wild horse gather operations. Ironically, for the Tuscarora Mustangs the issue was not the presence of, but rather, access to available water resources. Forced to navigate a myriad of new livestock fences and cattle gates, the horses were separated from the water holes that for decades had sustained their existence. Once again, humans were the greatest threat to the Mustang's survival.

As July came to a close and with twenty-one horses deceased at the resumed Tuscarora gather, fifty-four bipartisan members of Congress forwarded a letter to then secretary of the interior Ken Salazar calling for immediate action. Referencing the Calico and Tuscarora tragedies, the letter stated: "We are concerned by the inability of your agency to acknowledge these disturbing outcomes, change what seems to be deeply flawed policy, and better manage the gathers so as to prevent the unnecessary suffering and

death of these federally protected animals." The corre-
spondence concluded: ". . . we request that the Tuscarora
Complex roundup be suspended, along with any pending
gathers, until the agency demonstrates that it has addressed
the failings of the current program and can ensure the safety
and well-being of the animals you are charged with protecting." Samson's previous warnings and predictions were
accurate; the BLM was anything but a ship on a new and
changed course.

When I ventured out to the farm the first week of October, my ever-enthusiastic pupil seemed fully cognizant that
it was our one-year anniversary. Once I was seated atop his
back, and with little hesitation, he unloaded three swift bucks.
Samson the volcano had sat dormant for several months, but
to my surprise his eruption was little more than a hiccup.
This wasn't an act of defiance; this was a reminder: *You mount
and ride me because I let you mount and ride me. Just remember
that fact* the words that I imputed to his hard, unyielding gaze.
His message sent and received, Samson then walked off and
gave a perfect ride under saddle.

The truth, the reality, was that I had long since understood that if Samson didn't want me on his back, then I
wouldn't have been there. Perhaps he was too much horse for
me, or possibly I was too little trainer for him. But in truth,
I didn't really see it that way. In reality, despite my time,
patience, and understanding, I knew that Samson would
always be part authoritarian stallion, part untrained and
undomesticated wild horse, and part abused and brutalized victim. This is who Samson was, and this is what he
would remain.

Unable to change any of these things, I had to work

around Samson's many issues. I needed this horse to desire my attention, voluntarily comply with my mandates, and crave my approval. I needed Samson to want the "us." As Xenophon had instructed centuries before, horse and horseman needed to be partners. And that is exactly what we had become. For the better part of my career, I had advocated that true horsemanship rests upon a partnership between horse and human, and this horse had put my beliefs, my ways, and my abilities to the test. Through all of his moods, ghosts, and demons, his violent PTSD fits and rigid ways, Samson had unquestionably made me a better horseman.

This much I had already come to understand. But Samson had also taught me a great deal about patience and empathy. Our time together had shown me the true power of mutual understanding, mutual admiration, and mutual respect. What I didn't know, what I couldn't have foreseen, is that my time with Samson had made me a better person. He had turned me into a better version of myself. Samson was a partner in the truest sense of the word.

The winter of 2011 was cold, wet, and record breaking. While animals and humans alike battled the elements, Samson and his combat-tested winter blanket weathered the season's storms without worry. As the month of February came to a close and as winter prepared its exit, over a period of several days the BLM released a series of noteworthy press releases. In its first statement, and after battling two separate lawsuits, the BLM announced that it was abandoning its plans to round up Colorado's West Douglas wild horse herd. To the west in Nevada, having already captured fourteen hundred wild horses, the BLM declared the Antelope Complex wild horse gather concluded after determining that the herd's numerous pregnant mares were at risk. It was a story that could have been, but thankfully was not, the next Calico.

And last, on February 24 the BLM unveiled its long-awaited accelerated reforms to the Wild Horse and Burro Program. In the words of BLM director Abbey, "We've taken a top to bottom look at the wild horse and burro program and have come to a straightforward conclusion: we need to move ahead with reforms that build on what is working and move away from what is not. . . . [W]e need to enlist the help of partners, improve transparency and responsiveness in the program, and reaffirm science as the foundation for management decisions."[35]

For wild horse advocates, it was the trifecta of announcements and evidence of change that had been a long time coming. With an updated 2008 GAO analysis that reported that the BLM was starting to clean shop and assurances of "reform" and "new ideas," the agency that oversees our free-roaming Mustangs was promising a "new chapter in the management of wild horses, burros, and our public lands."[36] Whether or not they could follow through on these promises was an entirely different story.

The following weekend, as the soil started to thaw and the air turned warmer I ventured out to work Samson. Exiting my truck, I was perplexed by the sight of Valley Girl standing alone in the south pasture. Samson was nowhere to be found. Jumping up on my truck's front bumper, I located Samson, in the grass, prone on his right side, beside his mare. No one had ever seen him down before, so I knew that I was living my worst nightmare. I ran to the back of my truck and grabbed my trauma kit, but I knew that I had lost him.

As I passed through the gate and entered the south pasture, my concerns were amplified when Valley Girl failed to run up and excitedly greet my arrival. At this point, the ever-vigilant defensive sentry Samson should have been up and guarding, protecting his territory and his mare. He wasn't. Running toward the motionless and seemingly lifeless Samson, I was moving at a full clip, but it seemed as though I were stuck in slow motion. Part of me felt nauseous; the rest felt numb.

"After all we've been through," I said, kneeling beside the unmoving Mustang. Suddenly he opened his eyes, jumped up, and stomped at the ground, as if to say, *Can't a horse take a damned nap around here?* Put off by my rude intrusion, he trotted over to the fence line where Ike was standing. Expecting violence and bloodshed, I held my breath.

"Ike, get away from there, *now!*" I yelled from across the pasture to no avail.

But instead of losing his famous Barb temper, Samson simply sniffed at Ike, who returned the greeting. I looked hard but saw no sign of Samson's curled upper lip or his flesh-shredding incisors. Absent were the high-pitched stallion-like squeals of battle; gone were the wails of a miniature horse being scalped alive. Without my realizing it, Samson had adopted the ragtag bunch of farm animals. He now had a family; he now had his herd.

As I gazed across at Valley Girl playing with Ike, I realized the profound impact that this easygoing youngster had on my combative student. While I had trained Samson to survive in the human world, Valley Girl had taught him how to live in hers. Where I had failed to convince Samson to unconditionally accept the human species, Valley Girl had persuaded him to embrace another. Valley Girl's gift to Samson was far greater than mine, for she returned him to a world and a life from which he had been torn and distanced. She returned him to his world, the world of the horse.

Looking back upon our many ups and downs, successes and failures, moments of joy and instances of disappointment, I realized that my Samson Experience had been quite the ride. Life is chock-full of choices and littered with decisions, and I wouldn't have changed a single thing when it came to this wayward Mustang. For horse and horseman, it was simply meant to be. And for Samson, fate and luck had given back to him the good fortune that life had taken away.

Days later, while I was out on the trail working another horse, a beautiful young woman on an oversized warmblood rode up beside me. Her name was Alison; her ride, pleasant but antsy. My horse was calm and collected and Alison wanted to know my secret. A year earlier, I might have given her a gracious answer, shrugged her off as yet another horseperson seeking free advice, and then moved on to finish my ride. But on this day, with the thought of Samson and his adopted herd on my mind, I stayed and talked.

No one can do it all alone, I thought to myself. While I hadn't previously realized it, I too, in my own way, had been closed off. With me in my forties and single, the small voice inside my head had counseled that a wife and family were no longer in the cards. Like Samson, I had accepted being alone and solitary, and I had grown indifferent. But my Mustang pupil changed all of that. Samson the beaten-down Mustang who never let go of hope had taught me well.

Months later, this very same horsewoman would come to the farm and calmly hold Samson while I tended to a serious wound. Both Samson and I knew a good apple when we saw one.

In my head, the question that my clients had been asking for months, "What exactly is it with you and that Mustang?" echoed through the empty space. With each of my horses, the glue, the bond that binds horse and horseman, is always different. When it came to Alexandros, the horse who had cast in his stall, I was undeniably a strict and authoritarian dictator. For Sky, I was a calming agent who guided her into a new and strange world. And for Samson, I was a friend. In fifteen years of working with damaged and troubled equines, I don't know that I have ever occupied such a role. And as I thought long and hard on this, I came to understand that I wasn't just Samson's friend, but he in turn was mine. Our relationship was reciprocal, our friendship mutual.

Like true friends, Samson and I had each compromised and sacrificed so that our relationship could flourish. We each had our good days, and we both had our bad. On many occasions, Samson had made it quite difficult for me to call him a friend. And on other days, I am certain that I deserved the swift kick that he wanted to deliver to my back end. We were a dangerous mix of different and contrasting personalities. He was volatile, moody, and explosive; I was static, even-keeled, and easygoing. No matter how hard Samson tried to punch my buttons, I, for the most part, remained indifferent.

Samson and I were opposites that attracted. We were a truly original odd couple. But as in any good friendship, we each more or less understood and respected the other. Trust, loyalty, and respect were traits both horse and horseman admired, understood, and employed.

As true friends, Samson and I had each provided the other with lasting gifts. I gave him a new lease on life and taught him how to discard years of hatred, contempt, darkness, and despair. He allowed me to brush shoulders with the most elemental horse I had ever come across and opened my eyes to *Equus caballus* in its truest, purest, and most noble sense. From the moment that I put eyes on him, I knew that he was different. His bloodlines had survived the deserts of the East, scaled the mountains of the West, traveled the high seas, and discovered the Americas. Samson, the modern era's version of his ancient and storied ancestors, had shown me the true nature of the horse, returned my love for training, and given me a gift that I could never repay.

As for what made this horse tick, like a prized diamond there were many facets to Samson, and my understanding of him merely scratched the surface. Ironically, over the years many have voiced similar observations of my personality. Perhaps this is why he and I clicked. Maybe we really were more similar than dissimilar—two complicated, determined, enigmatic aging warriors past their prime. Maybe the Old English saying "show me your horse, and I will tell you who you are" had it right. Either way, for me a part of Samson would forever remain the imposing, barely visible, pedestaled beast lurking in the shadows of a dark stall. A part of Samson would forever be the mysterious and free horse of the wild whom nature and nurture had created.

Looking out at Samson, I saw something more than a horse, a pupil, and a friend. He was, like all Mustangs, a living and breathing history of the horse and history of the world. His blood carried the genetic code of the first dawn horse. His lungs held the stamina of the fabled desert horses of the East, his legs possessed the speed of the noble Conquistador mounts, and his mind embraced the intelligence and determination of the great Native American warhorse. Nearly every horse that walks this earth carries his bloodline. He has galloped across continents and floated across oceans. He conquered the Old World and discovered the New World. His hooves have carried the sands of the East, the soils of the West, and the salt of the oceans.

When I looked at Samson I saw greatness.

I also saw an animal who knew how to survive. He had escaped the devastation of the Ice Age and somehow managed to avoid becoming dinner for mankind's earliest citizens. The brutal, sadistic training methods of the Old World failed to dent his armor. He was a prized possession to kings and a symbol of certain defeat to the vanquished. He was a trusted mount in life and a necessity for the afterlife. He had chased countless buffalo, dodged the never-ending hail of cavalry bullets, outwitted the Mustangers, and outrun the BLM helicopters.

And now he had outlasted his abusers and silenced his critics.

Samson had weathered the storm. He had entered the world to adversity and led a lifetime of adversity. With greatness in his heart, survival in his blood, and determination in his soul, he was the horse of the centuries and the steed that time and history had built. Samson was a tried-and-true American wild Mustang and he had made his herd proud.

So when I thought of Samson and his proud and prideful ways, I found myself saying, *Why not?*

Samson was no longer maladjusted, no longer socially dysfunctional, and no longer hateful, but when I looked at him I still saw sadness, darkness, and despair. I pictured the thousands of Indian buffalo-catchers and painted war ponies dispatched under the aim of cavalry rifles. I envisioned the endless array of wild horses who had their tendons sliced by trip wires and eyes shot out by Mustanger bullets. I thought of every Mustang who suffered at slaughter to fill canned tins. I closed my eyes, but all I could see was pain, suffering, and death.

All I could see was the forever damaged and hardened, hated, abused, victimized, and brutalized Mustang horse.

As Samson slowly patrolled the perimeter fence line, I gazed at his freeze mark and thought of all the Mustangs the BLM had chased, culled, and captured. I saw horses at trap sites consumed with frenzied fear and once-spirited wild Mustangs standing spiritless in BLM mud lots. I pictured all the wild horses who were adopted by unscrupulous buyers and inexperienced horse owners, jammed into stock trucks, and shipped off to slaughter. And, I saw the cursed horse, the allegedly protected free-roaming modern-day wild Mustang that has been the target of countless unlawful, random, and sadistic acts of terror in a decades-long sportless hunt.

Samson wasn't just a historic and majestic steed; he was also the long forgotten and hated wild horse of the West. He was the horse that has survived centuries of inclement weather and millions of years of predation only to continually fall victim to man—his greatest predator. Decades' worth of scientific research has exonerated him of a major role in rangeland degradation and resource depletion, yet he has remained loathed and despised. Through no fault of his own, he has spent a lifetime misunderstood and mistreated where pain, suffering, and hardship was his one true constant. His fight to survive was indeed an epic battle to persevere.

I thought about Amy's random naming of her lawless, wayward horse. Similar to the biblical character, Samson the Mustang was a victim and a martyr, a fighter and a survivor. With strength, resilience, and fortitude they had each defeated their many enemies and slew their countless demons. Neither character was perfect. Both were heroic warriors and tragic figures. Each had persevered through adversity and hardship so that his story could be told.

Willful single-mindedness, stubborn determination, and a rigid resolve fueled their fight. One Samson was caught between the Hebrew and Philistine societies, the other stuck in limbo unable to live in either the world of the wild horse or the domestic horse world. Neither had a home. Though Amy's choice of name for Samson had been arbitrary, it couldn't have suited him any better.

It, like everything else in this story, was simply meant to be.

And like the great biblical figure, this Samson's story had become symbolic. His pain, suffering, and sacrifices spoke volumes as to what the wild Mustang was, what it had become, and what it could be. His story represented all that was right with the Mustang horse and all that was wrong with man. Samson the epic biblical character and his name-sake shared much more than just a name. Their lives, their trials and tribulations, had been the same. Perhaps Samson the Mustang horse, like the biblical Samson, would deliver his kind from their oppressors' hand.

Condensed into fourteen tumultuous years, Samson's long and storied journey was metaphorically the story of his kind. His struggles had been the Mustang's struggles. His victories had been the Mustang horse's victories. Samson's saga was in fact the saga of the American wild Mustang. And despite years of hardship, Samson has found peace from little more than a glimmer of hope. While abuse, sadness, and despair were fixtures of the Samson story, hope was this tale's theme.

Samson's saga is a tale of pain, suffering, resilience, sacrifice, compromise, and understanding. It is the chronicle of a horse who had nearly given up on man, and a man who would not give up on a horse. It is the story of an allegedly hopeless, worthless Mustang whose heart and soul forever changed the lives of those tasked with changing him. It is the story of one horse, one horseman, and one last chance.

Samson's long and arduous journey demonstrates the true power of hope, friendship, love, and redemption. And where there was hope for Samson, there is renewed hope for the Mustang horse—now homeless, displaced, forgotten, and rejected. Optimism, for the horses who still gallop across the western frontier—roaming their ancestral lands, our ancestral lands, the land of the free and spirited wild horse. There is still hope for the majestic, historical, timeless American wild Mustang.

Through years of persecution, violence, and near mass
extinction, the Mustang horse, much like Samson the Mustang, has fought for its very existence. It has survived in places
like Nevada's Lincoln and Nye counties, where despite 1,357
and 3,377 acres respectively per horse, it was removed and
zeroed out from its native habitat. This was the horse that
lived through the 1973 Howe, Idaho, massacre only to re-
live the experience again in 1989 when five hundred head
were shot dead in Nevada. It was an animal that outran the
hail of bullets in 1998 when thirty-four horses were gunned
down in Reno, only to have the process repeated in 2000
when thirty-seven Mustangs were massacred in Wyoming.
And it was a horse that fought for its life in 2003 when five
hundred captured Mustangs starved to death locked in BLM
holding corrals awaiting relocation.

Beat-down after beat-down had only stiffened Samson's
resolve and tragedy after tragedy has only hardened the Mustang character.

With its hooves imprinted in American culture and
American history, the Mustang is a uniquely American horse.
It is a fighter and a survivor—a steed commanding and demanding of respect. Forever wild and craving liberty, it is a
proud animal, and an animal the American people should
be proud of. It is a horse that has persevered through hardship and rebounded from despair. It has made countless sacrifices, and it has paid its dues. The Mustang way is indeed
the American way. It is an animal and a legacy that should
be admired, revered, and preserved.

No longer an essential component of our postmodern society, the wild Mustang's significance has faded much like
the old gold rush towns of the Wild West. Once a tool of

exploration that first discovered North America's virgin soils and then constructed American culture, the wild horse has become a mere historical footnote. Formerly a symbol of the American spirit, sadly, the Mustang is now deemed by many a plague upon the land. As to what role the few and ever-decreasing wild Mustangs can play in modern American society, this is a question that only the American people can definitively answer.

My arrival at the farm mid-March brought the all-too-familiar sight of Samson standing in the north pasture's far northwest corner, facing and gazing west. After all of this time, it was a sight that still broke my heart. It was a picture that said that this was still a homeless horse. Only on this day, something different happened. As I approached Samson from the rear, at twenty yards and closing on his position, he spun and faced me head-on. He didn't stand transfixed by the Sirens' westerly song and he didn't revert his gaze back in the direction of his former home.

Instead, on this day Samson rotated around, faced me, and turned his back on the memories and longings that had fueled his survival through his darkest moments. For Samson, it was a simple act that said that he was finally at peace and ready for a new start. For me, it was a monumental act that left me surprisingly touched.

The moment was bittersweet. In his book *The Mustangs*, American folklorist J. Frank Dobie observed: "If a really good Mustang is captured, the only way to keep him good is to gentle him with a care and kindness seldom practiced. Then he'll likely become a one-man horse."[36] Affirming this and recognizing that no one else would mount or ride her Mustang, Amy had sent an e-mail offering Samson to me. I was faced with the most agonizing decision of my career.

Selfishly, my heart wanted to grab Samson and trailer him off. But my head knew better. I knew better.

"I am going to leave you here," I told Samson, "with your new herd, with your family—where you belong. But I will be back next week, and the week after that, and the month after that. I will never leave you, old boy."

Standing twenty yards from my pupil, I looked Samson over with an admiring gaze. Like most wild Mustangs, he would never win a race, travel the show circuit, or sire a champion. But this didn't mean that he wasn't destined to make a name for himself. Samson didn't just have greatness in his blood; Samson was a great horse.

I gazed upon him in much the same fashion as I had nearly two years earlier in that dark prison cell of a stall. Where seven years' worth of hateful, derogatory, presumptive, and doubting labels had once sat atop his back, now there would only be a saddle and rider. Descriptive adjectives such as "hopeless," "belligerent," "crazy," "angry," and "antisocial" were no longer fitting for this animal. Conversely, terms such as "willful," "proud," "prideful," and "dominant" still described this steed to a T and I wouldn't have had it any other way.

Now free of his burden, Samson's gait had turned fluid and animated, his posture erect and proud. After so many years of darkness and despair, this horse was alive and free: free from the beat-downs, free of the Samson Rules, and relatively free from the ghosts and demons that had tormented his soul. And as for our contract, the covenant entered into between horse and horseman in that dark and damp stall one July afternoon, neither Samson nor I have ever tried to void, rescind, cancel, or nullify this agreement. Unlike the hundreds of broken contracts I have been hired to litigate, the agreement between Samson and me has, to this very day, remained in full force and effect. It was an understanding premised upon mutual trust, loyalty, and sacrifice.

It was a contract of friendship, an agreement in perpetuity, and a bond for life.

Dating back to our first encounter, and like the Plains tribes and their horses, Samson and I had forged an unbreakable, lasting bond. He was my loyal Indian warhorse and I his dedicated warrior brave.

Gazing out across the pasture, I strained and listened intently for the sound of waves crashing against and then receding from the shore. Only on this day, all I could hear was the sound of the warm spring breeze barreling through the otherwise quiet, picturesque rural Midwest glacial valley. And as I looked at Studs, Ike, and Star off to my left and Valley Girl standing to my right, I realized that Samson now had a herd, a harem, an owner, and, last, a loyal friend. This wayward, lost, lonesome, and solitary horse had returned to the glacial lands of his ancestors and he had found a home.

ENDNOTES

1. Xenophon, *Xenophon in Seven Volumes*, ed. E. C. Marchant (Cambridge, MA: Harvard University Press, 1984), p. 7.
2. Elwyn Hartley Edwards, *The Encyclopedia of the Horse* (New York: DK, 2009), p. 216.
3. J. Frank Dobie, *The Mustangs* (Lincoln: University of Nebraska Press, 2005), pp. 58–59.
4. Ibid., p. 59.
5. Hope Ryden, *America's Last Wild Horses* (Guilford, CT: Lyons Press, 2005), p. 57.
6. Ibid., p. 74, quoting from *Washington Irving's Astoria*.
7. Ryden, *America's Wild Horses*, p. 106, quoting from John A. Hogwood, *America's Western Frontiers*.
8. Ryden, *America's Last Wild Horses*, p. 177.
9. Dobie, *The Mustangs*, p. 144.
10. Ibid., p. 219.
11. David Cruise and Alison Griffiths, *Wild Horse Annie and the Last Mustang: The Life of Velma Johnston* (New York: Scribner, 2013), p. 59.
12. Ibid., p. 13.
13. Ibid., p. 13.
14. Ibid., p. 43.

15. Ibid., p. 7.
16. The Wild Free-Roaming Horses and Burros Act of 1971, Public Law 92-195 as amended, 85 Stat. 649 (1971), codified at 16 U.S.C. §1331-1340.
17. National Academy of Sciences, *Wild and Free-Roaming Horses and Burros: Final Report* p. 44 (Washington, DC: National Academy Press, 1982).
18. Ibid., p. 43.
19. The Wild Free-Roaming Horses and Burros Act of 1971, 16 U.S.C. §1331, Public Law 92-195 as amended.
20. Ibid.
21. Ryden, *America's Last Wild Horses,* p. 306.
22. United States General Accountability Office Report to the Secretary of the Interior, *Rangeland Management Improvements Needed in Federal Wild Horse Program,* August 1990, p. 3.
23. Ibid, pp. 2–3.
24. Ibid., p. 3.
25. Ibid., p. 3.
26. Ibid., p. 4.
27. Transcript deposition testimony of Glenna Eckel, in the matter of Western Watersheds Project v. BLM (May 13, 2009) p. 810.
28. Stephen Long, *U.S. Humane Society Head Quietly Meeting with BLM Officials,* reprinted in Equine Welfare Alliance Email Newsletter (February 2010).
29. Cruise and Griffiths, *Wild Horse Annie,* p. 76, quoting Charlie Johnston.
30. Dobie, *The Mustangs,* p. 201.
31. Stephen Long, *BLM Calls Death Stampede at Calico "Humane,"* quoting BLM spokeswoman JoLynn Worley, reprinted in Equine Welfare Alliance E-mail Newsletter (March 2010).
32. BLM Press Release, June 3, 2010.
33. BLM Press Release, June 3, 2010.
34. Humane Society of the United States Press Release, July 14, 2011.
35. BLM Press Release, February 24, 2011.
36. Dobie, *The Mustangs,* p. 197.

BIBLIOGRAPHY

Books

Cruise, David, and Alison Griffiths. *Wild Horse Annie and the Last Mustangs: The Life of Velma Johnston*. New York: Scribner, 2013.

Dobie, J. Frank. *The Mustangs*. Lincoln: University of Nebraska Press, 2005.

Edwards, Elwyn Hartley. *The Encyclopedia of the Horse*. New York: DK, 2009.

Ryden, Hope. *America's Last Wild Horses*. Guilford, CT: Lyons Press, 2005.

Stillman, Deanne. *Mustang: The Saga of the Wild Horse in the American West*. New York: First Mariner Books, 2009.

Xenophon. *Xenophon in Seven Volumes*. Edited by E. C. Marchant. Cambridge, MA: Harvard University Press, 1984.

Journal Articles

Hanggi, Evelyn B. "The Thinking Horse: Cognition and Perception Reviewed." *AAEP Proceedings* 51, 2005.

McDonnell, Sue M., and Samantha C. Murray. "Bachelor and Harem Stallion Behavior and Endocrinology." *Biol. Reprod. Mono.* 1, 570–90. University of Pennsylvania School of Veterinary Medicine—Kennett Square, 1995.

Magazine Articles

Fuller, Alexandra. "Spirit of the Shrinking West Mustangs." *National Geographic,* February 2009.

Reports and Studies

National Academy of Sciences. *Wild and Free-Roaming Horses and Burros: Final Report.* Washington, DC: National Academy Press, 1982.

United States Government Accountability Office. *Bureau of Land Management: Effective Long-Term Options Needed to Manage Unadoptable Wild Horses.* GAO-09-77, October 2008.

United States Government Accountability Office. *Rangeland Management: Improvements Needed in Federal Wild Horse Program.* GAO/RCED-90-110, August 1990.

Statutes

The Wild Free-Roaming Horses and Burros Act of 1971, Pubic Law. 92-195 as amended, 85 Stat. 649 (1971), 16 U.S.C. §1331 et seq.

The Federal Land Policy and Management Act of 1976, Public Law. 94-579 as amended, 43 U.S.C. §1701 et seq.

The Animal Welfare Act, Public Law 89-544, 80 as amended, Stat. 350 (1966), 7 U.S.C. §2131 et seq.

Web sites

www.blm.gov/wo/st/en/prog/whbprogram.html
www.humanesociety.org
www.saveourwildhorses.org
www.thecloudfoundation.org
www.wildhorsepreservation.org